Algorithmic Trading Systems and Strategies: A New Approach

Design, Build, and Maintain an Effective Strategy Search Mechanism

Viktoria Dolzhenko

Apress®

Algorithmic Trading Systems and Strategies: A New Approach: Design, Build, and Maintain an Effective Strategy Search Mechanism

Viktoria Dolzhenko
San Jose, Costa Rica

ISBN-13 (pbk): 979-8-8688-0356-7   ISBN-13 (electronic): 979-8-8688-0357-4
https://doi.org/10.1007/979-8-8688-0357-4

Copyright © 2024 by Viktoria Dolzhenko

This work is subject to copyright. All rights are reserved by the Publisher, whether the whole or part of the material is concerned, specifically the rights of translation, reprinting, reuse of illustrations, recitation, broadcasting, reproduction on microfilms or in any other physical way, and transmission or information storage and retrieval, electronic adaptation, computer software, or by similar or dissimilar methodology now known or hereafter developed.

Trademarked names, logos, and images may appear in this book. Rather than use a trademark symbol with every occurrence of a trademarked name, logo, or image we use the names, logos, and images only in an editorial fashion and to the benefit of the trademark owner, with no intention of infringement of the trademark.

The use in this publication of trade names, trademarks, service marks, and similar terms, even if they are not identified as such, is not to be taken as an expression of opinion as to whether or not they are subject to proprietary rights.

While the advice and information in this book are believed to be true and accurate at the date of publication, neither the authors nor the editors nor the publisher can accept any legal responsibility for any errors or omissions that may be made. The publisher makes no warranty, express or implied, with respect to the material contained herein.

    Managing Director, Apress Media LLC: Welmoed Spahr
    Acquisitions Editor: Malini Rajendran
    Development Editor: James Markham
    Coordinating Editor: Gryffin Winkler

Cover designed by eStudioCalamar

Cover image designed by Freepik (www.freepik.com)

Distributed to the book trade worldwide by Apress Media, LLC, 1 New York Plaza, New York, NY 10004, U.S.A. Phone 1-800-SPRINGER, fax (201) 348-4505, email orders-ny@springer-sbm.com, or visit www.springeronline.com. Apress Media, LLC is a California LLC and the sole member (owner) is Springer Science + Business Media Finance Inc (SSBM Finance Inc). SSBM Finance Inc is a **Delaware** corporation.

For information on translations, please e-mail booktranslations@springernature.com; for reprint, paperback, or audio rights, please e-mail bookpermissions@springernature.com.

Apress titles may be purchased in bulk for academic, corporate, or promotional use. eBook versions and licenses are also available for most titles. For more information, reference our Print and eBook Bulk Sales web page at http://www.apress.com/bulk-sales.

Any source code or other supplementary material referenced by the author in this book is available to readers on GitHub (https://github.com/Apress). For more detailed information, please visit https://www.apress.com/gp/services/source-code.

If disposing of this product, please recycle the paper

This book is dedicated to all those who are constantly in search of new ideas. These tireless adventurers are undeterred by any difficulties or failures and have been looking for something new all their life to improve both their lives and the lives of the people around them. I admire such people immensely. It is thanks to them that the world continues to improve at least a little bit.

Dare and create. This is the purpose of life.

Table of Contents

About the Author xi

About the Technical Reviewers xiii

Introduction xv

Chapter 1: Popular Approaches to Developing Trading Systems 1

    Manual Trading 2

    Ready-Made Signals and Algorithms 2

        Signals 3

        Third-Party Algorithms 5

    Specialized Services 9

    Independent Creation of a Trading Platform 10

        Testing a Single Strategy 10

        Various Developer Approaches 12

    Hiring Third-Party Developers 12

    My Approach 13

    Summary 15

Chapter 2: Introduction to Developing Trading Systems 17

    General Theory 18

        Order Execution 21

        Margin and Leverage 24

    Composition of the Trading System 25

        Trading Theory 27

TABLE OF CONTENTS

    Capital Management 39
    Risk Control 49
    Testing 58
    Performance Indicators 59
    Optimization 63
Summary 67

Chapter 3: Architectural Solution Part 1: Identifying the Requirements 69

Requirements Elicitation 71
    Signals 72
    First View of the Process 74
Theory Generator 78
    Strategies Searching 82
    Selection and Forward Testing 97
    Selection of Financial Instruments 98
    Setting Up a Search for a Profitable Strategy 99
    The Logic of Searching for Profitable Strategies 100
    Real Trading 101
Important Questions 103
    Life Cycle of a Position 103
    Capital Management 106
    Risk Control 107
    Scalability of Indicators 114
Summary 116

TABLE OF CONTENTS

Chapter 4: Architectural Solution Part 2: Services and Subsystems 117
Microservice Architecture 118
    Kubernetes 122
Subsystems 124
Strategy Search Subsystem 125
    Processing Generators 126
    Queue 130
    Finite State Machine 134
    Concept of Theory Processing Steps 135
    Calculation of Subtheories 140
    Core 149
    Sandbox Exchange 150
Real Trading Subsystem 151
    Integration with Exchanges 152
    Launch and Operation of Strategies 156
    Enabling and Disabling Strategies 158
    Checking the Type of Financial Instrument 160
    Master Data 167
Summary 169

Chapter 5: Technology Stack and Libraries 171
Choosing a Framework 172
Application Architecture 172
    Spaghetti Code 173
    Clean Architecture 174
    Domain-Driven Design vs. Anemic Model 177

TABLE OF CONTENTS

Object Relational Mapper 178
    How to Use Dapper 179
    Migrations 184
Finite State Machine 185
    Principle 186
    Hosted Service 189
Backworker 207
Summary 213

Chapter 6: Optimization Algorithms 215

Formulation of the Problem 216
Population Algorithms 217
Genetic Algorithms 220
    Mutation Operators 222
    Crossover Operators 224
    Filtering Operators 228
    Selection Operators 234
    Restrictions 238
    Local Unconstrained Optimization Algorithms 249
Summary 264

Chapter 7: Implementation of Optimization Algorithms 265

General View 266
Brute-Force Algorithm 270
    Getting Info 272
    Getting a Set of Values 277
    How to Use 282
Genetic Algorithm 285
    Steps 286

TABLE OF CONTENTS

- Getting Info 287
- Getting a Set of Values 294
- Initialization Step 303
- Mutation Step 306
- Filtering Step 309
- Breeding Step 314
- Test Functions 321
- SubTheory Example 322
- Summary 325

Chapter 8: Implementation of the Core Module 327
- Use Cases 327
- Context 331
- Update Candle Event 332
- Check Signals 335
  - Strategy Model 337
  - Calculate Signal 343
  - Calculation of Indicators 351
  - Average True Range (Atr) 357
- Process of Positions 362
  - Process Bot (Lite Version) 364
  - Process Steps 373
  - Events 376
  - Process Acts 390
- Summary 396

TABLE OF CONTENTS

Chapter 9: Approaches to Final Implementation 397
    Binance Adapter 397
        Implementation 398
    Docker 403
        History 403
        Why Is This Needed? 405
        Docker Components 406
        Launching the Application 408
    Kubernetes 415
        Components 416
        Pods 417
        Deployments 419
        Services 424
        Helm 426
    Summary 429

Index 431

About the Author

Viktoria Dolzhenko My dream of becoming a programmer started the moment a computer first appeared in my home. As a child I loved programming and started regularly participating in programming competitions. And now, I have more than 10 years of experience in developing complex systems from scratch.

My professional passion is the complex design of various applications, while personally I am interested in algorithmic trading. To bring these two ideas together, I decided to build a system that would search for and find profitable strategies on its own. At that time, developing such a system for algorithmic trading was an interesting and difficult task.

Now I am sharing my findings and conclusions in this book so that everyone who wants to build their own algorithmic systems will not waste time creating ineffective systems. Readers can learn from my experience to gain the maximum benefits from their creations.

About the Technical Reviewers

Ganesh Harke is a seasoned technology leader working with a multinational investment bank. Over the past 14 years, Ganesh has channeled his expertise in design, architecture, and development of scalable and low-latency systems into various industries.

In his current role as technical lead at Citibank, Ganesh is at the forefront of developing a cutting-edge e-commerce platform. His professional journey extends beyond Citibank, with previous impactful roles at esteemed organizations such as Barclays and Siemens. He has contributed to and thrived in dynamic environments at each juncture, leaving an indelible mark on projects ranging from intricate financial solutions to cutting-edge technological innovations.

Ganesh has a master's degree in financial engineering and a bachelor's degree in information technology and has passed all three CFA levels.

Ganesh is also a mentor who helps fellow professionals and colleagues with his technical expertise. Ganesh was recognized for his work inside and outside of his career network.

ABOUT THE TECHNICAL REVIEWERS

Vadzim Zylevich is a certified Microsoft Solutions Developer with a strong background in software development, focusing on technologies like C# and ASP.NET. Over his 10-year career, he has led several important projects and has been recognized for his technical skills and leadership. Currently, he works at Maersk, the leading global logistics company, where he continues to apply his expertise to innovate and improve their technological capabilities. Beyond programming, he is a technical writer at Code-Maze and mentors aspiring developers, sharing his knowledge and experience. His interest in the impact of AI on software development led him to discuss this topic in a TickerNews interview, highlighting his commitment to both innovation and education in the tech field. His goal is to not only advance in technology but also support the growth of the tech community by making complex concepts accessible to all.

As a senior portfolio performance and risk expert, **Samantha** delivers multi-asset expertise within her area and clarifies the strategic solutions to global asset managers and sell-side players leveraging Bloomberg's suite of solutions and models. Specializing in liquidity stress assessment, fixed-income analytics, and customized indexing within the context of various investment vehicles, Samantha has a wealth of knowledge of the ever-shifting investment landscape and the relevant world-class solutions to address the regulatory and industry challenges.

Introduction

If you start researching algorithmic trading, you will notice a general pattern in the logic of creating trading systems. That pattern is to find a few high-profit strategies and use them in the trading. Often the search is carried out using a lot of manual labor. There is one big drawback in this approach: there is a low probability that a profitable strategy will be found.

Also, because of the amount of manual labor in this process, excessive demands are placed on the strategies found. They require a lot of support and configuration.

I remember when I tried many different strategies, most of which showed low performance. I was increasingly frustrated with myself and the approaches I was using. One day, I remembered some work I did with a teacher at my university. We were looking for optimal parameters for launching and adjusting the movement of artificial earth satellites to launch them into the target orbit with the least amount of fuel consumed. I thought, how does this task differ from the task of finding a profitable strategy? I realized that they were the same, which meant my knowledge in that area could be applied in a completely new direction.

As a result, I combined my knowledge of creating high-load systems and the field of engineering to create a new approach for finding and using profitable strategies. The solution lies not in looking for dozens of highly profitable strategies. The solution is to quickly find hundreds of strategies, albeit with more modest results, with minimal manual labor.

In this book, I not only describe a system that continuously searches for and runs strategies but also show an option for implementing the fundamental parts of such a system using the .NET Framework. In this book you will learn how you can build a trading system that finds profitable strategies with a higher probability than with conventional approaches.

CHAPTER 1

Popular Approaches to Developing Trading Systems

Before you start creating your own system, you must first look for possible ways to implement it. Perhaps someone has already implemented your idea and there is no need to create your own program. Even if there is nothing like your idea on the market, you can still glean valuable insights from existing products.

Currently, there are many approaches to creating trading systems, ranging from using conventional manual trading systems on the stock exchange to hiring third-party developers or a company to implement your ideas. In fact, you can not only find ideas for trading systems on the Internet, but also find their implementations.

In this chapter, you will learn about the main approaches to creating trading systems and consider their advantages and disadvantages. I will also describe my approach and explain why I chose it.

CHAPTER 1 POPULAR APPROACHES TO DEVELOPING TRADING SYSTEMS

Manual Trading

The most famous traders earned their fortunes through their knowledge, effort, and vast experience. If you want to follow their path, you need to hone your trading skills and increase your knowledge every day.

The essence of a trading system based on manual trading is an independent search for successful strategies, gaining experience from daily failures and successes. I am fascinated by successful traders who do not use third-party assistant programs to trade. Naturally, these people use classic charts provided by brokers, but they do the main work of analyzing their strategies on their own. No matter how popular artificial neural networks are, they do not yet have intuition and subconsciousness—an undeniable advantage of humans.

However, it is worth noting that this plus is also a minus. Emotions and greed have long plagued humanity, and traders are no exception. Often, when an important decision needs to be made, a person succumbs to the crowd effect, or even panic, and thoughtlessly takes on unnecessary risk. That is why, in manual trading, human error is high. Mistakes, in turn, lead to undermining the human nervous system.

Emotions will never get the best of a trading robot. In addition, it is capable of making decisions much faster than a human, and it does not require rest or sleep; therefore, the number of trading transactions it can complete is significantly greater than that of a human.

Ready-Made Signals and Algorithms

The easiest trading system to understand and implement can be based either on trading signals from other trading participants or on the signals or automatic trading of a trading robot that you have purchased. Both of these approaches can generate income, but only if used correctly. Don't be duped by what their sellers promise. That is, you need to use them as tools and not all-encompassing solutions.

CHAPTER 1   POPULAR APPROACHES TO DEVELOPING TRADING SYSTEMS

Signals

Signals in trading are hints or recommendations from a *signal provider* to make purchases and sales of financial instruments. That is, a signal tells you to buy or sell. In practice, if this signal is in the form an alert, it could look like a short text message, as shown here:

TSLA. Buy price 203, Sell price 208

Signal providers can be both ordinary traders and serious experienced analysts at specialized companies. There are a huge number of signal providers on the market; the main problem is finding a high-quality and honest company.

Signals are convenient because they require absolutely no time to develop and test. When you buy one, you receive a ready-made solution; all that is required is to follow the instructions. But as they say, the devil is in the details. Despite the apparent simplicity of the signals, suppliers often hide or provide partial information about the logic of the decision-making involved, so users do not know exactly what logic the signal is based on. Therefore, to decide whether to work with a certain provider and its signal, you need to carefully study its analytics.

Signals come in different types depending on the control and price. These divisions are somewhat superficial, but here are the distinctions:

- **Hand signals.** These are signals that the supplier provides using manual trading. They are often the result of sitting in front of a monitor for a long time and studying the instrument for a long time. Most likely, there will not be very many of these signals from one supplier.

- **Automatic signals.** These are signals based on the trading algorithm of the supplier. That is, these signals are generated automatically. Naturally, with this approach, the number of generated signals will most likely be higher than with manual signals.

- **Copy trading.** When copying a trade, the seller's account and the buyer's account are linked, and when the seller's account opens a transaction, it is automatically opened in the buyer's account. This is a simple principle that allows the buyer not to spend a lot of time trading. But the biggest disadvantage of this case is the lack of sufficient control over your account.

- **Alerts.** These are signals in the form of text messages that tell the user what to do. I showed an example of an alert earlier. This is one of the safest types of signals, since the decision for action and position size always remains with the account owner.

- **Account management.** With this option, the client completely transfers control of their account to the supplier. For this, the supplier will most likely take a certain percentage of the profit. When choosing this option, you should carefully read the information about the company providing such services. Also, there is a high risk of fraud here.

- **Free.** Free signals are generally of lower quality than ones that cost money. This is logical as almost no one wants to share the results of their work for free.

At first glance, the task of creating a trading system based on ready-made signals looks simple. The user creates a portfolio of such signals from different suppliers and works on it. The main difficulty here is that it is necessary to spend quite a lot of time on analytics and on testing such signals, constantly adding new ones and eliminating outdated ones. This means that the relative simplicity of creating such a system results in enormous difficulties and costs to maintain it.

CHAPTER 1   POPULAR APPROACHES TO DEVELOPING TRADING SYSTEMS

Third-Party Algorithms

The global trend to automate and algorithmize everything has now come to trading, and every year the number of algorithmic systems that help traders or that even trade independently is growing. Anyone can buy an algorithmic robot; you don't need to be a programmer.

There are so many of trading robots that the question becomes, why haven't the people who created them used them to make themselves millions? Some may have, of course, but ironically it's not so much thanks to trading, but rather thanks to the proceeds from selling the robots to consumers.

My point is that you need to understand that no one would be selling a trading robot if trading with it could bring in more money than the sales from the robot itself. This does not mean that there are no helpful robots, just that robots can only do so much with search and analytics.

You should also pay attention to the rather high price of robots. That is, you'll want to get a profitable trading algorithm but also earn back the money you invested in the robot. In fact, finding a decent robot that will work consistently is quite difficult. At the time of writing this book, one of the popular sites for selling algorithmic robots sells about 4,000 "expert" robots. Imagine how hard it is to analyze them all and make sure they work! You should not only be looking at the reviews but also analyzing the indicators yourself before buying one.

That said, anyone who does not want to create all this from scratch can easily buy a robot. In fact, some people have hundreds of such robots in their portfolio and yet they don't spend a second of their time creating them.

There are different types of algorithms used in robots. The types differ not only in the logic of decision-making but also in money management, average trading time, trading method, price, and many other parameters. In addition, any trading robot must contain the analytical data of its work, which is valuable information for the buyer.

CHAPTER 1   POPULAR APPROACHES TO DEVELOPING TRADING SYSTEMS

The following is a short list of indicators that can be used to analyze a robot's performance; I will talk about them in more detail in the next chapter:

- **Expected value.** This is an estimate of the average expected return of a strategy during its long-term use. Essentially, it tells you how successful a strategy can be over the long term.

- **Profit factor.** This is an indicator of the effectiveness of a trading strategy, which is the ratio of the amount of profit to the amount of losses. This shows how your profits compare to your losses.

- **Absolute drawdown.** This represents the change in funds in a trading account from the beginning to the end of the trading period.

- **Relative drawdown.** This drawdown is the trader's largest loss as a percentage relative to the previous maximum balance.

- **Maximum drawdown.** This shows the maximum decrease in capital from the highest level it has ever been to the lowest it has ever been.

- **Recovery factor.** The recovery factor is equal to the absolute value of net profit divided by the maximum drawdown. The higher the recovery factor, the faster the system recovers after a drawdown.

As you can understand, there are many types of robots. The following are some of them:

- **Long-term, medium-term, short-term.** This is a classification based on the average time a position is held.

CHAPTER 1 POPULAR APPROACHES TO DEVELOPING TRADING SYSTEMS

- **Short-term ones, in turn, are divided into arbitrage and scalping.** Arbitrage robots open positions not on one exchange but on several, but their positions are always short-term and last literally milliseconds. In this they are similar to scalping ones, but the latter trade on only one exchange.

- **Automatic and semi-automatic.** While automatic systems carry out activities without human assistance, semi-automatic ones require constant attention. This is because semi-automatic systems have much less functionality and are replaced by human labor. For example, such a system may require information about the size of the position being opened.

- **Expert advisors based on the Martingale principle.** This is a money management system in which after each unprofitable closing of a position, it is necessary to double the size of the next position. If the outcome is profitable, you can cover losses from the previous transaction and return to the original position size.

- **Trend and oscillator.** These are systems based on technical analysis.

- **Nonindicator.** These are specific algorithmic robots. Examples are systems that make decisions based on the analysis of news sites or forums.

For short-term signals, one of the most important analytical indicators is the average time of holding a position. After all, if this indicator is equal to or less than one minute, this means you are dealing with scalper or arbitrage signals. These signals are extremely sensitive to ping, and most likely you will not have a chance to trade them in time. Therefore, I advise you to consider signals only with a holding position of at least several

CHAPTER 1   POPULAR APPROACHES TO DEVELOPING TRADING SYSTEMS

minutes or more. Lengthy deals are also a bad sign. Perhaps the robot is trying to wait out the accumulated losses on transactions and the decision-making logic contains a serious flaw, reflected in an untimely exit from the position.

In addition, you should absolutely be scared off by Martingale advisors. Despite its apparent simplicity, this system will almost always lead you to losing all your capital. With a long series of losing trades, your capital will be reset to zero. It is quite easy to determine whether a system belongs to Martingale by looking at the balance chart and the funds chart. These graphs for normal systems should be as close as possible and naturally tend to grow. A uniform alternation of open and closed positions also indicates the reliability of the system. But large gaps between charts and an increase in the number of open positions and a decrease in closed ones indicates Martingale.

Automatic robots are generally considered more reliable than semi-automated ones. After all, the human factor is completely excluded from them. But it should also be noted that they are much more complex in development than semi-automatic ones, and the price for the highest quality ones is, accordingly, higher. It is also worth noting the need for total control over the operation of such a system so that you or the monitoring system can detect a problem in a timely manner and stop trading.

The market for algorithmic robots is dominated by trend and oscillatory systems. And this is logical, because the formulas of technical indicators can be easily transferred into the program. They are easy to see on stock charts and easy to analyze.

The undeniable advantage of any algorithmic robot is its ability to trade different instruments. In fact, this feature alone suggests that the robot is quite reliable; it is obvious that this robot does not work by adjustment, which means that it will give good results in the long term and respond well to market changes.

Someone who wants to create their own trading system based on purchasing algorithms can take the path of diversification and risk reduction. Buy a large number of robots for your portfolio, preferably working on different principles, and use them comprehensively. In essence, the principle is similar to creating a portfolio from trading signals. Here, too, most of the time will be spent on constant analysis and testing. But this approach, unfortunately, is more expensive.

Specialized Services

All the previous options have one drawback—they do not implement your ideas for trading strategies exactly. Of course, you can create your own trading system using your own ideas. But what do you do if you have no programming skills? In this case, special services can come to the rescue, where it is possible, without any special knowledge, to assemble your robot step-by-step. You can simply implement the decision-making logic and then test and analyze the resulting strategy. Some services even allow you to set up the money management rules and risk control, and others allow you to complicate the logic using a special scripting language.

Unfortunately, it's difficult to create something specific with these types of services. For more advanced strategies, you need to learn at least an easy scripting language to go beyond simple logic. Some services provide programming capabilities using languages such as Python or C#, both of which allow you to create more complex algorithms. In addition, there are many more such services other than "constructor" services. They usually have a large number of users and thus a developed learning environment.

Difficulties arise when you want to create something unique to test a theory that does not fit into the standard framework. This is the time to switch to independent development or to hire third-party developers.

CHAPTER 1   POPULAR APPROACHES TO DEVELOPING TRADING SYSTEMS

Independent Creation of a Trading Platform

Having your own trading system has a big advantage over other approaches—you have the ability to test any of your theories since you are not limited by the functionality included in a ready-made solution. The prospects for this direction are enormous, because they are not limited in any way, by anyone, or by anything. The process is surprisingly creative and unique to each developer. Moreover, the developer is not tied to any specific programming language; you can use the technology stack that you know. Most likely, once you choose this course, you will never switch to another, simpler one.

The division into different approaches in this category is arbitrary. After all, adding or removing a functionality to/from a program changes the system every time, and it becomes completely different. But still, let's look at some different approaches so that you have an idea of what suits you best.

Testing a Single Strategy

Let's imagine that you have a brilliant idea and want to test it. You will quickly program the logic and test it through your own or some third-party service. Everything that your trading system will contain is a single strategy. At the same time, the functionality of your trading platform is not important; it may or may not contain a testing or optimization module. All your platform does is trade according to a single given scenario.

The undeniable advantage of this approach is its high development speed. You don't need to worry about the optimal value of your strategy parameters or the impact of any indicator on performance.

The obvious disadvantage is the lack of understanding of what can be improved in the strategy or how the performance would change if you added or removed some condition or changed some indicator parameter.

CHAPTER 1   POPULAR APPROACHES TO DEVELOPING TRADING SYSTEMS

Roughly speaking, the main disadvantage is a lack of searching for the optimal strategy for your theory. But there is a theory in your strategy; you just immediately set certain parameters for it.

Here is an example of this strategy.

>   Input signal:
>
>   >   BBW > 0.05
>   >
>   >   WMA < Open Price
>
>   Output signal:
>
>   >   BBW < 0.01
>   >
>   >   RSI > 30

You can, of course, evaluate this strategy in terms of performance indicators, but it would be much better to consider how these indicators change if the specific parameters of the strategy also changed. The brute-force method will be the easiest to implement here.

The brute-force method, although ancient and elementary, has always helped humanity in incomprehensible situations. It can also serve an excellent purpose for a simple developer. If you implement the brute-force method into the previous strategy, you can see how the specific value of each parameter affects performance. That is, by setting a specific range and step, you can build a graph of changes in any performance indicator depending on changes in the parameter.

The brute-force method does an excellent job of analyzing the influence of specific values of indicator parameters on the effectiveness of the theory. Thus, by sequentially or comprehensively going through all the possible options for parameters, you can conduct an accurate analysis of the theory. But this method is effective only on a small number of parameters. If the theory contains a large number of possible strategy options, then finding the optimal value will take an incredibly large amount of time.

CHAPTER 1   POPULAR APPROACHES TO DEVELOPING TRADING SYSTEMS

Various Developer Approaches

Basically, those who really take the matter seriously develop entire trading platforms with a lot of functionality. Some write their own analog of the exchange to have their own independent testing. Optimization modules, modules for searching for optimal strategies, real trading module, money management module, and much more. Some write their own analog of the exchange to have their own independent testingTrading system developmentindependent testing, optimization modules, modules for searching for optimal strategies, real trading module, money management module, and much more.

The theories that cannot be verified by standard auxiliary services can be verified in your own system. For example, say you want to test the market psychological theory that the stock price of a certain company directly depends on mentions of this company on social networks. You can create a parser that could analyze the mood of the masses using hashtags and generate signals when a critical mass is reached in a positive or negative direction. Or you have the idea that some stocks are directly dependent on other stocks. Or that a certain company's stock goes up when it rains. Crazy? Maybe, but you can test all your ideas when you do independent development.

Hiring Third-Party Developers

At some point, a mechanical trading trader may decide to automate their system, in whole or in part, which will allow them to free up more time for deeper analysis and improvement of trading strategies and theories. However, if the trader has no programming experience, this can be intimidating. After all, no one wants to spend months or even years studying this when it's unclear whether the time spent will pay off.

Therefore, despite that there are many services on the market that help you create a full-fledged trading robot, it is still a very labor-intensive task. As a result, it is often the successful traders who consider hiring an experienced engineer to design and develop their own trading system. That is, when someone has a great theory but neither the time nor the opportunity to implement the idea programmatically, they often hire third-party developers.

The first disadvantage of this approach is the need to share your profitable idea with other people. This may lead to the emergence of competitors who then start working according to your theory. So, you need to protect your intellectual property. A special contract may help with this, but it still may not help. In any case, you definitely shouldn't trust the developers' word. It may seem right to share only part of your idea with the developer, but in this case, the developed system may not work as you originally planned. Therefore, if you decide to hire programmers, then it is better to draw up the detailed technical specifications yourself.

The second disadvantage is that it is unclear whether you will recoup your development costs. You spend a lot of money to bring your theory to life, but it might not lead to any profit.

Another important question is where to find a good developer for your system. There are also many paths here. The route of hiring a third-party company seems to be the most suitable, and most likely your intellectual property will remain yours. After all, a company's reputation is worth a lot. But be prepared to spend more money than if you hired a freelance developer.

My Approach

Each of the previously discussed approaches has its place, and each of them is capable of bringing profit to the trader. In this book, I will describe my approach and how I created a trading platform without hiring third-party developers, without using specialized programs, and so on.

CHAPTER 1   POPULAR APPROACHES TO DEVELOPING TRADING SYSTEMS

In the beginning, I analyzed the existing approaches of developing trading robots, studied the robots for sale at that time, read blogs of successful practicing algorithmic traders, and so on. As a result, I realized almost all traders were looking for super-profitable strategies. It had to be a strategy that brought 1,000 percent per month and had a drawdown of 1 percent and no more. Of course, each trader had their own concept of an extremely profitable strategy, but most of them would not even look at a strategy with a very modest result of 3 percent per year.

I didn't initially understand this concept. After all, even if a person is very smart, there is a possibility that they will not be able to find such a strategy even if they spend their whole life searching. I understood that the likelihood that I would find a super-profitable strategy was very low. So, I decided to try the diversification approach. I thought, what if I create strategies that are fundamentally different, with modest indicators, for example, 0.5 to 1 percent per month, but use them in real trading in hundreds? Most likely, there are many more such strategies than super-profitable ones, and, naturally, they are much easier to find.

As a result, I chose the option of completely independent development with the idea of automatically searching for many profitable strategies, but with modest indicators. Of course, if the system finds a super-profitable strategy, then good; if it doesn't find it, it's OK. Thus, I wanted to create a system that every developer could do independently and that could almost 100 percent of the time generate additional income. Yes, it may not be millions of dollars, but it will work consistently and will require low operating costs.

The big disadvantage of this approach is that it takes a huge amount of time to implement. In fact, this process will never end. I constantly want to improve something or add some functionality. But this is a very creative and interesting process that I advise for everyone.

CHAPTER 1   POPULAR APPROACHES TO DEVELOPING TRADING SYSTEMS

Summary

In this chapter, I briefly discussed the types of trading systems and how to create them, and I discussed their advantages and disadvantages.

- **Manual trading.** The main advantage of this approach is the complete absence of labor costs for creating a trading system, as well as the use of human intelligence and experience. Among the shortcomings, the most striking are instability due to the emotional state of a person, as well as a relatively low number of open positions.

- **Trading using ready-made signals.** The advantage of this approach is that there is no need to implement a trading system. The main disadvantage is that you must trust the experience of others, with a possible lack of understanding of the logic of how the signals work.

- **Trading using purchased algorithmic robots.** Again, the undeniable advantage of this approach is that there is no need to create a trading system. You will be working using someone else's system. This also entails disadvantages: you will understand the real capabilities of system only *after* the purchase. And often you will misunderstand the internal logic of such systems.

- **Independent development of individual strategies.** This is a popular approach primarily because of its simplicity and flexibility. You can implement your own unique strategy, but speed comes at the cost of limited functionality.

- **Hiring third-party developers.** With this approach you can get almost anything, including implementing my approach in developing a trading system. The main disadvantages are the difficulty of finding good developers, the need to share your ideas, and the high cost.

- **Independent development of a trading system.** With this approach, you either independently or in a circle of a small number of partners independently implement not a single strategy but an entire system with automatic search, testing, and launch strategies. The obvious advantage of this idea is the flexibility of strategy implementation. The big disadvantage of this approach is the large labor costs for implementing such a system.

CHAPTER 2

Introduction to Developing Trading Systems

To move on to the next chapters, which contain specific information about the architecture and technical solution of my system, we must consider the basic concepts related to stock trading. If you know what types of markets exist, how limit orders work, and what anti-Martingale money management is, you can skip this chapter and move on to the next one. But if you want to create your own trading system and don't know where to start, then I strongly recommend reading this chapter so that you don't have questions when studying further topics.

In this chapter, we will briefly review the general theory of exchange trading, consider the approximate composition of a trading system, and dwell in detail on the formation of a trading theory, since this is the main topic of this book. We will also study the main approaches to capital management and risk control and touch on the topic of testing and optimization a little. This chapter, in fact, is just a bit of the knowledge that is necessary to start creating your own trading robot but without which the further steps are impossible.

CHAPTER 2   INTRODUCTION TO DEVELOPING TRADING SYSTEMS

General Theory

First, we need to understand what stock trading is. To do this, let's look at the basic concepts in simple terms.

- An **exchange** is a kind of organized trading platform where buyers and sellers meet to make purchase/sale transactions in financial instruments such as stocks, bonds, commodities, and currencies.

- A **broker** is an intermediary between the investor (trader) and the exchange. It provides access to stock trading, fulfils customer orders, provides market information, and provides various financial services.

The relationship between the broker and the exchange consists of two main points. First, this is the order execution chain. This is when a broker executes various orders from investors, sending them to the exchange for processing by the exchange itself, thereby ensuring that traders interact with the real market. It is worth noting that the broker can provide access not only to one specific exchange but to many different ones, which allows the trader to expand their working hours and the list of financial instruments with which they can work.

Second, the broker provides traders with current information on the state of the market, analyst reviews, news, and other data that can help make a trading decision. The broker also conducts a technical analysis of the trader's transactions, showing the status of orders and the movement of funds in the account.

In addition, some brokers provide advice and counsel to clients regarding their investment strategies and portfolio state. Or they can even directly manage clients' financial accounts. Thus, the broker and the exchange are closely interconnected in the process of exchange trading, where the broker acts as an intermediary, providing traders with access to real exchange markets and providing them with the necessary services and facilities for successful participation in trading.

When people talk about financial instruments, they mean anything that can be bought or sold to make or save money. For example, company stocks, bonds, debt obligations, and even cryptocurrencies such as Bitcoin and Ethereum are all financial instruments. These tools help people invest and manage their finances.

Let's take a closer look at the main types of these financial instruments.

- **Stocks.** In short, a stock is ownership in part of the company's property. Traders who hold shares are called *shareholders*.

- **Bonds.** These are debt securities that represent some kind of promise by a company or government to repay the trader's borrowed funds with interest. But unfortunately, they may not keep their promise.

- **Commodities.** These are the most tangible assets—real physical goods such as gold, oil, or grain—which can be bought and sold on the market.

- **Currencies.** The simplest asset is the monetary units of various countries that have the right to be traded on the foreign exchange market.

- **Derivatives.** These are financial instruments whose value depends on changes in the price of another financial instrument, called an *underlying asset*. Simply put, derivatives "derive" from another asset and allow investors to bet on changes in its value. Examples include futures, options, and swaps.

- **Indexes.** They can easily be thought of as a portfolio of stocks or other financial instruments that represent the overall performance of a market or sector.

- **Investment funds.** These are funds that pool money from different traders to invest in a variety of assets.

- **Cryptocurrencies.** This is the newest type of asset. Cryptocurrencies are decentralized digital currencies that use cryptography to ensure transaction security.

It's also worth mentioning **dividends**. Some companies pay out a portion of their profits to their shareholders. Dividends are paid to attract new shareholders and reward old ones. The amount paid is directly proportional to the number of shares held by the holder. Overall, dividends are an important aspect for investors, providing them with additional income from owning shares in a company. Finally, it is worth adding that dividends are not only paid to stockholders; some types of bonds, investment funds, exchange-traded funds (ETFs), and derivatives can also be a source of this income.

The concept of a financial instrument goes hand in hand with the concept of a ticker, which is a unique symbolic code. It is used to identify a specific asset in the financial market. A ticker usually consists of several letters that are associated with a specific company, currency, commodity, or other type of financial asset. They make it easier to identify and track price changes in the market because they are a compact and unique designation for each asset.

The following are some examples of tickers:

- **TSLA:** Tesla Inc. stock ticker

- **JPYUSD:** Ticker for the Japanese yen to U.S. dollar currency pair

- **CC1!:** Ticker for the commodity Cocoa
- **ADAUSD:** Ticker for the Cardano cryptocurrency against the U.S. dollar

Order Execution

Now that you know what a financial instrument is, you need to understand how to sell and buy it. To carry out these actions, the broker provides us with such a tool as an order. In trading, an **order** is an instruction sent from a trader to a broker or trading platform to execute a trade in a financial market. The order specifies what operation the trader wants to perform (buy or sell) and also determines the main parameters of the transaction, such as volume (number of assets) and price. Any order contains special characteristics, such as order type, order direction, instrument ticker, and volume.

Let's take a quick look at what each characteristic means.

- **Order type.** This determines the way a trader can interact with the market and implement their trading strategies. The main types are Market, Limit, Stop Order, Stop Limit Order, Take Profit Order, Stop Limit For Sale, Market On Open, Market On Close, Market If Touched Order, and One Cancels The Other Order.

- **Direction of the Order.** This indicates the trader's desired action in relation to the asset. It determines whether the trader wants to buy or sell an asset. Two possible directions are Buy Order and Sell Order. Buy expresses the trader's desire to purchase an asset, and Sell expresses the trader's desire to sell.

- **Volume.** This is the quantity (of shares, bonds, etc.) that the trader wants to buy or sell

- **Price.** For limit orders, this is the price level at which the trader wants to carry out a transaction, for stop orders, upon reaching which the order is activated.

- **TimeInForce.** This indicates the duration of the order's relevance.

In fact, there are only two main types of orders: market and limit. **Market** reflects a trader's request to buy or sell an asset at the current market price. **Limit** is the same request, but the purchase or sale must be carried out at the price level specified by the trader. To better understand the difference between them, let's look at what happens after an order is created.

After it is created by the trader, it is sent to the so-called Depth of Market order book (order book). The order book is a representation of the interaction of all orders for the current financial instrument. Market orders make instant changes to the order book, while limit orders form a display of it, providing information about the price levels, resistance, and support levels at which market participants are willing to trade.

This happens because the nature of a market and limit order is different. The market order is immediately executed at the current buy or sell price, changing the level of supply and demand, and the limit order fixes the specific price at which the trader is ready to buy or sell a specific asset. Let's take a look at Figure 2-1.

CHAPTER 2　INTRODUCTION TO DEVELOPING TRADING SYSTEMS

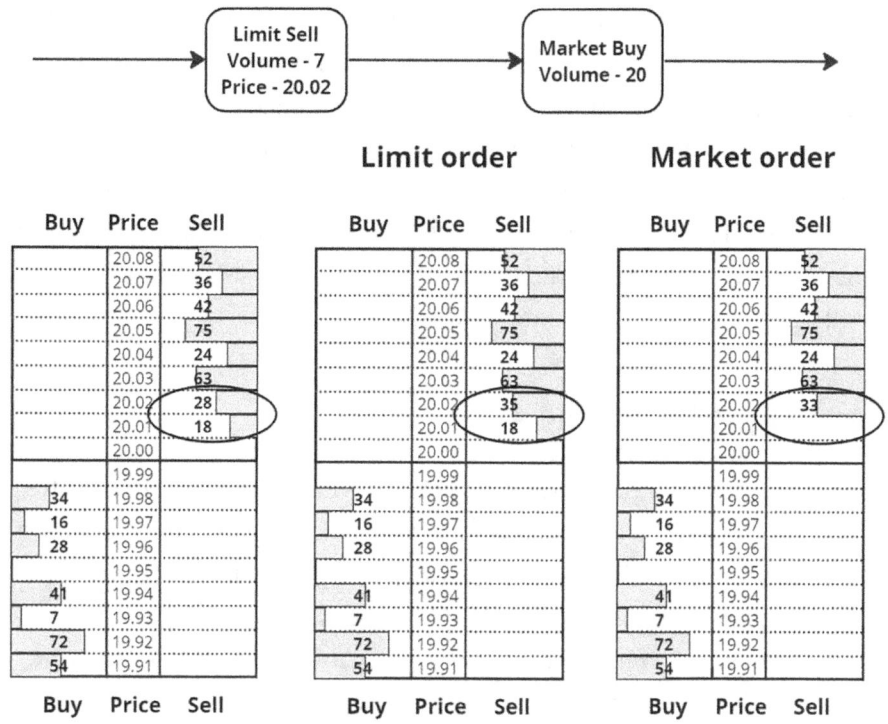

Figure 2-1. *Limit and market purchase and sale process*

First, we see the order book before the trader creates any orders. Then the trader created a limit sell order with a volume of 7 lots at a price of 20.02. On the second order book you can see how the total volume in the exchange order book at the level of 20.02 increased by exactly 7 units. It's easy to guess that our trader's limit order contributed to this. Next, the trader decides to create a market buy order with a volume of 20 lots. This order will work immediately: first, 18 lots will be purchased at a price of 20.01 and then another 2 lots at a price of 20.02. The example is given only from the point of view of the nature of order execution. It is unlikely that a real trader will make such a chain of orders on one instrument at the same time.

As you might have guessed, a financial instrument essentially has two prices; one is the maximum buy price (bid), and the other is the minimum sell price (ask). The combination of these two prices is called the *quote*. That is, a **quote** means the current price of a financial instrument at which a trader can buy or sell this instrument. The difference between these prices is called a *spread*, which depends mainly on the liquidity, volatility of the financial instrument and the cost of order processing at the broker. I'll talk more about volatility later in this chapter.

Margin and Leverage

Some traders use a broker's service such as leverage to increase potential profits. Leverage gives them the ability to trade larger volumes than their own funds allow. It shows the ratio of how many more funds can be used in a transaction compared to your own funds. For example, with a leverage of 1:50, a trader can trade 50 times more than they have in their account. This allows the trader to invest in more expensive assets that they would not have enough money for using only their personal funds.

Leverage implies the use of another concept: margin. Both of these concepts relate to the use of brokerage leverage but are expressed in different forms. Thus, **margin** is a specific amount of money that a trader is required to provide to participate in trades, while **leverage** determines how much these funds increase their purchasing power in the market. It turns out that the trader deposits margin as collateral, which ensures the execution of transactions and covers potential losses, and the broker provides the remaining funds.

There are two main types of margin.

- **Initial margin.** This is the minimum amount to open a new position.

- **Maintenance margin.** This is the minimum amount to maintain an open position.

It is worth noting that when using margin and leverage, the trader pays the broker a commission for providing borrowed funds. These expenses may reduce the overall profit from transactions. But the main drawback is the greatly increased risk in conditions of strong market fluctuations, since the losses can exceed the trader's own funds. Therefore, it is important to use these tools with caution.

Composition of the Trading System

For a trader to begin to think through the architecture of their trading system, they still need to know what it consists of and what its main purpose is. Let's start with the goal.

The goal of any trading system created will most likely be to obtain a main or additional source of income. But bad news—we will not be able to assess the potential of the system either at the idea stage or at the testing stage. The efficiency will be visible only when the minimum set of necessary functionality is developed and when the system is tested in real trading. Therefore, the stage of determining the financial goal for the trading system being developed can be a thankless task.

But this minus more than outweighs the plus that the more time we invest in developing and thinking about the strategy and functionality itself, the higher the potential efficiency. It turns out that our main goal is the continuous improvement of the system. This is our guiding star and our motivation. After all, our financial results will be directly related to this strategic goal.

With this goal figured out, what's next? The trader needs to come up with their own trading strategy, test it, think through risk control and money management, and evaluate the effectiveness of the system. For each of these tasks, the trading system should have its own separate module. Each of these key modules will perform specific functions.

CHAPTER 2 INTRODUCTION TO DEVELOPING TRADING SYSTEMS

Moreover, these modules must work interconnectedly, providing a full cycle of trading operations. Effective interaction between them is the key to the successful operation of the trading system.

Now let's look at these main modules:

- **Formation of a trading theory.** This module is based on a multistep process that includes various steps such as choosing an approach (technical analysis, fundamental analysis, etc.), choosing a market structure to trade (volatile, bearish, bullish, etc.), choosing a time frame, choosing a trading strategy, and creating rules trading and specific signals generated based on these rules.

- **Testing.** This is an important step before using the system in real markets. This includes the selection of market data, determination of evaluation criteria, preliminary testing, backtesting, forward testing, and evaluation of results.

- **Capital management.** The main goal here is to ensure sustainability and minimize risks in trade. This includes choosing an approach to determine the optimal position size.

- **Risk control.** This module closely intersects with money management and is responsible for ensuring financial stability and protection against potential losses. The purpose of the module is to determine the maximum level of risk, use stop-loss orders, diversify the portfolio, and reassess risks when market conditions change.

- **Efficiency mark.** This is an important stage to determine its quality and potential success in the market. The main task is to calculate performance indicators such as profitability, Sharpe ratio, maximum drawdown, profit factor, and other metrics.
- **Optimization.** This module is based on a dynamic process, the task of which is to find the best parameters and settings of the strategy to achieve maximum efficiency and profitability. Great importance is paid to optimization algorithms.

In my opinion, each of these modules is desirable but not required. After all, each algorithmic trader has their own path, and they can create a trading program that is completely unique in structure.

Trading Theory

If we do not want to play roulette, then before real trading, we must formulate our trading theory: the idea on which all deals will be based. The purpose of trading theory is to create a system of rules and strategies that allow a trader to make reasoned decisions about entering and exiting the market. Based on these rules, specific signals will be generated in the future. This is one of the most important stages of creating your system, so we will start with it.

Just as a plant cannot grow without a seed, a trading system will never become profitable without a quality theory. But how is one formulated? Where do ideas come from? There are actually a lot of options, and first, let's highlight the main approaches in the formation of trading theories, and then I will talk in more detail about some of them.

- **Technical analysis.** This method of analyzing financial markets relies on examining and interpreting price and trading volume charts to identify trends and predict future price movements.

- **Fundamental analysis.** This method of analysis is based on the study of financial, economic, and other fundamental data to make trading decisions.

- **Mixed approach.** This is a combination of technical and fundamental analysis. This approach uses both fundamental data and technical indicators to more fully and informedly predict market movements.

- **Automatic theory formation in algorithmic trading.** In this approach, a trading strategy is created and optimized automatically using algorithms and/or machine learning. This method allows algorithms to analyze historical data, identify patterns and trends, and then generate trading signals and strategies based on this data.

- **Event trading.** This is a sibling of fundamental analysis, but while the fundamental approach is primarily focused on the long term, event trading focuses on short-term price changes associated with specific events or news. Traders using this approach often seek to make a quick profit on the volatility caused by the market's reaction to news. Event trading is a dynamic and fast-paced approach to trading that requires the trader to be alert to news and events occurring in real time and to respond quickly to create profitable trading opportunities.

- **Own unique theories.** This is an interesting and creative approach where everyone can see a connection or pattern that has not previously been noticed by other traders.

As a result, the choice of a specific approach or a combination of them is a personal matter for everyone. Now let's look at some of them in more detail.

Technical Analysis

Technical analysis is perhaps the most popular. This is easily explained by the fact that it uses graphs, making it relatively easy to understand. Graphs can be easily understood and interpreted by most traders, making technical analysis accessible even to beginners. Additionally, technical analysis techniques are applicable to a wide range of financial instruments and markets, including stocks, commodities, and others. It turns out that this is one of the most universal trading tools. And its easy automation makes it easy to use in the development of robotic trading systems. This helps traders use strategies without constantly monitoring the market. Another advantage is that technical analysis uses historical data for testing, which makes it possible to easily analyze strategies.

Technical analysis includes different areas, each of which focuses on different formats of price movement.

These are the main functions of technical analysis:

- Graphical analysis
- Indicators and oscillators
- Trend analysis
- Geometric analysis
- Fibonacci retracement and extension

CHAPTER 2　INTRODUCTION TO DEVELOPING TRADING SYSTEMS

Graphical Analysis

Graphical analysis means using visual representations of price activity to make trading decisions. The basic idea is that price information is reflected in charts, and analyzing these charts can help traders predict future price movements and come up with the right strategies. This allows you to identify trends, resistance, and support levels, as well as patterns and optimal entry and exit points. Graphical analysis mainly uses candlestick, bar, line, point, figure, and Renko charts. You can see examples of these charts in Figure 2-2.

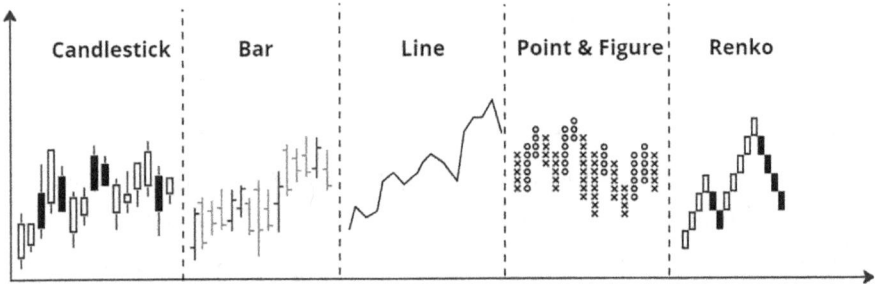

Figure 2-2. *Types of charts*

Indicators and Oscillators

Indicators and oscillators are mathematical expressions that are based on price and volume activity in the market. They can be visualized on a chart and can be conveniently used for analysis when making trading decisions. Indicators and oscillators help traders assess the current market situation, identify potential reversal points or continuation of a trend, and determine overbought or oversold levels of an asset.

Indicators also help traders determine general trends, the direction of market movement, and the strength of the trend. They are often represented on charts as lines or curves, plotting values on a price axis or separate scale. Indicators are varied and can be classified according to their main functions.

CHAPTER 2   INTRODUCTION TO DEVELOPING TRADING SYSTEMS

The following are several main types of indicators:

- **Trend indicators.** Examples are Moving Average (MA), Moving Average Convergence Divergence (MACD), the Bollinger Band (BB), and Parabolic SAR. They help determine the general direction and strength of a trend.

- **Oscillators.** They are typically used to measure whether a market is overbought or oversold and provide signals about possible turning points. They usually fluctuate around a central line (such as the zero line) and are charts often located below the main price chart. Examples including Relative Strength Index (RSI), Stochastic Oscillator, Commodity Channel Index (CCI), and MACD.

- **Volume indicators.** Examples include On-Balance Volume (OBV), Chaikin Money Flow, and Volume Price Trend (VPT). Their function is to analyze trading volumes and help in assessing the strength of a trend and confirming its direction. And some still depend not only on volume but also on price such as Volume Weighted Average Price (VWAP) and Money Flow Index (MFI). They combine price and volume information to help determine the average price based on trading volume.

- **Volatility indicators.** Examples are Bollinger Bands and Average True Range (ATR). They reflect price volatility, allowing you to identify support and resistance levels, as well as when the market is overbought or oversold.

CHAPTER 2 INTRODUCTION TO DEVELOPING TRADING SYSTEMS

- **Momentum indicators.** Examples include Relative Strength Index (RSI), Momentum, and Stochastic Momentum Index. Their function is to measure the momentum of price movements and help identify possible turning points.

- **Cyclical indicators.** Examples include Detrended Price Oscillator (DPO) and Schaff Trend Cycle. They highlight cyclical components in price data, which can help predict future trend changes.

- **Other indicators.** Examples include Ichimoku Cloud, Elliott Wave Theory, and Gartley Pattern. Their function is to identify certain formations and structures on charts, providing signals about possible price movements. The list of indicators and their possible functions does not end there.

Indicators are also divided into leading and lagging indicators. Leading indicators seek to predict future price changes and trends before they happen. Examples are RSI and Stochastic Oscillator. Lagging indicators reflect past price changes and trends, confirming the current state of the market. Examples include MA, Bollinger Bands, and MACD.

The choice between leading and lagging indicators depends on the trading strategy and style of the trader. Some prefer leading indicators to try to identify potential market changes in the early stages, while others prefer lagging indicators to more reliably confirm the current trend.

It is important to remember that no single indicator guarantees success in the market, but combining them and analyzing supporting factors may be a more effective approach.

Trend Analysis

Trend analysis is aimed at identifying the general direction of price movement of a particular financial instrument. The essence of this method is to determine the current trend and understand whether it will continue or change in the future. Traders are looking for optimal points to enter a trade in the direction of the trend and exit it before its possible change. Trends can be divided by duration: short-term, medium-term, long-term. But still, the main division occurs in the direction of the trend (see Figure 2-3).

- **Upward.** There is a gradual increase in price. The graph looks like a staircase going up when viewed from left to right.

- **Downward.** There is a gradual decrease in price. The graph looks like a staircase going downward when viewed from left to right.

- **Sideways.** Prices move in a horizontal range without a clear dominant direction.

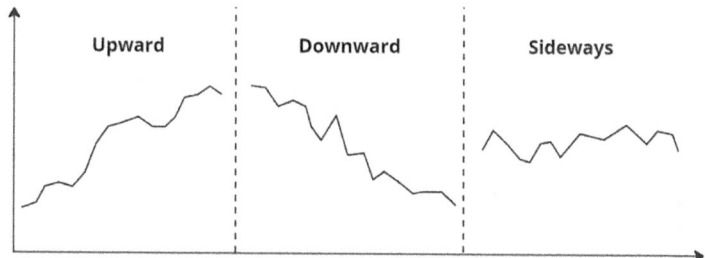

Figure 2-3. Types of trends

Geometric analysis is mainly represented by the study of graphic patterns, searching for them in market data and predicting future price movements based on them. Basic geometric shapes: triangles (ascending and descending), diamond, wedge, flags, double peaks, head and shoulders, and others.

Fibonacci Retracement and Extension

Fibonacci retracements and extensions are technical analysis tools based on Fibonacci numbers. They are used to determine potential support and resistance levels in financial markets. Fibonacci retracement uses levels based on the Fibonacci number sequence (e.g., 23.6%, 38.2%, 50%, 61.8%, 76.4%). After the price of an asset rises or falls, traders can use the Fibonacci retracement tool from the initial move to identify possible levels at which the price may change direction. For example, 38.2%, 50%, and 61.8% are often used as potential support and resistance levels (50% is not a Fibonacci number but is often used). If the price of an asset rises and then experiences a correction, a trader can apply Fibonacci retracement from the start of the move to the end of the correction to identify support levels. Fibonacci extensions also use Fibonacci numbers, but instead of retracement levels, they are used to determine the levels at which the price can complete a move or continue in the same direction.

Traders can use Fibonacci extensions to determine possible future levels where the price may go. The 161.8%, 261.8%, and 423.6% levels are some of the Fibonacci extension levels often used by traders. If the price begins to move higher after a correction, a trader can apply a Fibonacci extension from the beginning of the movement to the end of the correction to identify potential resistance and support levels.

Fundamental Analysis

Fundamental analysis in trading is a method of market analysis based on the assessment of fundamental factors affecting the value of financial assets. The basic idea is to estimate the intrinsic value of an asset and then compare it to the current market price to identify potential overvaluations or undervaluations.

CHAPTER 2   INTRODUCTION TO DEVELOPING TRADING SYSTEMS

To make a decision to buy/sell the financial instrument in question, a trader needs to analyze the company's financial indicators, such as profit and loss statements, balance sheets, and cash flow statements; evaluate the company's management; and of course evaluate the trends and prospects of the industry in which it operates this company. Also, an important stage is the assessment of competitors and their market shares, assessment of the impact of global and political events on the company's activities, and assessment of profitability and dividend payments. As you can see, a colossal amount of work is being done. Therefore, given the volume of data being studied, fundamental analysis is widely used by investors to make long-term decisions.

It is important to emphasize that fundamental analysis can be combined with other methods, such as technical analysis, to gain a more complete understanding of the market.

Mixed Approach

Technical-fundamental analysis in trading is an approach that combines elements of technical and fundamental analysis to make trading decisions. This method allows traders to evaluate assets, taking into account both their current value and trends obtained from technical analysis tools and the main factors influencing their value, obtained from fundamentals. This combination gives a more complete picture of the direction of price movement. Combining the two methods can help not only minimize the risks associated with a limited view of only the technical or fundamental side of the market but also provide more accurate forecasts and informed trading decisions. A trader can use technical indicators to confirm or refute fundamental signals and vice versa.

Volatility

It is worth mentioning such an important concept as volatility. Volatility in trading is a measure of price volatility in financial markets. This concept reflects the degree of fluctuation in asset prices over a certain period of time. The higher the volatility, the more significant the up and down price movements can be.

Volatility shows the following to a trader:

- Describes how much asset prices can change in a short period of time. High volatility may indicate unstable times.

- Serves as an important risk indicator. Higher volatility can mean greater potential gain but also greater potential loss. For example, with higher volatility, larger stop loss levels should be set.

- Affects the choice of strategies. Volatile markets can provide more opportunities for profit, but they can also be riskier.

- Affects the choice of analysis period, which may depend on the degree of volatility. For example, when volatility is high, traders may prefer shorter time frames to respond more quickly to market changes.

This concept refers to aspects of two main types of analysis: technical and fundamental. In the context of technical analysis, volatility can be seen as a key parameter for making decisions about entering and exiting trades. Thus, many technical indicators and strategies take volatility into account when generating signals. In fundamental analysis, fundamental factors such as news, economic events, and data can influence market volatility. For example, important announcements about large companies

CHAPTER 2   INTRODUCTION TO DEVELOPING TRADING SYSTEMS

or changes in a country's economic policies can cause prices to change dramatically. Thus, volatility is not a separate type of analysis but rather a factor taken into account within analytical approaches, be it technical or fundamental analysis.

In practice, volatility is assessed by a trader using volatility indicators. Examples are Volatility Index (VIX), True Average Range (ATR), Bollinger Bands, Chaikin Volatility, Volatility Stop, Volatility Momentum, and Market Facilitation Index (MFI).

Signals

We have dealt with the approaches to forming a trading theory. That is, by now the trader knows the necessary theory to generate their own trading strategy. Next, to the trader needs to define clear trading rules according to which the signals will be generated.

1. Selecting one or more financial instruments for trading
2. Choosing an approach for developing a trading strategy
3. Formulating the conditions for opening a position
4. Formulating the conditions for closing a position

Formulating entry and exit conditions in trading is the process of defining clear rules on the basis of which a trader makes a decision to enter the market (buy or sell an asset) or exit a position. These terms are based on the various aspects of market analysis that we have already covered. They must be clearly defined and are often subject to optimization and backtesting.

They can be roughly described as follows:

- **Entry conditions.** First, we determine which condition or event will serve as a signal to open a position; then we determine which time chart the strategy will work; and at the end, if necessary, we need to receive confirmation of the signal through some additional indicator.

- **Exit conditions.** First, we determine which signal or event indicates the need to close the position; and then we look for confirmation indicating a change in the direction of the trend, set the level at which the position is automatically closed to limit losses and the level at which the position is closed to take profit.

Let's look at an example:

- **Conditions for opening a position:** Buy when the price touches the lower Bollinger band on the daily chart and its width is at a relatively low level. Confirmation of the signal is the presence of oversold conditions on the RSI indicator on the four-hour chart.

- **Conditions for closing a position:** Sell when the price touches the upper Bollinger band on the daily chart and its width becomes relatively high. Confirmation of the signal is the presence of overbought conditions on the RSI indicator on the four-hour chart.

Great, now we can generate trading signals based on these trading conditions. While entry and exit conditions are more general concepts, trading signals are specific instructions indicating the need to take certain actions in the market, such as buying or selling an asset.

For example, trading signals based on the conditions from the example earlier would look like this:

Signal to input

> Daily chart
>
>> Price <= lower Bollinger Bands
>>
>> BBW < 0.05
>
> 4 hour chart
>
>> RSI < 30

Exit signal

> Daily chart
>
>> Price >= upper Bollinger Bands
>>
>> BBW > 0.08
>
> 4 hour chart
>
>> RSI > 70

In practice, traders begin to follow the path taken by many and start with the now classic crossing of moving averages and then gradually learn more complex strategies and test them in practice. I think this is the right approach; without basic knowledge of indicators, it will be difficult to do anything worthwhile.

Capital Management

Let's say a trader comes up with a promising trading theory and starts trading on the stock exchange without thinking about the size of each position. What could this lead to? The answer, it seems to me, is serious financial losses. Let me give you a clear example. Let's say an experienced trader has $10,000 in capital and is engaged in short-term trading in the stock market. They decide not to follow any capital management strategy and instead invest their entire amount in four large and high-risk orders. Market conditions unexpectedly go wrong, and all four orders lose money due to sudden price declines. As a result, the trader loses up to 70% of their capital.

If the trader had decided to use even a simple capital management strategy, such as a fixed interest rate, the trader would have retained most of their capital. That is, we see that capital management not only helps reduce losses but also helps preserve capital in difficult market conditions. It turns out that the goal of capital management is to maintain and grow a trading account, avoid large losses, control risks, and help avoid emotional decisions.

Oddly enough, the most banal and effective way to manage capital is to divide capital into parts. Yes, you don't need to put all your eggs in one basket. This is already clear to everyone, but what makes this management effective, unfortunately, is not for everyone. That same efficiency primarily follows from the optimal position size, and this size, in turn, depends on the method of capital management. There are quite a few of these methods.

Here are the main ones:

- Fixed position size
- Kelly criterion
- Optimal f
- Martingale
- Anti-Martingale
- Fixed proportional position sizing

Fixed Position Sizing

The fixed position sizing method implies a fixed position size for each trade, regardless of the current capital amount or risk level. This means the trader always risks the same fixed amount, or a fixed amount or a fixed percentage of their capital on every single trade. If a trader decides to work on a fixed volume (amount), then they need to set each time the exact and constant number of units (money) in which the financial instrument is measured, which they will always buy or sell. If they choose a fixed percentage, then they need to make a transaction for a constant fixed percentage of their current capital.

The first method is simple and straightforward, but it does not depend on the amount of capital and the volatility of the asset. With little capital, it becomes very risky. The second method automatically adapts to changes in capital, but volatility is also not taken into account and requires constant recalculation of the position size when the account changes.

For example, let's say a trader has $10,000 in capital. At a fixed volume, after purchasing shares at $60 per share and a constant volume of 100 shares, they would be risking $6,000, which is more than half of their capital. This is not normal and about the same thing will happen if you wait for a fixed amount! The picture is different for a fixed percentage. If they decide to risk 1.5% of their capital on each position, then the maximum amount they can lose on one trade is $150. At a stock price of $60 per share, they can afford to buy 2 shares ($150 / $60). As you can see, this approach is more secure.

Kelly Criterion

The Kelly criterion is a formula proposed by American mathematician and statistician John L. Kelly in 1956, used to determine the optimal bet size under conditions of uncertainty or risk in money management. Most often, traders use this criterion for trading using leverage.

CHAPTER 2 INTRODUCTION TO DEVELOPING TRADING SYSTEMS

The basic Kelly formula looks like this:

$$f^* = x - \frac{y}{z}$$

f*: The optimal share of capital to invest in each transaction

x: The probability of winning

y: The probability of loss (y = 1 - x)

z: The average win relative to the average loss

Based on the proposed formula, it is always necessary to risk a certain percentage of the total capital on each order. For example, if x is 0.05, then your bet on each order should be 5% of your total capital.

Let me give you a small example. Let's assume that a trader trades using a strategy where for every 100 positions, 52 positions were losses and 48 were profits. This means our x = 48% and y = 52%. Substituting into the formula, they will take the following form:

x = 0.48, and y = 0.52

In monetary terms, the total profit was $7,000, and the loss was $3,000. Then z will be equal to this:

$$z = 7000/3000 \approx 2.33$$

Then:

$$f^* = 0.48 - \frac{0.52}{2.33} = 0.2268$$

It turns out that f* = 0.2268, or 22.68%. The risk on each position can be a maximum of 22.68% of capital.

We will also change the amount of profit and loss for clarity. Now the profit will be $3,800, and the loss will be $3,600.

CHAPTER 2   INTRODUCTION TO DEVELOPING TRADING SYSTEMS

Then: $z = 3800/3600 \approx 1{,}055$

$$f^* = 0.48 - \frac{0.52}{1.055} = -0.01289$$

This definitely means the account will go to zero.

Since this method has quite a few disadvantages, such as the need for a history of positions for a specific strategy, the need for constant recalculation (preferably after each trade), the lack of forecasting, or the frequent recommendation of using large bet sizes, many traders modernize it or use f* in a reduced form or consider the Kelly criterion as the size of the optimal leverage.

Optimal f

The main developer of the optimal f system is Ralph Vince. He was able to modernize the Kelly criterion, where he took into account different sizes of winnings and losses. This strategy operates on the assumption that a trader's profit directly depends on how much capital they use in each transaction. The optimal f-ratio is the dynamically optimized percentage of capital used in each trade that maximizes the strategy's overall profit. To find f, Vince introduced a concept called TWR, which stands for *terminal relative wealth*. TWR is an indicator characterizing the relative final capital, or, more simply, how many times the initial capital increases.

It is calculated by the following formula:

$$TWR = \prod_{i=1}^{N}(1 + f^*(\frac{-Trade_i}{BiggestLoss}))$$

where N is the total number of transactions:

$$1 + f^*(\frac{-Trade_i}{BiggestLoss})$$

- profit for a certain period,

CHAPTER 2 INTRODUCTION TO DEVELOPING TRADING SYSTEMS

f* - share of capital,

$$-Trade_i$$

- profit or loss on that trade (with the opposite sign so that the loss becomes a positive number and the profit a negative number)

$$BiggestLoss$$

- largest loss per trade (this is always a negative number)

When the optimal f deviates by only insignificant values, the value of TWR changes sharply, and the trader's task is to find such f* so that TWR is maximum. TWR itself is maximized by searching f* from 0 to 1 with a step of 0.01.

This method is much closer to optimal position sizing in real life than the Kelly criterion. But at the same time, its main drawback is the impossibility of determining the optimal f during live trading, since it is based on past data. The optimal share for one trading period may be 25%, while for another period it may be 20%, and so on. A precise determination of the optimal share for the current situation remains impossible.

Martingale

Martingale is a capital management method used in stock trading that uses the principle of increasing position size when losing in order to compensate for losses. This can involve significant risks and is not recommended by many professional traders. The Martingale principle is to double the position size after each losing trade so that on the next profitable trade the trader can cover previous losses and even make a profit.

This method is based on the assumption that a winning trade will eventually occur and will offset all previous losses. However, it should be noted that Martingale does not take into account capital limits and can lead to significant losses if the market does not move in the desired direction and can create the risk of quickly losing all capital, especially with prolonged streaks of losing trades. For these reasons, most professional traders prefer more conservative capital management methods.

Consider an example where a trader sets an initial bet of 1% of their total capital, which is $10,000. If the first trade ends in a loss, the trader doubles their bet and risks 2% of their capital on the next position. In case of additional losing trades, the trader continues to double the bet size. When a trader closes a profitable trade, they return to the initial rate of 1% of capital.

These are examples of positions:

- In the first position, the trader uses 1% of $10,000 ($100). The position is closed at a loss.

- In the second position, the trader uses 2% of $10,000 ($200). The position is closed at a loss.

- In the third position, the trader uses 4% of $10,000 ($400). The position is closed at a loss.

- In the fourth position, the trader uses 8% of $10,000 ($800). The position is closed with a profit.

In this example, even after three losing positions, a successful fourth position allows the trader to return to the initial level. However, it should be remembered that with a long series of unprofitable positions, you can simply destroy your capital. Therefore, to reduce risk, some traders use lower odds instead of doubling the bet. But personally, I still advise you never to use it.

Anti-Martingale

The key element for both Martingale and anti-Martingale is changing the bet size. In Martingale, the rate increases after a losing position, while in anti-Martingale it increases only after a profitable position and decreases after a losing one. The essence of anti-Martingale is also simple, as simple as one, two, three. If the first position in the series brought a profit, then the next position is opened in the same direction, but in double volume; if the position brought a loss, then we reduce the volume accordingly.

The price level at which a new position is opened is chosen by each trader himself, following their trading strategy. But it is not recommended to open more than three orders. As in Martingale, you can use a smaller coefficient to increase the position (for example, not 2 times, but 1.3 times) or completely change the progression from geometric to arithmetic (that is, for example, change the position by 20 percent).

Anti-martingale is insidious in that if the forecast is unsuccessful, the profit on the first orders is very quickly covered by the loss on the last, most voluminous order. This can happen when a trader is mistaken in believing that they have caught a trend.

Fixed Proportional Position Sizing

Economist Ryan Jones proposed fixed proportional position sizing as a capital management technique. This strategy was developed to effectively balance risk control and profit maximization. The fixed proportional method is a kind of variation of the anti-Martingale strategy.

The concept of this method is that in the initial stages of trading, profits may be small, but at the same time, more stable results are provided over time. As the deposit increases, the profit margin also increases, which reduces overall risk. The main idea of the method is to determine a certain level, upon reaching which the trader can increase the traded volume by a certain number of lots.

Jones proposed using the concept of "delta" to define a fixed value, a certain proportion, upon reaching which a trader can increase the working size of a position. When the delta is reached, the traded lot size increases, and when losses exceed the specified delta, the lot size decreases. The Jones method allows you to simultaneously control both

CHAPTER 2 INTRODUCTION TO DEVELOPING TRADING SYSTEMS

risks and profitability. Delta is a variable value in the calculation and is determined according to the trader's trading method or style. The degree of aggressiveness of a trader's trading depends on its size; the smaller its size, the more aggressive capital management is.

The formula for determining levels is as follows:

$$Capital_{i-1} + (i * \delta) = Capital_i$$

where:

i: The level number (often coincides with the number of lots)
$Capital_i$: The next level capital
$Capital_{i-1}$: The previous level capital
δ: Delta

Let's imagine that the trader's initial capital is $5,000. They select a delta of $4,000 and trade one lot. Then to move to the next level, you need to solve this:

$$5000\$ + (1 * 4000\$) = 9000\$$$

Upon reaching this level, they will be able to trade two lots. This is the next level:

$$9000\$ + (2 * 4000\$) = 17000\$$$

At level 3, they will be able to trade three lots. And so on. As you can see, a trader can only influence the delta. It reflects the trading style: aggressive or less risky. There is also a situation when a trader begins to incur losses. In this case, to reduce the growth rate of losses and maintain the resulting profit, the reduction delta should be reduced (compared to the delta when the account grows). That is, the delta used to calculate the level of increased position size may exceed the delta required to reduce the position size in the event of a drawdown. For example, you can use a delta half as large as the growth delta or set it as a separate and independent reduction delta. Formulas for decline levels can be different and depend on the style of the trader. Figure 2-4 shows one way to reduce levels.

CHAPTER 2　INTRODUCTION TO DEVELOPING TRADING SYSTEMS

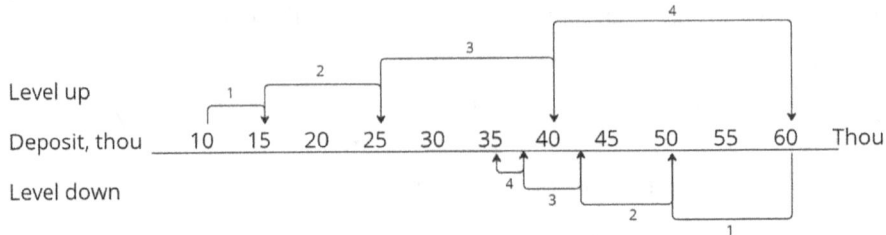

Figure 2-4. *Example of the process of changing levels*

For example, if the delta of decline is half the delta of growth, then the decrease in the traded lot during the period of drawdown will occur twice as fast as its growth during the period of rise. Then the formula for calculating the reduction level will look like this:

$$Capital_i - (Capital_i - Capital_{i-1} * 0.5) = Capital_{new}$$

where $Capital_{new}$ is the capital of a new level.

Let's imagine that a trader rose to level 8 and their account became equal to $150,000, the previous level was equal to $115,000, and they initially chose a delta equal to $5,000. The reduction level will be equal to the following:

$$150000\$ - ((150000\$ - 115000\$) * 0.5) = 132500\$$$

Like any method, the fixed proportional method has its pros and cons. One of the main advantages of this strategy is the possibility of geometric profit growth if all conditions are met. Reinvesting profits and increasing trading volume can significantly increase profitability using this method, especially due to the use of delta. The degree of aggressive or conservative trading is determined by the chosen delta, where a small delta leads to a faster increase in volume.

However, the disadvantage of the fixed-proportional method is the long recovery from drawdown periods. The decrease in trading volume occurs much faster than its increase. However, this circumstance allows you to save profits received during periods of successful trading series.

In addition, even such an aspect as choosing the optimal delta can take a long time. However, by thoroughly testing your strategy using the fixed proportional method, a trader will be able to optimally adjust all the variables to suit their needs.

Risk Control

Risk control in trading is a system that gives the trader control over possible losses. Simply put, this is a set of actions and calculations aimed at one goal: preventing the loss of a deposit and preserving profits as much as possible. Effective risk management in stock trading allows you to wait out difficult periods associated with unprofitable transactions. Each successfully passed period of losses without significant losses of the deposit indicates how effectively the trader manages risks. In this regard, capital management and risk control go hand in hand; they are closely intertwined, and often one means the other. This is easy to explain, since position size management plays a key role in risk control. By managing risks, a trader decides how many times they can close a position in the red and how much they can lose. That is, they strive to save money first and only then think about profitability.

Perhaps the main rule of risk control is to recognize that there are no 100% results and there will always be unprofitable trades. And its root is the permissible drawdown. Thus, deliberately reducing the average loss, for example reducing it by $100 per trade, has the same positive effect on the account as increasing the average profit by $100. That is, risk control directly affects the trader's final profit.

There are several main approaches to risk control:

- Maximum loss amount
- Stop loss orders
- Take profit orders

CHAPTER 2   INTRODUCTION TO DEVELOPING TRADING SYSTEMS

- Trailing stop orders
- Portfolio diversification
- Monitoring market volatility

Maximum Loss Amount

To effectively manage losses during trading operations, it is critical to first determine the maximum percentage of risk that a trader is willing to bear for each individual position. As mentioned earlier, good capital management helps with this. An equally significant factor here is the limitation on the number of simultaneously open positions. For example, given that the established risk per position can be, for example, 0.3%, and the maximum risk per deposit is 6%, the number of simultaneously open trading transactions cannot exceed 20. This is a simple but effective method that is suitable even for a beginner.

Risk control for a certain time period (for example, a day, a week, or a month), which also includes a certain strategy for exiting a drawdown, is similar in nature. So, if a trader is faced with a series of unprofitable positions over the period under review, it is advisable for him to take a break. This makes it possible to limit losses and reassess the situation. For example, if the maximum loss for a day has been reached, it is recommended to end trading for the current day and resume it the next. The same applies to weekly and monthly limits, allowing you to effectively manage risks across different time frames.

Let's look at an example. The trader has $10,000 on deposit. If they have an acceptable daily drawdown of $200, then the entire deposit will be lost after 50 trading days with losses. If the allowable daily loss is $100, then the trader will be able to survive 100 days with unprofitable transactions. With a maximum drawdown of $50, these periods increase to 200 days, with $25—up to 400 days.

CHAPTER 2   INTRODUCTION TO DEVELOPING TRADING SYSTEMS

Stop Loss Orders

A stop loss is a type of order that allows a trader to determine the highest level of potential loss while trading a single position. In practice, this means that when the price reaches the level at which the stop loss is set, this order is closed at a loss. Setting a stop loss order allows the trader to determine in advance the maximum amount of possible losses for a specific position, and this determination is made at the stage of opening the position. Pre-set stop orders are an effective tool for controlling risk and minimizing losses in rapidly changing markets.

Applying a strict stop loss rule, such as exiting a position if it loses 3% to 10%, is a common practice. But in turn, I will immediately make it clear that not everyone uses stop losses. My personal observations and analysis showed that for many strategies the use of stop losses was inappropriate. But if you use a stop loss as part of your strategy, it is important to honor the obligation to exit a position if the market does not move as expected.

Depending on whether the trader has opened a buy or sell order, the stop loss will be placed differently (see Figure 2-5).

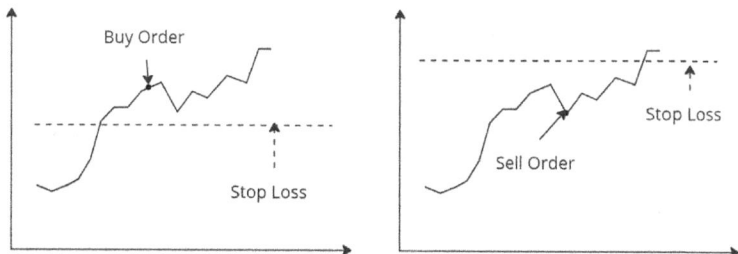

Figure 2-5. Examples of stop-loss levels

Some traders prefer to use several types of stop signals for more flexible position management.

The main types of brake lights include the following:

- **Initial stop.** This signal is related to the position's entry level and can be expressed as a percentage or a fixed amount.
- **Trailing stop.** This stop signal follows the price movement in the direction desired by the trader, changing as profits increase.
- **Take profit.** This stop signal causes the position to be closed when a predetermined profit amount is reached.
- **Breakeven.** This means moving the stop loss to the price where the breakeven level is. Often traders set this stop loss in an arbitrary place, which is fundamentally wrong. All movements must be carefully considered and should not be taken at random.
- **Timed stop signs.** In case market behavior does not meet expectations, some professionals recommend exiting the position even if there is no financial loss. Timed stop signals remind you to exit the market if it is unclear what is actually happening.

In conclusion, setting initial stop losses is a special form of trading art. The ability to recognize false or true breakouts of resistance and support levels plays a key role in this skill.

Take Profit Orders

Take profit, as a type of stop loss, is a preset price level, upon reaching which the trader automatically closes their position with a certain profitable result. That is, the specified take profit level always exceeds the current market price (if the trader has placed a Buy Order) of the asset, and if the market price rises to a predetermined value, the broker automatically places a limit order to sell (see Figure 2-6).

CHAPTER 2 INTRODUCTION TO DEVELOPING TRADING SYSTEMS

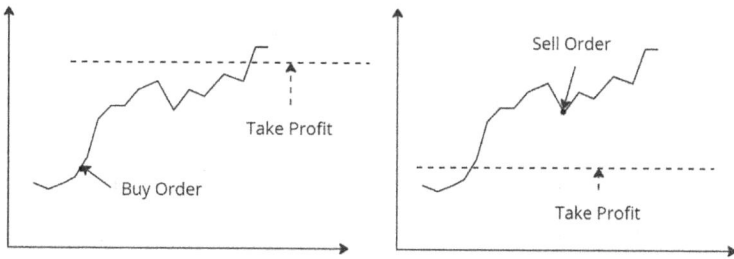

Figure 2-6. *Examples of take profit levels*

Many traders determine the take profit level based on key resistance and support levels. Another approach is to use Elliott wave theory, which suggests that markets move in cycles consisting of waves of different orders. Additionally, many traders prefer a customized approach to determining profit levels based on their own comfort level with risk management.

Trailing Stop Orders

A trailing stop is a dynamic order that is used in trading to automatically update the stop loss level in accordance with changes in market prices. This mechanism is similar to a regular stop loss but differs in that it is not set at a fixed price. Instead, it continuously monitors the current price of the asset and automatically changes the stop loss level when the price changes in a direction favorable to the trader; it also works like a regular stop loss if the price changes in an unfavorable direction.

Let's look at an example. If a trader opens a position at a price of $50 (Buy Order) and sets Take-Profit (TP) at $55 and Stop-Loss (SL) at $45, then TP and SL will be automatically activated only when the levels are reached at $55 or $45, respectively. By setting limit orders at $55 and $45, the trader formally agrees to a maximum potential profit and acceptable loss of 10%. If a trader entered a trade at $50 with a target of $55 and the

CHAPTER 2   INTRODUCTION TO DEVELOPING TRADING SYSTEMS

price moves up to $60, they do not receive the full profit from the move up. Or you can imagine the opposite situation, when the price reached $54 and instead of taking a profit, the trader decided to wait for the upward movement to continue, but as luck would have it, the price went down and dropped below $45. It's also sad. It turns out that instead of a realistically achievable profit of several percentage points, the trader received a 10% loss. Figure 2-7 illustrates these situations.

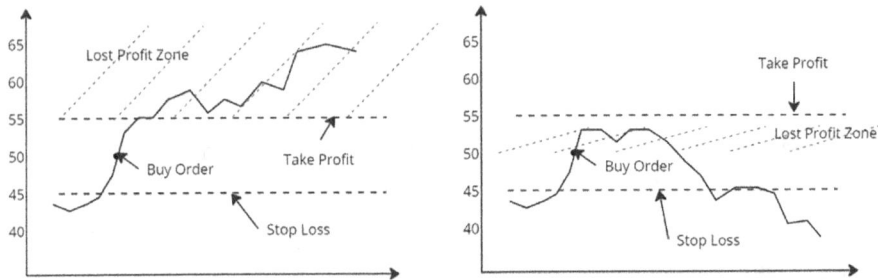

Figure 2-7. *Examples of profit losses without trailing stop order*

To avoid such scenarios, you can set Take-Profit higher or not use it at all. However, in this case, the trader will have to constantly monitor the market and close manually. At the same time, Stop-Loss will remain at $45.

A trailing stop order prevents such situations. So in the previous example, a trailing stop would automatically raise the stop loss level when the market rises. For example, if we set the trailing stop to maintain the stop order at a distance of $5 from the current price, when the price rises, it will move it according to the upward movement of the price. For example, if the price increases from $50 to $52.5, the stop loss moves from $45 to $47.5. If the price further rises from $52.5 to $62.5, the stop loss rises from $47.5 to $57.5. Trailing stop can be considered as a certain safe level, or as periodic profit taking. At the same time, the trailing stop does not decrease if the price goes down. The Variable Stop Loss value is attached to the last mark and remains there until the price reaches its level. Figure 2-8 shows one example of how a trailing stop works.

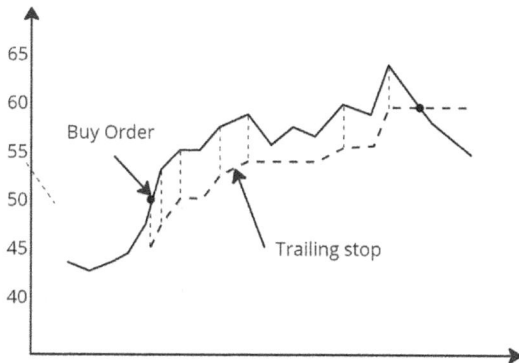

Figure 2-8. *Changing the trailing stop level*

This is certainly an incredibly useful tool for a trader. Only outwardly it seems difficult, but after trying it several times, you will definitely like it. Plus, I have been convinced more than once that if you use it on some strategies, their effectiveness noticeably increases.

Portfolio Diversification

Diversification of an investment portfolio is a method of reducing risks and ensuring stable income. It consists of distributing funds between different types of exchange instruments, such as stocks, bonds, precious metals, currencies, and others. This strategy helps protect against losses in the event of a decrease in the profitability of one of the assets, while compensating for the losses of unsuccessful investments through profits from others. However, it is important to note that simply buying shares of different companies does not always count as diversification. For example, owning shares in several oil companies will not create a diversified portfolio because all of these companies belong to the same industry, even though they may be located in different countries. If oil prices fall, the profitability of all these assets may decline.

CHAPTER 2 INTRODUCTION TO DEVELOPING TRADING SYSTEMS

Therefore, let's look at diversification methods that actually work:

- **Division by asset class.** Thus, bonds are considered the most predictable and stable instruments, including corporate and government securities. But investing in stocks, although they are riskier, can bring good profits when prices rise. Savvy investors also consider futures and options, although these instruments tend to be more unpredictable.

- **Sector division.** Each sector of the economy undergoes its own unique development path, and even during periods of crisis, when some of them experience decline, others continue to demonstrate steady growth. Therefore, it is important that the investment portfolio is diverse and includes various sectors, such as the oil and gas industry, aviation manufacturing, pharmaceuticals, information technology, and others.

- **Separation by countries and currencies.** Spreading your investments across different currencies provides protection against sharp exchange rate fluctuations. And investing in assets from different countries helps avoid exposure to political and economic problems in one of the unstable countries, since losses can be offset by securities of other countries. Experts advise limiting the share of investments in one asset to 10% of capital and not exceeding a total of 20% for assets belonging to one sector of the economy.

- **Correlation.** This shows to what extent the dynamics of the value of one financial instrument correlates with the dynamics of another. To ensure effective diversification, it is important to include instruments with low or inverse correlations in your portfolio. That is, the less the financial instruments are correlated, the more profitable the portfolio. This means that changes in the prices of one asset will be offset by changes in the prices of other assets. In this way, the risk of the investment is spread across different assets, which helps reduce the overall risk level of the portfolio.

Monitoring Market Volatility

The risk of positions can also be assessed by analyzing the volatility of a financial instrument. You can estimate this volatility using the standard deviation. If the standard deviation of an instrument is high, it indicates high risk and uncertain returns. A low standard deviation, on the contrary, implies less volatility and stability of returns. This indicator is especially useful when comparing different instruments.

The formula for calculating the standard deviation can be calculated as follows:

$$StandardDeviation = \sqrt{\sum_{i=1}^{N} \frac{(Price_j - MA(N,j))^2}{N}}$$

$Price_j$: Price value on the j-th candle
$MA(N,j)$: Moving average value on the j-th candle
N: Sample size

Let's look at an example. The trader plans to invest each month in one of two funds. Both funds have an average return of 10%. The first fund has a standard deviation of 5, which means its return can vary from 5% to 15%. A second fund with a deviation of 12 could have a return of -2% to 22%. If a trader prefers to avoid excess volatility and reduce their risks, they are better off choosing the first fund, as it offers the same returns with less volatility.

CHAPTER 2   INTRODUCTION TO DEVELOPING TRADING SYSTEMS

Testing

Testing the chosen trading strategy on historical data allows you to evaluate its effectiveness without the risk of real financial investments. This practice is based on the assumption that a strategy that has been successful in the past has a high probability of being effective in the present. And receiving positive results during such testing strengthens the trader's confidence in the prospects of their chosen approach. Negative test results may require changes to parameters or a review of strategy.

One of the challenges associated with backtesting is the possibility of creating a strategy that looks successful on historical data but fails in real trading. For example, often when adjusting a profitability graph obtained during testing or over-optimization, it is possible to create a system that would demonstrate success in tests for a certain historical period, but retesting over a long period would show its uselessness. Therefore, it is important to follow certain rules and not use results adjustment.

For example, the choice of testing period is extremely important. The testing period depends on the time scale of the chart on which the moment of entering the market is determined. There are general recommendations in this matter. For example, when planning to trade on the daily chart, it is recommended to backtest at least the last five years. If you select a shorter time scale, such as less than a day, it is recommended to test for at least one year to account for seasonality. These recommendations are based on statistical requirements for a minimum amount of data. It is important that testing covers not only periods of strong economic growth but also the latest crisis or recession. The longer the period of testing, the more reliable the results obtained will be. This is important because during the economic recovery phase, almost any trend trading strategy brings a good profit, while during a recession or crisis the situation may be different.

You also need to distinguish between different testing approaches. Thus, it is possible to use a complex multistep testing algorithm, starting from preliminary testing, when the trader conducts a quick check without

CHAPTER 2   INTRODUCTION TO DEVELOPING TRADING SYSTEMS

spending a lot of time on tests, and ending with forward and multicurrency multiperiod testing, or you can limit yourself to just classic backtesting.

Classic backtesting involves testing a strategy against historical data, while forward testing gives a more realistic idea of how the strategy will perform in reality, since it uses data that the strategy has never seen before. Multicurrency multiperiod testing, as you might guess from the name, includes testing on different financial instruments and different historical periods, which allows you to assess the stability of the system. The choice of testing stages, as always, depends on the trader and their desires.

Performance Indicators

Of course, after testing, the obtained performance indicators should be adequately assessed. For this, it is important for the trader to determine what results and assessments can be considered acceptable or desirable. It is often considered that the main goal is to achieve high returns, taking into account transaction costs. However, in this case, it would be reasonable to compare returns with other alternatives, such as placing funds on a bank deposit with lower risks and similar returns.

This leads to the first criterion of effectiveness: comparing the profitability of the strategy with the profitability of a bank deposit. After all, taking into account all the risks of exchange trading, active trading makes sense only with significantly higher profitability.

The second criterion is comparison with a long-term buy-and-hold strategy. This strategy involves an investor purchasing financial instruments and not selling them for a long period of time. The investment horizon ranges from several years to several decades. With this approach, it is also important to evaluate the return and risk of active trading with the return and risk of a buy-and-hold strategy.

Thus, the effectiveness of the strategy is assessed not only by the profitability achieved in testing and real trading but also by the return to risk ratio, especially in comparison with alternative long-term strategies.

Creating a strategy that improves this ratio is the designer's task to provide more beneficial results relative to alternative approaches.

The previous two criteria are mandatory to understand, so I highlighted them separately from the rest. They are basic; without them, it is impossible to understand the real picture of your system. But besides them, the effectiveness of any trading strategy can be assessed by more than 50 other parameters. Let's look at some of the key ones.

Profitability is a percentage return that reflects how much capital is earned in a trading account over a given period. For example, if you had $10,000 at the beginning of the year, and by the end of the year the amount grew to $20,000, then the profitability for the year will be 100% (in the absence of additional infusions or withdrawals of funds). The best calculation method is to calculate profitability over a long period of time and based on a large number of positions. Since earnings of 10% for one position or week are not of much importance if the trader loses 30% in a month, profitability for the year is more significant than the profitability for the month.

The **profit factor** is calculated as the ratio of absolute income to absolute loss (without taking into account the minus sign). If your system's profit factor is greater than 1, this indicates its ability to generate profit. However, simply having a profit factor > 1 is not enough. It is important to understand the internal mechanism of the system. Perhaps only one position made a significant contribution to the overall income, while most of the time the system was in the red. A profit factor with a value > 6 is more indicative.

A **drawdown** is a temporary decrease in the available funds in a trading account caused by the opening of a losing position. Simply put, this is a trader's loss, which is shown on the chart as a falling yield line and is most often expressed as a percentage.

CHAPTER 2 INTRODUCTION TO DEVELOPING TRADING SYSTEMS

The following types of drawdowns exist (see Figure 2-9):

- **Current drawdown.** This type of drawdown occurs when opening any trading position. When a position is opened, it always starts with a loss equal to the commission established by the brokerage company. Brokers typically make money from the difference between the bid and ask prices they provide on trading platforms. These prices are usually disadvantageous for the trader but are always profitable for the brokers themselves. Therefore, until the position overcomes the distance corresponding to the size of the commission, it will be in a state of drawdown.

- **Recorded drawdown.** This drawdown represents the trader's closed position, which turned out to be unprofitable at the time the decision was made to close the position. This recorded, or, as it is also called, actual drawdown, negatively affects the total volume of the deposit, since it reduces it by the percentage of the loss resulting from the completion of this position.

- **Maximum drawdown.** This represents the maximum reduction of your deposit. Simply put, this drawdown shows the maximum loss you have incurred in monetary terms.

- **Absolute drawdown.** This drawdown can be equal to zero if the trader immediately began to make a profit from the first positions. This indicator is defined as the difference between the initial capital and its minimum reduction.

CHAPTER 2　INTRODUCTION TO DEVELOPING TRADING SYSTEMS

- **Relative drawdown.** This drawdown represents the maximum loss in percentage terms. The determination method is similar to the maximum drawdown, except that the most significant percentage is considered, not the absolute monetary value.

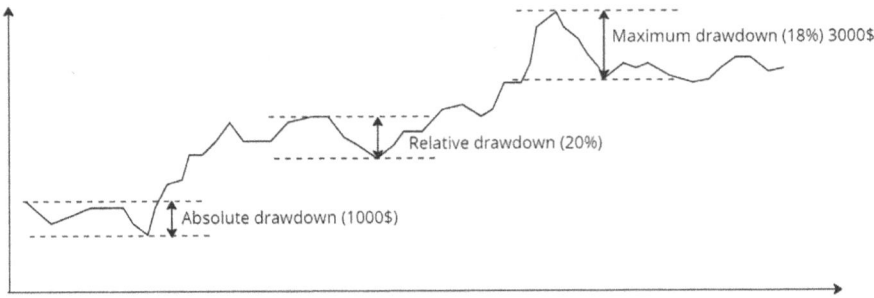

Figure 2-9. Types of drawdowns

Sharpe ratio is a characteristic of income per unit of risk. The higher the Sharpe ratio, the better the return/risk ratio.

Here's the formula for calculation:

$$Sharpe\,Ratio = \frac{R_p - R_f}{\sigma_p}$$

R_p: The profitability

R_f: The risk-free profitability rate

σ_p: The standard deviation of profitability

This indicator shows how much profit an investor receives for each unit of risk. The higher the value, the more favorable the return in relation to risk is considered. A high Sharpe ratio greater than 1 is generally assessed as "positive," indicating that the portfolio's return exceeds its volatility and therefore suggesting excess return relative to the level of risk.

For the **average winning trade size and average losing trade size**, sum up the results of all profitable positions for a certain period, and then divide this sum by the total number of profitable positions. The resulting value represents the average size of a profitable position. Also add up the results of all losing positions for the same period and divide this sum by the total number of losing positions. This way you will determine the average size of a losing position.

Although most traders strive for the average size of winning positions to be greater than the average size of losing positions, this is not a prerequisite for a successful strategy. But if the average size of positive positions is still greater than the average size of negative positions, trading can remain profitable even with a low ratio of profitable to unprofitable positions. If the average loss exceeds the average profit, a higher ratio of winning to losing positions is required to ensure a profitable trading system.

Expected value is a composite metric that combines the two previously mentioned parameters and provides information on how much a trader can expect to earn on each trade. The formula for calculating the mathematical expectation is as follows:

$$EM = (Prob.Win * AvgWin) - (Prob.Loss * AvgLoss)$$

Prob.Win: The percentage of profitable positions
AvgWin: The average winnings
Prob.Win: The percentage of losing positions
AvgWin: The average loss

Essentially, the expected value provides information about the average dollar amount of profit or loss that can be expected over a long-term time horizon.

Optimization

Optimization is the process of tuning the original trading system by adjusting its parameters or group of parameters. This process consists of considering all variations of parameter values within specified boundaries on a time range of historical data for a specific financial instrument. It

CHAPTER 2   INTRODUCTION TO DEVELOPING TRADING SYSTEMS

follows that the main goal of optimization is to determine the optimal parameters of the system for a given time period and take into account the characteristics of a particular financial instrument. And since the trading algorithm mainly determines the opening and closing points of trading positions, changes in the rules for entering and exiting a position entail changes in the overall efficiency of the trading system. Also, the effectiveness of the algorithm may change as market conditions change. This highlights the importance of optimizing a trading system to achieve better results in the current market condition or in the limited future.

The optimization results are evaluated by the values of system performance indicators for each set of optimized parameters. In other words, each set of parameters is tested on a specific period of historical data, and the test results provide information about what results were achieved under these different sets.

Optimization may include various procedures, such as choosing the optimal time frame, choosing optimal stop order values, choosing brokerage trading conditions, choosing the trading algorithm itself, adding confirmation filters, or finding optimal parameter values for an existing system. The choice is certainly great and is limited only by the trader's capabilities.

To optimize a trading strategy, the following sequence of steps is proposed:

- Fully describing the strategy. First, describe the entry and exit conditions, a list of financial instruments, time frames, etc. Also take into account the characteristics of the selected asset, the size of the spread, the possible lot sizes, the volatility, and other trading conditions.

- Preliminary testing of the system for performance to identify possible errors or shortcomings in the description of the trading algorithm.

CHAPTER 2   INTRODUCTION TO DEVELOPING TRADING SYSTEMS

- Selecting a source and period of historical data for testing. This can be a unique period for each period.

- Testing the strategy on a selected interval of historical data.

- Preparing the system for optimization, including identifying parameters to be optimized.

- Determining the boundaries of parameter values for optimization, excluding absurd options.

- Determining performance indicators in the optimization stage. Optimization occurs using some optimization algorithms, such as grid search, random search, genetic algorithms, and simulated annealing. These algorithms systematically work across parameter ranges and evaluate the strategy's performance for each combination.

- Selecting the most acceptable parameter values and, if necessary, retesting the system with narrowing the boundaries of the values n number of times.

After completing the optimization process, it is recommended to check the performance of the system under real market conditions.

It is worth mentioning that during the optimization process, various problems are possible that may arise at different stages of its implementation. Let's look at them in more detail.

- **Optimization time.** This is directly related to the number of parameters, the ranges of their possible values, and the volume of historical data. To reduce optimization time, it is recommended to divide it into several stages. In the first stage, all parameters are selected within wide reasonable limits with a large search step. Then, after rough selection, in the second stage the search boundaries are narrowed around the obtained values, and the step is reduced. This approach allows you to find more accurate settings.

- **Inadequate results.** These often arise due to the lack of clear restrictions on parameter combinations. Defining commonsense, well-defined constraints on possible parameter combinations helps avoid absurd results.

- **Errors in historical data.** Quotation errors cannot be completely avoided, and their presence should be taken into account when evaluating system performance.

- **Human factor.** This includes a wide range of possible problems associated with the presence of emotions and irrational assessments of the system. Consideration of the human factor includes constant awareness of the emotional influence on decision-making and the desire for a more objective assessment of the performance of the trading system.

Yet, how can a trader determine whether a trading strategy is optimal? As already noted, the optimization process comes down to systematically changing the values of the parameters of the trading algorithm within a given range to improve the efficiency of the system. For each unique set of parameters, the trading system is tested on a specific financial instrument, time frame, and time interval of historical data. The results of such testing are expressed in the values of certain system performance indicators, some of which we have already reviewed. Based on these values, an optimal set of parameters is selected, which is considered the best for further use.

It turns out that the efficiency of the system when used in real conditions and the efficiency obtained after optimization will depend on the efficiency indicators chosen by the trader or their combination. The goal of proper optimization and analysis is to minimize this difference.

Summary

In this chapter, we looked at the basic concepts of exchange trading, how the process of order execution occurs, and what types of orders there are. We also looked at approaches to developing a trading strategy, the main ones being technical and fundamental analysis. In addition, we examined how the process of generating trading signals takes place based on the formulated trading rules.

We studied the basic methods of capital management and risk control. We learned a little about the process of testing and optimizing a trading strategy.

In the next chapter, we'll dive right into my approach to creating an automated trading system. We'll start with the architectural solution.

CHAPTER 3

Architectural Solution Part 1: Identifying the Requirements

In the previous chapter, we discussed the general theory of creating trading systems and talked about the modules that are present in such systems and their functionality. In this chapter, we will put this knowledge into practice and build our product. We will draw up a high-level plan of the system, describe the subsystems and their services, and also determine how those parts will interact with each other.

In most cases, creating the architecture of our application consists of the following steps:

1. **Identifying the requirements**

    At this stage, we must understand what the system should be able to do. What behavior do we expect from our system? What technical expectations and limitations do we have of it? This step lays the foundation of our application. The first diagram is drawn. We understand how many users will interact with our system and how they will do it. The result of this stage should be a list of technical tasks.

2. **Making architectural decisions**

    At this stage, we decide how the assigned tasks will be solved. For example, will we use a queue or create some kind of service? What architectural patterns and templates will we use to solve the problem? Here we can superficially discuss whether we will use databases and how our services will interact with each other. The result of this stage is a list of architectural solutions for each of the assigned tasks.

3. **Identifying subsystems**

    At this stage, we determine the list of subsystems of our future system. We briefly define its input and output. The result of this stage should be a list of the subsystems of our future system with a description of the functionality for which it is responsible.

4. **Identifying the services of all the subsystems**

    At this stage, we must clearly understand the composition of services. How will they scale? Will they have their own databases? What will the API of each service look like? How will caching be carried out? Let's discuss what kind of applications will be built on the basis of these services. How will our services scale and make decisions to optimize performance? The result of this stage will be a service diagram for each subsystem.

This sequence of actions is conditional and may include other steps. It is also worth keeping in mind that the process of building an architectural solution is iterative. It often happens that even when describing a service, the architect understands that their higher-level solution is not optimal and has to go back and redo the overall solution scheme. Sometimes these shortcomings become visible after the prototyping stage, when a prototype of the future system or its individual components is quickly created to more accurately determine the weaknesses of the architectural solution and check with the customer's expectations. It is much more unpleasant if the shortcomings of an architectural solution are revealed at the development stage, when the cost of an error increases significantly. Therefore, creating an architectural solution is one of the key stages in the development of any system.

After thoroughly going through all the stages of building an architectural solution, we will create a comprehensive diagram of our future application. In this chapter, I will show how a general vision of the system is created and describe the processes that will occur. Of course, for this it is necessary to identify the requirements.

Requirements Elicitation

This is the first and perhaps most important stage of creating a system. After all, a mistake in identifying requirements has a high cost. Therefore, it is important to determine them as accurately as possible. At this stage, we must not only identify the requirements for the functionality of our application but also decide on specific numbers. For example, we need to understand how many users will work with the application. How many strategies can the system support?

Let's first define general concepts and make a list of entities that will be used in our system. Entities are the main objects or concepts that the system operates on to achieve its goals. They have their own set of properties that we will manipulate.

CHAPTER 3   ARCHITECTURAL SOLUTION PART 1: IDENTIFYING THE REQUIREMENTS

Signals

Here I will show an example conversation between a customer and a system architect to help you understand this process as best as possible. For the sake of brevity, this conversation has been simplified.

> Architect: Why do you need a system? What purpose does it serve?
>
> Customer: To make money. As much money as possible.
>
> Architect: How will it make money?
>
> Customer: It will generate profitable strategies and use them in real trading. The more strategies and the better they are, the more money your program will bring me.
>
> Architect: What does it mean to "generate strategies"? How do you see the result of this generation?
>
> Customer: Well, it must create new conditions based on indicators, and the trading system, based on these conditions, will understand when it is time to enter a position and when it is time to exit it.
>
> Architect: How many new terms are there? Here we have a strategy, position, indicators and some conditions. The concept of an indicator is familiar to me. Do I understand correctly that an indicator is a certain formula, for example a formula for calculating the width of the Bollinger band or a function or anything, for example, the percentage of special words in a ChatGPT response, in general, something that gives us a number?
>
> Customer: Yes, that's absolutely right.

At this stage, we have the first entity of our future system: an **Indicator** (Figure 3-1). The purpose of this entity is to calculate a certain number according to its unique logic, based on the current situation on the market, for example, the appearance of new candles, changes in the order book, or news feed.

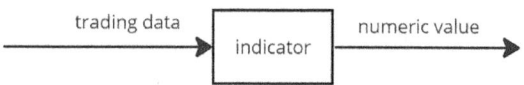

Figure 3-1. *Indicator entity*

> Architect: Fine. What do you mean by conditions? What is their purpose?
>
> Customer: This is a set of conditions taking indicators, processing their values, and giving a signal whether it's time to enter or exit a position or maybe neither.
>
> Architect: Do I understand correctly that, in fact, the purpose of a set of conditions is simply to return a yes or no value to us when passing trading data such as candles or the order book as input?
>
> Customer: Yes, that's right.
>
> Architect: Could this set of conditions be different for giving a signal to open and close a position?
>
> Customer: Yes, maybe.
>
> Architect: But in fact, are they the same thing? Are the parameters or formulas just different?
>
> Customer: Yes that's right.

> Architect: Do you mind if we call the set of these conditions "Signal" and continue to operate with this concept?
>
> Customer: Yes, I like it.

Here we have another entity: *Signal*. Its purpose is to give a yes/no answer in response to changes in trading data. To do this, the signal operates on indicator values. See Figure 3-2.

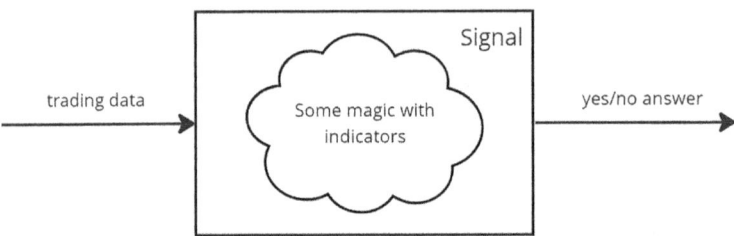

Figure 3-2. *Signal entity*

First View of the Process

The conversation continues:

> Architect: Great. Now let's turn our attention to our strategies. It turns out that a strategy is an entity that combines signals about opening and closing a position. That's all? How will the system understand how much money needs to be opened?
>
> Customer: Understanding position size is also part of the strategy. There are different methods of money management. One of the most primitive is to open a position for a certain percentage of the remaining capital; more advanced ones look at the historical or test indicators of the strategy and, based on them, decide on the size of the position.

CHAPTER 3   ARCHITECTURAL SOLUTION PART 1: IDENTIFYING THE REQUIREMENTS

> Architect: What about risk management? Will there be any protection in the case of unexpected market behavior?
>
> Customer: Undoubtedly! We must protect ourselves from sudden price drops and also be able to take profits. Here, too, there are simple methods and more complex ones. You can simply place a Stop Loss and Take Profit order, you can use a slightly smarter system and use trailing orders, or you can make a hybrid system with a trailing order, an additional signal, and even a limit on the number of open positions. But this does not change the essence. Yes, we need something that will monitor the current state of positions and close them in case of something unexpected or the need to take profits.

At this stage, we have one of the central entities of our system: a **strategy**. By strategy we understand that an entity combines the following:

- Signal to open a position
- Signal to close a position
- Capital management method
- Risk control method

The purpose of the strategy is to give a signal to open or close a position with the size of that position. The strategy also manages risks, namely, placing an order.

> Architect: What about indicator parameters? For example, Bollinger Bands Width (BBW) has several parameters, and one of them is the number of standard deviations. Are these parameters included in the strategy? Anything else?

Customer: Yes, the specific values of these parameters are part of the strategy. Also, please keep in mind that some theories use indicator values not only of the last candles, but also of the previous ones. For example, this is a simple condition: the closing prices of the last three candles must be greater than their opening prices.

Architect: I understood about the use of indicator values not only of the last candles. But what about the theory? What is it, and how does it differ from strategy? Better yet, tell us the process of your manual search for a strategy.

Customer: First, I come up with or read a theory on forums or from other sources. A theory is an idea for a future strategy. It does not contain specific parameter values for indicators. The theory is a description of the conditions of the signals, that is, the logic by which the signals will process the indicator values.

For example:

We open a position when the closing price crosses the WMA from bottom to top. We close when the closing price crosses the WMA from top to bottom. This strategy will work only if there is a strong trend, which we will check using the ADX indicator; that is, it must be greater than a certain value.

We open a position when the closing price breaks the upper Bolinger band and trading volumes increase. Exit a position at Stop Loss or Take Profit.

Next I test my theory. I take several variations of indicator parameter values, choose a capital management method, and test these strategies on historical data. If I understand that there is something in this theory, then I look for the most stable and profitable strategy for my instrument based on it. And after that I start trading on it.

Here we have a new entity: **Theory**. It consists of signals for opening and closing a position without indicator parameters, and it is on its basis that strategies are generated. The strategy includes data from the theory and specific values of the parameters that are necessary for the functioning of its components. See Figure 3-3.

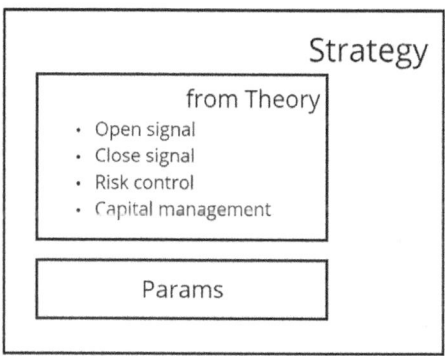

Figure 3-3. *Strategy entity*

Now it becomes clear what the whole process will look like:

1. The user creates theories in the system using a generator or independently.

2. Based on some algorithm, the performance of the theory is checked.

CHAPTER 3   ARCHITECTURAL SOLUTION PART 1: IDENTIFYING THE REQUIREMENTS

3. If, according to some criteria, the system understands that the theory is workable, then the process of searching for the optimal strategy begins.

4. If a strategy is found that meets the user's criteria, then it begins to participate in real trading. See Figure 3-4.

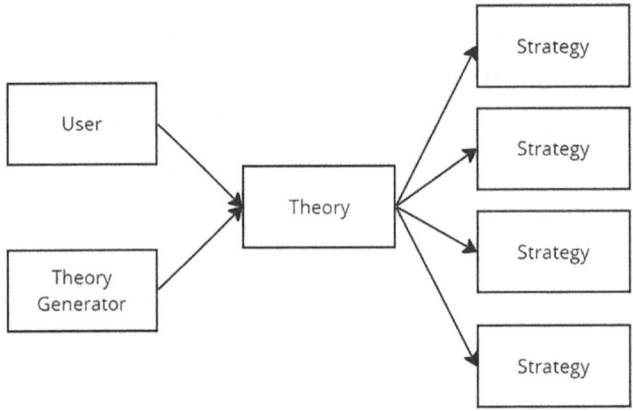

Figure 3-4. *First view of the process*

Theory Generator

We have identified the main stages of the strategy life cycle, from the moment of theory generation to the moment of using the strategy in real trading. Now let's look deeper and think about how each of these stages will work. The result of our discussions should be a complete understanding of the functionality of our system, as well as a list of tasks that need to be solved.

Let's start with generating theories.

First, theories can be created in two modes by the user: manually or using a generator.

CHAPTER 3   ARCHITECTURAL SOLUTION PART 1: IDENTIFYING THE REQUIREMENTS

Here we have two requirements for the system:

- It should provide the user with a tool for creating theories.

- It must implement a mechanism for generating theories.

If everything is clear with the first requirement, we implement it using a special form on the front end, and we understand that a user can create dozens of theories manually. Then, with the requirement about the theory generation mechanism, we need to work and understand how this process occurs and what data it requires.

Obviously, to generate a theory, we need to generate signals. To understand how to do this, we need to delve deeper into this concept. So, we know that the signal includes a set of indicators and, receiving trading data as input, returns a yes/no response using them. But how does this magic of working with indicators happen?

Basically, the signals look like this:

If

> Indicator_1 > Indicator_2

AND

> Indicator_3 < Indicator_4 on the last three candles

we should buy.

For example, here's the theory: the entry signal will be carried out by crossing the regression line (LRC) of the weighted moving average (WMA) from bottom to top and, accordingly, to the exit when LRC crosses the WMA from top to bottom. RSI is used as a confirmation factor for the transaction. That is, when we receive a crossover signal, we look to see if this candle or several previous ones have a corresponding RSI value. For example, if there is a buy signal, then the RSI value should be less than 30, and a sell signal should be greater than 70. We will also add an additional

CHAPTER 3   ARCHITECTURAL SOLUTION PART 1: IDENTIFYING THE REQUIREMENTS

condition to the input for the width of the Bollinger Band (BBW). If this becomes more than 0.04, then check the value of the ADX indicator; it should be more than 30.

In my presentation, this theory looks like this:

Signal to open a position:

> **AND** group:
>
> LRC > WMA on the current candle
>
> RSI < Const on the previous three candles
>
> BBW > Const on the current candle
>
> BBW on the previous candle < Const
>
> ADX > Const

Signal to close a position:

> **AND** group:
>
> LRC < WMA on the current candle
>
> RSI > Const on the previous three candles

Here we have the concept of **condition** and **condition group**. The condition contains left and right indicators and a comparison condition. *Time intervals*, candle intervals at which it is necessary to check the condition, become additional parameters in the strategy along with indicator parameters. The result of a condition being met is a yes/no response, but often we need to group these conditions.

For example, the following:

> Condition_1 AND (Condition_2 OR Condition_3)

can be expressed using groups like this:

> Group_1 = Condition_2 OR Condition_3
>
> Group_2 = Condition_1 AND Group_1

As a result, the root group of the signal will be Group_2. This is what will give us the long-awaited yes/no answer. See Figure 3-5.

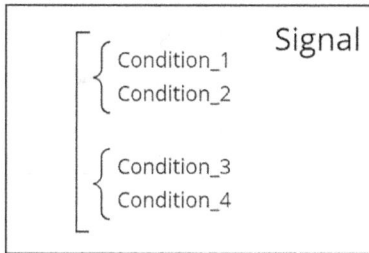

Figure 3-5. *Conditions*

Let's return to the theory generator. Somehow it must generate signals. From the logic of signal construction, it is clear that the number of combinations of conditions and their groupings can be infinite. This means we need to somehow limit this amount. I propose to do this by using signal templates, which will initially have condition layouts with groups, and the generator, substituting indicators in them, will create new signals.

It is worth noting here that this is not the only possible approach to creating signals. Conditions can also be created programmatically using the brute-force method with restrictions on possible options, for example, with a limit on the depth of nesting of groups and a number of conditions in each of them. Or you can use an optimization algorithm rather than a brute-force method, which will speed up the process of finding a profitable strategy.

Now imagine the beginning of the process of setting up the theory generator. The user first creates signal templates and then selects indicators. The generator, using the selected signal templates and substituting different combinations of indicators into them, will generate new signals.

At this stage, I will remind you what the theory consists of. These are signals for opening and closing a position, a capital management method, and a risk control method. We have closed the question of how signals will be generated, so now let's think about what to do with capital and risk management methods. In fact, there is nothing to invent here. We have a list of these methods, which is not large, so the user can simply specify a list of these methods when setting up the generator, and the generator will create theories where it will try each of them.

Strategies Searching

Theories are generated or created manually by the user. But one of the key requirements for our system is the search for profitable strategies and not the generation of theories. But how to look for them? And what does "searching for profitable strategies" even mean? The search process includes two important concepts: the search method and the criterion by which we understand that the search process is completed. We have a theory. We need to understand how to search for profitable strategies based on it and how we will carry out this search.

One-Step Approach

Let's start with the parameters that distinguish theory from strategy. They include indicator parameters and condition parameters, such as the depth of the candles at which the check takes place and time intervals. This means that to find a profitable strategy, we need to generate strategies by varying these parameters.

First, you need to understand that these parameters are limited. The depth of candles must clearly be greater than 0; for example, perhaps it cannot be greater than 50 and must always be an integer. And time intervals are generally limited to a finite list of values: 1 minute, 2 minutes, 3 minutes, 5 minutes, 10 minutes, 15 minutes, 30 minutes, 1 hour, 4 hours,

CHAPTER 3   ARCHITECTURAL SOLUTION PART 1: IDENTIFYING THE REQUIREMENTS

1 day, 1 week, 1 month, and 1 year. These restrictions greatly simplify our task, but there can be many parameters, and therefore there can be many possible variations of strategies.

For example, let's collect all the parameters and restrictions for the strategy we looked at earlier. For convenience, I have indexed the conditions and groups to make it easier to navigate their parameters.

Here's a signal to open a position:

GROUP_1	**AND** group:
CONDITION_1	LRC > WMA on the current candle
CONDITION_2	RSI < Const on the previous three candles
CONDITION_3	BBW > Const on the current candle
CONDITION_4	BBW on the previous candle < Const
CONDITION_5	ADX > Const

Here's a signal to close a position:

GROUP_1	**AND** group:
CONDITION_1	LRC < WMA on the current candle
CONDITION_2	RSI > Const on the previous three candles

What parameters does the LRC indicator from GROUP_1 CONDITION_1 signal for opening a position (SIGNAL_1) have?

83

CHAPTER 3   ARCHITECTURAL SOLUTION PART 1: IDENTIFYING THE REQUIREMENTS

First, we need to take into account the parameter of the `LookbackPeriod` indicator itself, which is how many candles this indicator will be calculated on. Second, we need to understand at what time interval (`TimeInterval`) this indicator will work. Third, what candle depth (`CandlesDeep`) will the signal use to calculate conditions? As a result, we get that the first INDICATOR_1 (LRC) from GROUP_1 CONDITION_1 and SIGNAL_1 has the following parameters:

```
GROUP_1
    CONDITION_1
        INDICATOR_1
            LookbackPeriod
            TimeInterval
            CandlesDeep
```

Remember when we talked about parameter limitations? Let's add them to our parameters:

```
GROUP_1
    CONDITION_1
        INDICATOR_1
            LookbackPeriod    from 2 to 300 step 1
            TimeInterval      limited to list of
                              12 values
            CandlesDeep       from 0 to 0 step 1
```

We can calculate how many strategy variations INDICATOR_1 from CONDITION_1 of the group GROUP_1 will cost us.

```
LookbackPeriod    (300 - 2 + 1) * 1 = 299
TimeInterval      12
CandlesDeep       1
Total             299 * 12 * 1 = 3588
```

84

CHAPTER 3 ARCHITECTURAL SOLUTION PART 1: IDENTIFYING THE REQUIREMENTS

Now let's do the same calculations with the remaining signal indicators for opening a position, SIGNAL_1.

```
GROUP_1
    CONDITION_1
        INDICATOR_1 (LRC)
            LookbackPeriod       from 2 to 300 step 1
            TimeInterval         limited to list of 12 values
            CandlesDeep          from 0 to 0 step 1
        INDICATOR_2 (WMA)
            LookbackPeriod       from 2 to 300 step 1
            TimeInterval         limited to list of 12 values
            CandlesDeep          from 0 to 0 step 1
    CONDITION_2
        INDICATOR_1 (RSI)
            LookbackPeriod       from 2 to 300 step 1
            TimeInterval         limited to list of 12 values
            CandlesDeep          from 0 to 10 step 1
        INDICATOR_2 (Const)
            Value                from 0 to 100 step 0.1
    CONDITION_3
        INDICATOR_1 (BBW)
            LookbackPeriod       from 2 to 300 step 1
            StandardDeviations   from 1 to 20 step 1
            TimeInterval         limited to list of 12 values
            CandlesDeep          from 0 to 0 step 1
        INDICATOR_2 (Const)
            Value                from 0 to 0.6 step 0.001
    CONDITION_4
        INDICATOR_1 (BBW)
            LookbackPeriod       from 2 to 300 step 1
            StandardDeviations   from 1 to 20 step 1
```

85

CHAPTER 3   ARCHITECTURAL SOLUTION PART 1: IDENTIFYING THE REQUIREMENTS

```
            TimeInterval            limited to list of 12 values
            CandlesDeep             from 0 to 10 step 1
        INDICATOR_2 (Const)
            Value                   from 0 to 0.6 step 0.001
    CONDITION_5
        INDICATOR_1 (ADX)
            LookbackPeriod          from 2 to 300 step 1
            TimeInterval            limited to list of 12 values
            CandlesDeep             from 0 to 0 step 1
        INDICATOR_2 (Const)
            Value                   from 0 to 100 step 0.1
```

If we count all the possible variations of strategies, we get the following:

```
SIGNAL_1=
   CONDITION_1 (299 * 12 * 1   *   299 * 12 * 1)
 * CONDITION_2 (299 * 12 * 10  *   1000)
 * CONDITION_3 (299 * 20 * 12 * 1  *  600)
 * CONDITION_4 (299 * 20 * 12 * 10 *  600)
 * CONDITION_5 (299 * 12 * 1   *   1000)
= 12,873,744 * 35,880,000 * 43,056,000 * 430,560,000 *
  3,588,000
= 3.072395344219699e+35.
```

This is the number of variations based only on the signal to open a position! This is an incredibly large number.

If we use even a very powerful server cluster and ignore the fact that working with such large numbers in any programming language is difficult, then it will still take millennia to run such a large number of strategies on historical data. For example, if our cluster calculates thousands of strategies per second, then it will take $9.742501725709345*10^{24}$ years to calculate all the options. This is completely unacceptable for us.

CHAPTER 3   ARCHITECTURAL SOLUTION PART 1: IDENTIFYING THE REQUIREMENTS

This means we need algorithms that are smarter than simply searching through all the possible options for parameters.

Simply distributing strategies evenly across the space of all possible options is not a bad idea, but it is not enough, because there may be a strategy with much more impressive results very close by. See Figure 3-6.

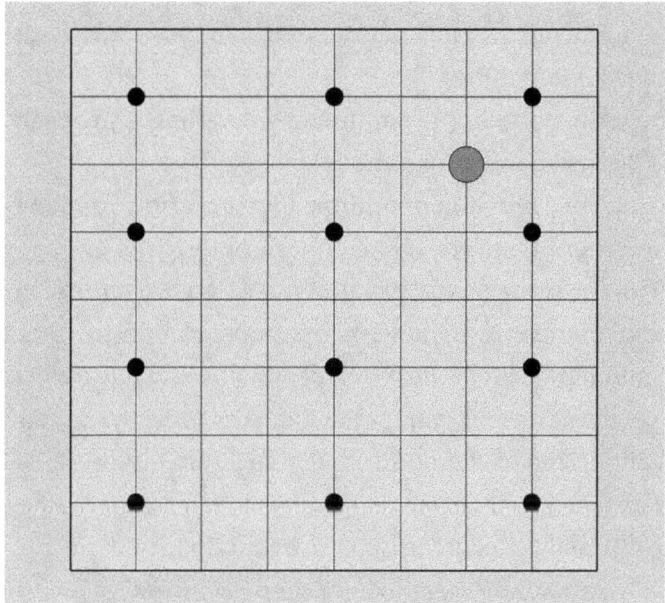

Figure 3-6. *Local extremes*

Fortunately, we are not the only ones faced with the task of finding the optimal solution in a vast space of possible variations. There is a special section of engineering that deals with this problem, and we can take advantage of the results of the work of a large number of scientists who have devoted many years to this branch of science. Optimization algorithms are the central part of this area. We'll talk about them in more detail in Chapter 6, but for now it's important to understand the general logic of how they work.

CHAPTER 3　ARCHITECTURAL SOLUTION PART 1: IDENTIFYING THE REQUIREMENTS

The task of optimization algorithms is to maximize the value of a function by selecting its parameters.

$$\max_{|X|} f(X) = f(X^*) = f^*$$

In this formula,

X is a vector of our variable parameters, in other words, a set of values for the strategy parameters.

|*X*| is the set of permissible parameter values and is precisely the restrictions imposed on our parameters.

f is the objective function or optimization criterion. In relation to a strategy, this criterion may be equal, for example, to the average monthly profitability of the strategy. It is usually calculated using the formula (ending balance − opening balance) / opening balance. In other words, this is how much percent of the initial capital the strategy earned.

X* is a vector of variable values at which the objective function reaches its optimal, in our case maximum, value. These are just the specific values of the constant LookbackPeriod or TimeInterval for each indicator.

f* is the optimal value of the objective function.

It is also worth noting that most modern optimization algorithms have not been proven to have absolute convergence. This means they have not been proven to find the most optimal result, but they do find a fairly good value of the objective function in a more acceptable time than millennia.

The following algorithm for finding the optimal strategy is obtained as shown here:

1. We pass a set of parameters with their constraints to the optimization algorithm. In response to this, they generate for us sets of parameter values, based on which we can create a strategy. That is, the algorithm will give us what the `LookbackPeriod` should be equal to, for example, for a specific opening signal indicator.

CHAPTER 3   ARCHITECTURAL SOLUTION PART 1: IDENTIFYING THE REQUIREMENTS

2. Our system simulates real trading with this strategy using historical data and, based on the results, calculates the optimization criterion for each set of parameters.

3. Again, we go to step 1; that is, we transfer the sets of parameters with the calculated criterion for each of them again to the optimization algorithm and, based on this data, it again generates a set of values for us. This loop continues until the stopping condition occurs. Such a condition can be the number of iterations or the fact that we have gone through all possible variations, or, for example, search degradation. This is when new sets of values don't differ very much from each other. See Figure 3-7.

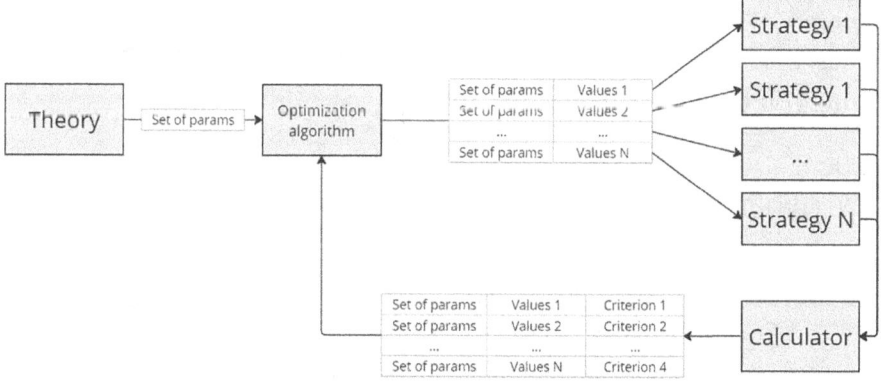

Figure 3-7. *One-step process*

Two-Step Approach

I showed how to implement a one-step system to search for a strategy, but I was not impressed with the results of its work. The fact is that optimization algorithms are evaluated by two criteria: the accuracy of

CHAPTER 3 ARCHITECTURAL SOLUTION PART 1: IDENTIFYING THE REQUIREMENTS

determining the optimal value and the coverage of all possible variations of parameters in their space. In practice, this means that if the algorithm is more tuned to coverage, then it will not find the most optimal solution, but the options that it will consider will be as varied as possible. And in the case of a bias toward optimization, the algorithm will find an extremum, but with a high degree of probability it will be local and not global.

So, I tried different optimization algorithms with a wide variation in their settings and was disappointed every time. Breadth-tuned algorithms did not find the best strategies because they did not include a local search algorithm, and the value space can be huge. Algorithms tuned in depth accurately found local maxima but often missed global ones. Also, the calculations took a long time and often had negative results when the theory turned out to be unviable.

As a result, I decided to complicate my system for finding profitable strategies. First, I wanted to quickly cut off bad theories; for this I used an algorithm configured in breadth and increased the step of parameter values. That is, for example, at the first step for GROUP_1 CONDITION_1 INDICATOR_1, I passed the following to the algorithm:

```
GROUP_1
    CONDITION_1
        INDICATOR_1
            LookbackPeriod      from 2 to 300 step 10
            TimeInterval        limited to list of 12 values
            CandlesDeep         from 0 to 0 step 1
```

I increased the step for LookbackPeriod by 10 times, which automatically reduced the number of variations by the same value.

An urgent question arose in the automatic determination of viable theories. I didn't like the strategy of simply selecting the best strategies sorted by the value of the optimization criterion, because the sample, for example, included strategies with 10 trades over five years or with a large number of losing positions and only a few, but large, winning ones. I consider such strategies unstable and do not work with them. Our task is to look for stable, albeit not very profitable, strategies.

Therefore, I came up with and developed another essence of my system, the **quality condition**. Its task is to analyze the calculated strategies and give a yes/no answer, that is, whether our theory is suitable for further research or not. Obviously, there is no point in analyzing all strategies, since they are already ranked according to the optimality criterion. This means that in the suitability condition it is necessary to specify a certain number or percentage of strategies that we are ready to consider. Next, we need to indicate the selection conditions by which the strategy can be classified as suitable. If at least one of the pool of strategies turns out to be suitable, then the entire theory is considered suitable, and we will continue to work with it. See Figure 3-8.

Figure 3-8. *Quality condition entity*

It is worth noting here that all these conditions can be included in the optimization criterion. For example, if maxDrawdown becomes more than 2%, then make it negative, and then the optimization algorithm will stop considering this strategy to generate the next set of variable values. However, I refused this because such strategies may be promising, but they just need to be optimized, which means they cannot be discarded from the field of view of the optimization algorithm.

CHAPTER 3 ARCHITECTURAL SOLUTION PART 1: IDENTIFYING THE REQUIREMENTS

Since in our sequence of searching for a profitable strategy, another operation appeared to vary the intervals and steps of parameters, there was also a need for another entity that contains data on these changes. I called it **SubTheory**. While the theory contains settings on the basis of which we will search for strategies, SubTheory will contain a specific optimization algorithm, rules for generating and calculating strategies. It is also obvious that SubTheories are generated based on theory. See Figure 3-9.

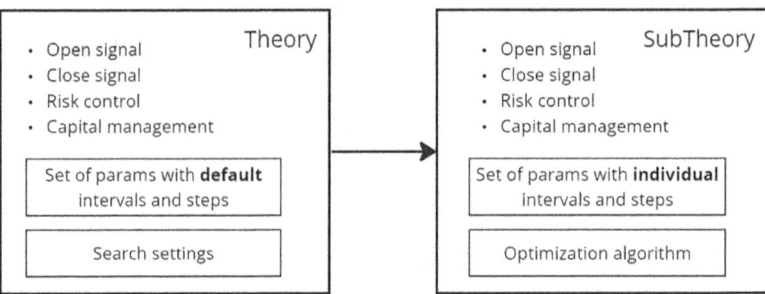

Figure 3-9. *SubTheory entity*

Based on theories, a set of SubTheory will be formed. And each SubTheory will generate strategies. That is, strategies are not built on the basis of theory. To test the theory, we created one SubTheory. See Figure 3-10.

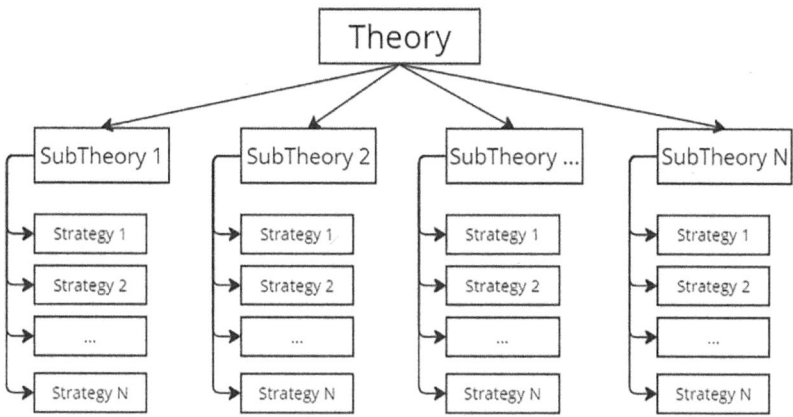

Figure 3-10. Relationship between Theory and SubTheories

Let's assume that one of our theories turns out to be suitable. That is, with a high degree of probability, one or even several good strategies can be obtained from our theory. All that remains is to find them. When determining suitability, we reduced the number of variations by increasing the parameter step. When searching for a profitable strategy, this approach will not suit us, because our task is to find the most optimal strategy possible and not one close to it. This means that the search accuracy should be as high as possible, and therefore the parameter step should be minimal. But let me remind you that in practice I realized that this approach does not work. Therefore, I decided to act iteratively. That is, reduce the step gradually while simultaneously narrowing the ranges of parameter values. In practice, this means that at each search step a new SubTheory will be created. Now the strategy search scheme looks like Figure 3-11 and Figure 3-12.

CHAPTER 3 ARCHITECTURAL SOLUTION PART 1: IDENTIFYING THE REQUIREMENTS

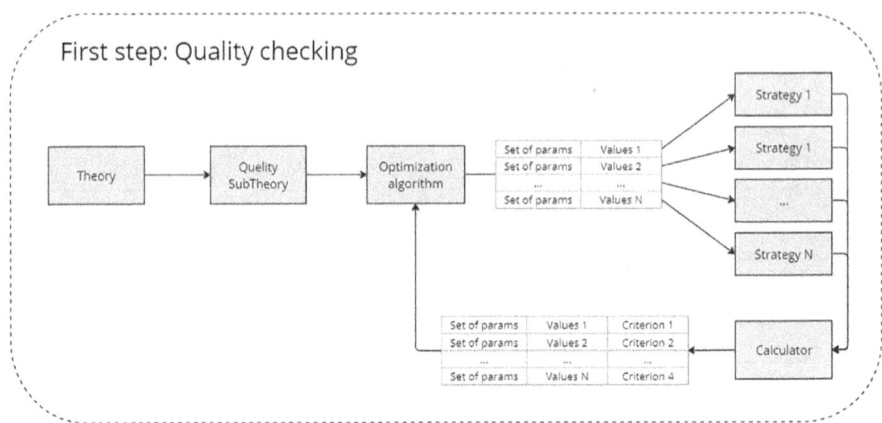

Figure 3-11. First step

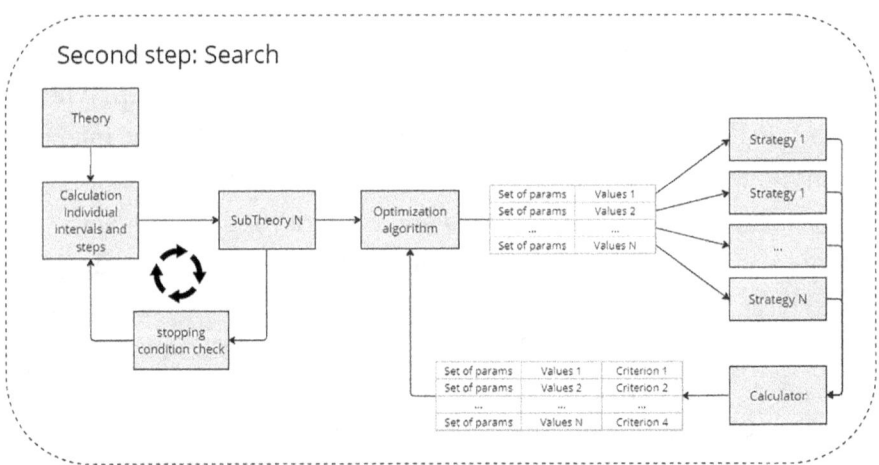

Figure 3-12. Second step

Let's look at the second step in more detail.

To simplify, let's imagine that our theory is characterized by only two parameters (Table 3-1).

CHAPTER 3　ARCHITECTURAL SOLUTION PART 1: IDENTIFYING THE REQUIREMENTS

Table 3-1. *Set of Params with Default Intervals and Steps*

Param	from	to	step
LookbackPeriod	1	300	1
Value	1	100	0.1

It is easy to calculate that this theory can have 300,000 strategies. This is not an impressive number that can simply be sorted out, but let me remind you that this is a simplified example and in real theories this number will be approximately $3.072395344219699 * 10^{35}$.

So let's get started. Before creating SubTheory, we need to decide on the step and interval of each parameter. For the first time, we will take the default intervals from theory and increase the step so that the number of parameter values is limited by the user settings. For example, let's take 20. We get the set shown in Table 3-2.

Table 3-2. *Set of Params with **Individual** Intervals and Steps*

Param	from	to	step
LookbackPeriod	1	300	300/20 = 15
Value	1	100	100/20 = 5

So, the first SubTheory has been created. Let's imagine that 20 strategies were generated and calculated on its basis. I understand that this number is lower than the number of all variations of strategies that can be generated based on this SubTheory, but I remind you that the optimization algorithm is not a brute-force method. The goal of these algorithms is to find the maximum value of the objective function in the least number of calculations.

Now, based on the results of these 20 strategies, you need to generate custom intervals and steps for the next SubTheory. The logic for defining the steps is clear, but what about the intervals? How to reduce them? Let's look at the `LookbackPeriod` parameter as an example. Let's take the values of this parameter from the five best strategies of this SubTheory. How many strategies do we take? And what rule (percentage or quantity) should be specified by the user at the stage of theory formation in the Search settings block? See Table 3-3.

Table 3-3. Calculated Strategies

Strategy	Value of LookbackPeriod
Strategy 1	91
Strategy 2	16
Strategy 3	196
Strategy 4	166
Strategy 5	16

From these values it is clear that the optimal value is in the interval 16 - 196. But since this is not the final solution, we will add one step in each direction. As a result, we will get an interval from 1 to 211. Next we need to reduce the step. And again we take 20 intervals. The step will then be equal to 211/20 = 10.55, but we know that the minimum possible step for this parameter is 1, which means it is necessary to round 10.55 to units. As a result, we get 11. We do the same with the second parameter.

This strategy for calculating new intervals and steps is not the only one. Better solutions can be devised, such as exploring multiple subintervals to more accurately probe these local extrema. You can also change the step size depending on the number of our iteration and/or the total number of strategies. Here I showed an example of the simplest implementation.

Now we need to discuss the conditions for exiting this cycle. I'm using a double condition. The first is the number of iterations. But it happens that the intervals narrow so much that the system has the opportunity to go through all possible strategy options in an acceptable time. Therefore, I also set the number of strategies after which the system could switch to the brute-force method. And after searching through all possible values, it stopped.

Selection and Forward Testing

The second step is complete, so now we'll select strategies for forward testing. I acted according to the following logic: I set the number of strategies I needed and the condition of suitability. My system followed a list of strategies sorted in descending order of the value of the optimization criterion; if any of them fulfilled the suitability condition, then the system allowed it to proceed to the next step. This should continue until either the required number of strategies is collected or the pool, the settings of which are specified in the suitability criteria, is exhausted.

We now need to test suitable strategies on stocks that were not included in the search process. This is necessary to make sure that the chosen strategies are truly profitable and not tailored to specific stocks. This test will also give us information about the operation of strategies, which can be applied in real trading in the risk control module. What is forward testing in relation to our system? This is simply modeling the operation of a strategy based on historical data and preselected instruments. Next, all results are checked according to the suitability condition, and if they all meet the condition, then the strategy is considered profitable and can be used in real trading. See Figure 3-13.

CHAPTER 3   ARCHITECTURAL SOLUTION PART 1: IDENTIFYING THE REQUIREMENTS

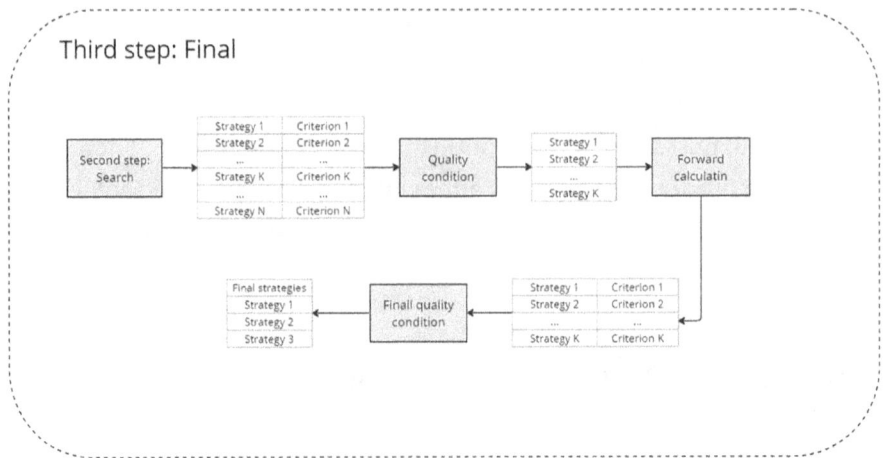

Figure 3-13. *Third step*

Selection of Financial Instruments

At this stage we have profitable strategies. But on what instruments are they profitable? On what instruments can they be used in real trading? There are many possible solutions to this issue. First, we need to divide all the tools we use by type. In the simplest sense, this is a division by price ranges and trading volumes. This division is necessary due to the widely used indicator theories based on price or trading volume.

This is not the only way to choose an instrument for real trading. There are many more options; for example, you can divide charts by type, highly volatile, trend, flat, and so on. Of course, to make the user's work easier, you can automate the creation of historical data with the automatic distribution of price charts into groups.

We all understand that the market situation can change, and this means that the instruments can change the group. So, we need to take care of two more things. First, we need to think about the distribution of instruments or the segments of their price charts into groups when connecting a new instrument. Second, we need to take care of a real-time monitoring system that will turn on or off strategies on instruments when the market situation changes.

So, charts or instruments are divided into types, which means that the system must check, search, conduct forward analysis, and conduct real trading on instruments of the same type. This is important, because a profitable strategy will cease to be profitable in completely new conditions. This approach looks like tweaking a strategy, but it's not at all because the types of tools can be broad rather than limited to one or two instances. Of course, if you set the conditions for a group that only one or two instruments fall under, then yes, this will be an adjustment. In this matter, it is important to maintain a balance between the breadth of coverage of tools or types of charts and understanding the specifics of how each of your theories works.

Setting Up a Search for a Profitable Strategy

In the previous steps, we talked a lot about the fact that the user must set some parameters to generate theories and find profitable strategies. Let's collect all this information in one place.

Obviously, the entire search process is governed by theory, which means that search settings should be stored in it. And since the theory can be created not only manually, the user must select these settings in the generator.

Also, the search settings should contain all the necessary information about the search parameters in all three steps and include a list of tools or segments of historical data on which strategy indicators will be calculated (see Figure 3-14 and Figure 3-15).

CHAPTER 3   ARCHITECTURAL SOLUTION PART 1: IDENTIFYING THE REQUIREMENTS

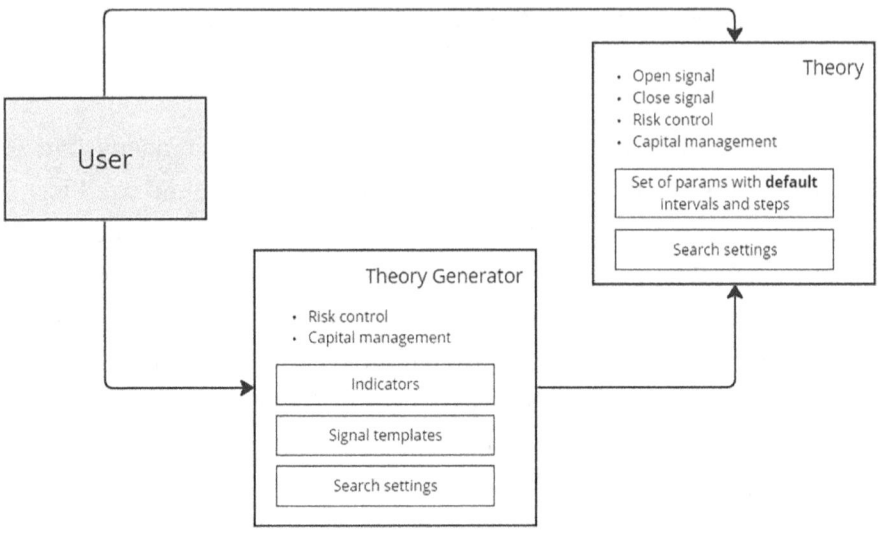

Figure 3-14.   Theory generation process

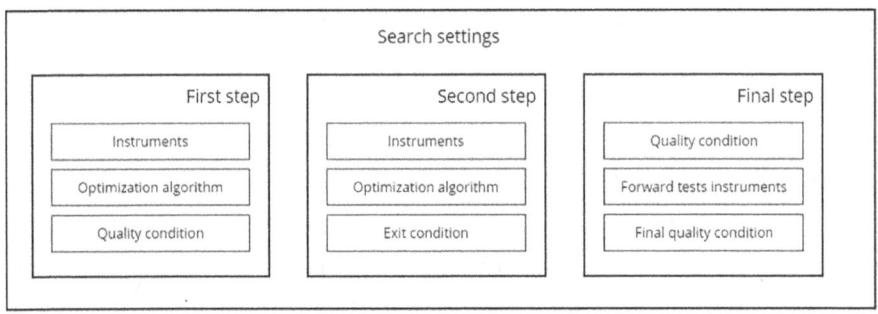

Figure 3-15.   Search settings at every step

The Logic of Searching for Profitable Strategies

Let's summarize and describe the general vision of the algorithm for finding profitable strategies:

1. The user creates a theory manually or using a theory generator. The user must make all the necessary settings to find a profitable setup, as well as signal templates and a list of indicators to generate strategies.

2. An initial check of the quality of the theory is carried out on a reduced field of possible parameter values using an optimization algorithm configured to cover a wide range of possible parameter values.

3. If the previous step is completed successfully and the theory is considered to be of high quality, then the optimal strategy is searched by iteratively narrowing the possible options for parameters with a gradual increase in their accuracy.

4. The required number of strategies is selected from the entire pool of counted strategies in step 3 using the quality criterion specified in the search settings.

5. Selected strategies undergo forward testing. Using the final quality condition, the required number of final strategies that are suitable for real trading are selected from them.

Real Trading

At the previous step, several promising strategies were found that performed well in forward testing. We also know what types of instruments or chart types each of these strategies can use.

This means that in a real trading system there should always be a robot running that monitors all available instruments and in real time determines their type or the type of their charts. As I said earlier, there are

CHAPTER 3 ARCHITECTURAL SOLUTION PART 1: IDENTIFYING THE REQUIREMENTS

many options. To keep things simple, I will use tool types in this book. For example, if a tool has increased in price from $15 to $50, then the robot must record this and change its type.

Another robot is also needed that constantly checks the strategies and types of tools. If one of the tools has changed its type, then you need to turn off the strategies that no longer correspond to it. Here it is necessary to pay special attention to the mechanism for disconnecting the strategy from the tool. Imagine a situation where a tool changes its type frequently. So, should the system constantly turn the strategy on and off? No, of course, this problem can be approached from two sides. First, correctly configure the definition of the tool type so that it has a reserve and the change of these types does not occur frequently. Second, do not turn off the strategy immediately, but wait for a certain time.

Also, this robot must include strategies on tools of the appropriate type. For example, if the tool has changed type or a new strategy has appeared, then it needs to be put into operation.

Our system works with money, which means that an external, additional audit of the strategy's operation is necessary. In practice, this means that not only the strategy itself, with the help of risk control, will monitor its work, but also an external robot will monitor its performance and, in case of any discrepancies, turn off the strategy. For example, if the balance of a strategy has dropped sharply, or vice versa, if the strategy has earned an amount of money that is not standard for it, then this robot should turn it off.

In real work, system stability is extremely important. This means we must have prepared scenarios for actions in case of unforeseen circumstances—a sudden shutdown of the exchange for some time, a planned system update when we are forced to stop all or part of the strategies, an unplanned lack of electricity or Internet.

It is necessary to understand that this system will trade on more than one exchange using dozens of instruments. This will be a large, full-scale program, integrated with dozens of exchanges, using hundreds of tools and thousands of strategies. This point will be critical at the design stage.

Important Questions

Previously, we defined the main essence of our future system and also described the main processes associated with the search and operation of profitable strategies. But there are still some points that should be examined in more detail.

Life Cycle of a Position

Each profitable strategy contains signals for opening and closing a position. But what is the position? What are its stages of existence?

First, I want to separate the concept of a position from the concept of a system (internal) order and an order placed directly at the broker. Let's start with the latter. This is exactly the order on the basis of which deals are executed and the broker notifies us about the change in status.

Many brokers provide functionality for placing not only market and limit orders but also such interesting types as stop loss or take profit, etc. But it is important to understand that not all brokers support all types of orders; therefore, we must implement them in our system. This is where the concept of a system order originates. This is the essence of our system, which "monitors" the state of the market, and if specific conditions are met, then it creates an order with the broker and monitors its execution (see Figure 3-16).

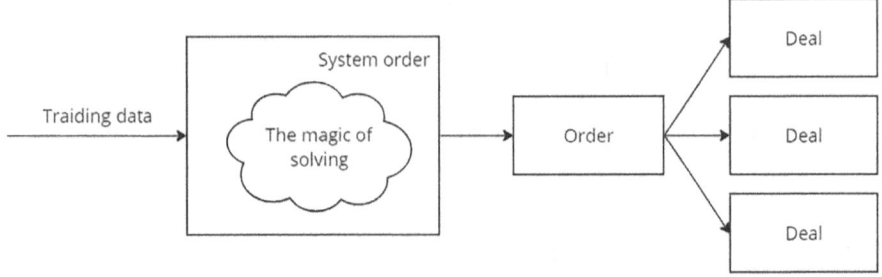

Figure 3-16. *System order process*

Position is one of the central entities of the system. It is this entity that initiates the creation of system orders. Each position can generate several system orders.

For example, one of the ways to control risk is to place take profit and stop loss orders. This means that when opening a position, we need to create three system orders: buy, take profit, and stop loss. However, not every one of them will generate an exchange order. See Figure 3-17.

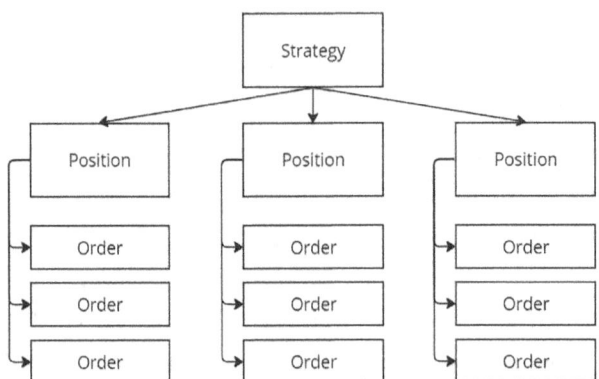

Figure 3-17. *Relationship between strategy and orders*

Let's describe the life cycle of a position. Here I will introduce one of the simplest position management processes. But I do not exclude the possibility of much more complex options. So let's get started.

A signal to open a position came from the strategy. This means we need to buy a certain amount of tools. We create a simple system buy order, which generates a market order.

Each order can have each of these statuses:

- **New:** Initial status. This means that the broker has successfully registered your request in the system.

- **PartiallyFill:** The order is partially filled. This is not the final status of the order; it only shows that one or more deals were made within the order, which do not cover the entire needs of the order.

- **Fill:** Final order status. This means that the order was successfully executed.

- **Canceled:** Final status. This status is set if you cancel your order yourself. It may come after PartiallyFill. It is normal when you cancel a partially filled order.

- **Rejected:** Final status. This status is set if the broker cancels the order for any reason.

Executing an order at a broker is not a synchronous process. There is also a time delay due to the mechanics of receiving order statuses. We must provide the correct logic for the position to take into account all these nuances. For example, a situation may arise when a market order switches to the Rejected status immediately after it is created or when the system sends a request to create an order and the broker returns an error.

This means we must provide a position-processing mechanism in the platform that will allow us to correctly process all these situations.

Capital Management

In the previous chapter, I described several ways to manage capital. Each method has its own characteristics, advantages, and disadvantages. But all these methods have one thing in common: at the input they must receive data about the operation of the strategy, and at the output they must say the maximum amount for the purchase of an asset and set a strategy for purchasing additional assets. See Figure 3-18.

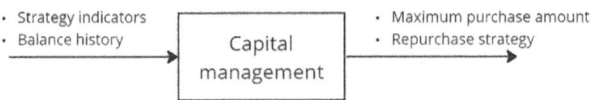

Figure 3-18. *Capital management entity*

This means the system will refer to the capital management method every time the price of an asset changes to obtain information about the need to repurchase or partially sell the purchased asset. That is, the purpose of this block is to answer the question, is it necessary to buy or sell part of the assets and for what amount?

To focus on the main thing, implementing a system for the mass search for profitable strategies, we will implement in this book only one method of money management, but we will focus on creating a mechanism that will make it easy to add more complex methods to the system.

Our first method will be the fixed interest method. This is perhaps one of the easiest methods to implement, as it has only one variable and some elementary logic. It was discussed in detail in the previous chapter, but I will remind you what it is. It specifies the percentage of the balance on the basis of which the maximum purchase amount of the asset will be calculated when opening a position. It is also worth noting that with this method, only one buy order is created for one position; that is, there is no provision for the additional purchase of an asset into the position.

CHAPTER 3   ARCHITECTURAL SOLUTION PART 1: IDENTIFYING THE REQUIREMENTS

Risk Control

There are many approaches to managing your risks, all of which come down to one goal: to prevent the system from losing or gaining too much. I chose three options for myself that can easily be combined with each other. This is the creation of a take profit, stop loss, or trailing system order.

Take Profit and Stop Loss

This system order does not immediately create an order with the broker. And it sets it only if the closing price of the candle exceeds the price specified during creation. To simplify, I introduced a parameter equal to the percentage of discrepancy in the average price of transactions when executing a system order during the opening of a position. That is, if the price exceeds this percentage, then an order is placed with the broker.

For example, the strategy gave a signal to open a position. According to the logic of position processing, a simple market system order to buy an asset was first opened. During its execution, the deals in Table 3-4 were made.

Table 3-4. List of Deals

Count	price	total
10	45.4	454
2	45.3	90.6

As a result, we get the average purchase price equal to (454 + 90.6) / 12 = 45.38. If the strategy settings indicate that it is necessary to create a system take profit order with execution when the price exceeds the 4% threshold, then the system order will give a command to open an order with the broker when the closing price of the candle exceeds the threshold price equal to 45.38 * 104% = 47.2.

CHAPTER 3 ARCHITECTURAL SOLUTION PART 1: IDENTIFYING THE REQUIREMENTS

Stop loss system orders act exactly the opposite. They create an order with the broker if the closing price of a candle falls below a certain level. Regarding the example given earlier, if you set a threshold of 3%, then such a system order will command the broker to sell if the asset price falls below 45.38 * 97% = 44.01.

Trailing System Order

A trailing system order is a dynamically changing order designed to maximize profits. In this section, I will present my version of the idea of implementing this type of order.

The components of a trailing system order are three lines: decision border, profit border, and stop border. The stop border and profit border depend on the trailing price, the change of which is controlled by the decision border. As in the case of take profit and stop loss, if the closing price of the current candle is higher than the profit border or lower than the stop border, then the system initiates the procedure for closing the position, but there is a significant difference: in a trailing order, these borders are dynamic since the trailing price on which they depend may change.

When creating a system order, the trailing price is equal to the average price of asset purchase transactions. The decision border is a price that is higher than the trailing price by a certain percentage. If the current price is above the decision border, then a special trailing signal is checked. This signal analyzes the current state of the market and shows whether we should expect the asset price to continue moving in the direction we need. If the signal returns "yes," then the trailing price becomes equal to the current one. This in turn entails a shift in the stop border and profit border prices. I have slightly modified the algorithm for determining the stop border and profit border. For me, they are not calculated using a simple formula that changes the price of the decision border by a certain, predetermined percentage. This formula also includes a factor for narrowing the acceptable price tunnel. When the stop border and profit border with each change the trailing prices become closer to each other. See Figure 3-19.

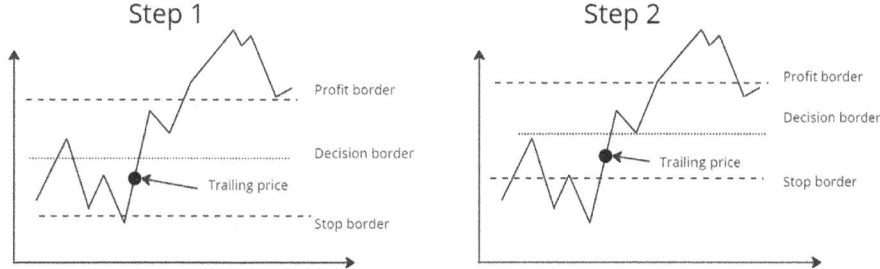

Figure 3-19. An example of how trolling order works

Let's look at the algorithm in more detail.

The following variables are necessary for a trailing system order to work:

- **TrailingPrice:** The price relative to which the boundaries are located. When creating a trailing system order, the trailing price is equal to the average price of transactions when purchasing assets.

- **ProfitBorderCoeff:** What percentage of TrailingPrice is the upper price border.

- **StopBorderCoeff:** What percentage of TrailingPrice is the lower price border.

- **BorderChangeCoeff:** What percentage the distance between the profit border and the stop border decreases by with each shift of the Trailing price.

- **DecisionCoeff:** What percentage of TrailingPrice is the decision line located at.

CHAPTER 3 ARCHITECTURAL SOLUTION PART 1: IDENTIFYING THE REQUIREMENTS

- **DecisionSignal:** The signal on the basis of which a decision is made to change the TrailingPrice.

- **DecisionCount:** The number of changes TrailingPrice.

The algorithm for processing changes in the asset price will look like this:

1. We check the penetration of the profit border. If we break through, then close the position.

2. We check whether the stop border has been broken. If we break through, then close the position.

3. We check the penetration of the decision border. If they hit, then we check the signal. If the signal returns "yes," then TrailingPrice becomes equal to the current price of the asset.

For example, if the price of an asset changed as shown in Table 3-5.

Table 3-5. *Change in the Price of a Financial Instrument*

Date	Price
2021/10/01 11:00	97
2021/10/01 11:05	95
2021/10/01 11:10	105
2021/10/01 11:15	107
2021/10/01 11:20	107.5

CHAPTER 3 ARCHITECTURAL SOLUTION PART 1: IDENTIFYING THE REQUIREMENTS

And the variables in the strategy are equal to the values in Table 3-6.

Table 3-6. Strategy Parameter Values

ProfitBorderCoeff	0.1
StopBorderCoeff	0.05
BorderChangeCoeff	0.3
DecisionCoeff	0.02
TrailingPrice	90
DecisionCount	0

Then our algorithm will work as follows:

1. 2021/10/01 11:00 CurrentPrice = 97

    a. Checking the penetration of the profit border. To do this, you need to calculate ProtectedPrice, which is the profit border price.

    ProtectedPrice = TrailingPrice * (1 + ProfitBorderCoeff * ((1 - BorderChangeCoeff) pow DecisionCount)) = 90 * (1 + 0.1 * ((1 - 0.3) pow 0) = 90 * (1 + 0.1 * 1)= 99

    The current price of 97 is less than the ProtectedPrice of 99. This means there is no need to close the position.

    b. Checking the penetration of the stop border. To do this, you need to calculate ProtectedPrice minus the stop border price.

ProtectedPrice = TrailingPrice * (1 - StopBorderCoeff * ((1 - BorderChangeCoeff) pow DecisionCount)) = 90 * (1 - 0.05 * ((1 - 0.3) pow 0) = 90 * (1 - 0.05 * 1) = 85.5

The current price of 97 is more than the ProtectedPrice of 85.5. There is no need to close such a position.

c. Checking the penetration of the decision border. To do this, let's calculate DecisionPrice.

DecisionPrice = TrailingPrice * (1 + DecisionCoeff) = 90 * (1 + 0.02) = 91.8.

The current price of 97 is greater than the DecisionPrice of 91.8, which means we check the signal. For example, the signal gave the answer "yes." It turns out that TrailingPrice becomes equal to 97, DecisionCount 1.

Results of the step: We do not close the position. TrailingPrice = 97, DecisionCount = 1.

2. 2021/10/01 11:05 CurrentPrice = 95

a. Checking the penetration of the profit border.

ProtectedPrice = TrailingPrice * (1 + ProfitBorderCoeff * ((1 - BorderChangeCoeff) pow DecisionCount)) = 97 * (1 + 0.1 * ((1 - 0.3) pow 1) = 97 * (1 + 0.1 * 0.7)= 103.79

The current price is 95 less than the ProtectedPrice of 103.79. This means there is no need to close the position. Please note that

CHAPTER 3 ARCHITECTURAL SOLUTION PART 1: IDENTIFYING THE REQUIREMENTS

not only has the upper price limit changed from 103.79 to 99, but also the distance between the upper and lower limits has decreased.

b. Checking the penetration of the stop border.

```
ProtectedPrice = TrailingPrice * (1 -
StopBorderCoeff * ((1 - BorderChangeCoeff )
pow DecisionCount)) = 97 * (1 - 0.05 * ((1 -
0.3) pow 1) = 97 * (1 - 0.05 * 0.7) =93.65
```

The current price is 95 more than the ProtectedPrice of 93.65. This means there is no need to close the position.

c. Checking the penetration of the decision border. To do this, let's calculate DecisionPrice.

```
DecisionPrice = TrailingPrice * (1 +
DecisionCoeff) = 97 * (1 + 0.02) = 98.94.
```

The current price 97 is greater than DecisionPrice 98.94, which means we check the signal. For example, the signal gave the answer "no." It turns out that TrailingPrice does not change.

Results of the step: We do not close the position. TrailingPrice = 97, DecisionCount = 1

3. 2021/10/01 11:10 CurrentPrice = 105

   a. Checking the penetration of the profit border.

   ```
   ProtectedPrice = TrailingPrice * (1 +
   ProfitBorderCoeff * ((1 - BorderChangeCoeff )
   ```

CHAPTER 3   ARCHITECTURAL SOLUTION PART 1: IDENTIFYING THE REQUIREMENTS

pow DecisionCount)) = 97 * (1 + 0.1 * ((1 - 0.3) pow 1) = 97 * (1 + 0.1 * 0.7)= 103.79. Obviously it has not changed since the previous step, because TrailingPrice has not changed

The current price is 105 more than the ProtectedPrice of 103.79. This means we give a signal to close the position.

Results of the step: Closing a position.

A trailing system order is a very powerful risk control mechanism because it changes its parameters depending on the market situation.

Scalability of Indicators

There is one big problem that I encountered almost immediately after the first attempt to implement this system: different scales of indicator charts that are compared in signals.

Imagine a situation where you need to compare ADX and the closing price of a candle, in some signal condition (see Figure 3-20).

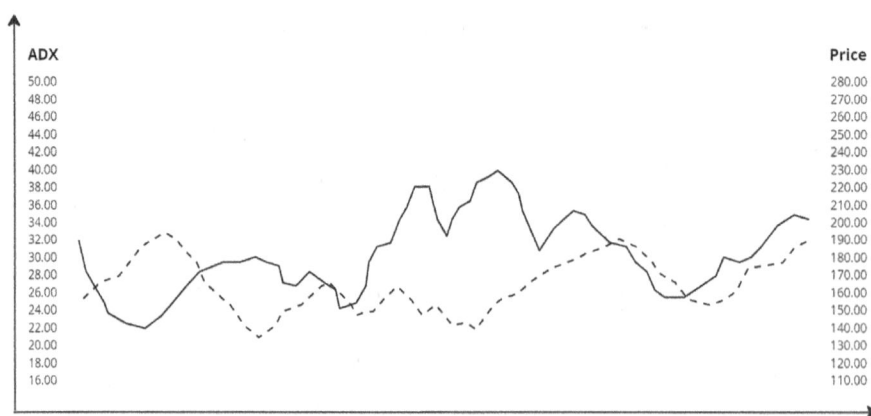

Figure 3-20.   *Scalability of indicators*

114

CHAPTER 3   ARCHITECTURAL SOLUTION PART 1: IDENTIFYING THE REQUIREMENTS

I propose solving this problem in a way that is standard for many trading platforms: scaling the indicators and bringing them to a single coordinate system. To do this, it is necessary to take the maximum and minimum values on the last segment of historical data for each indicator and equate them to 0 and 100%. As a result, each indicator value can be scaled from 0 to 100 using the following formula:

(currentValue - minValue) / ((maxValue - minValue) * 100)

It is worth noting here that as the strategy works, the values of minValue and maxValue should change as new data arrives. That is, the start of calculations will occur only after processing a given length of historical data.

Let's look at an example. As a result of analyzing historical data, the maximum value of the indicator was 20, and the minimum was 9. See Table 3-7.

Table 3-7. *Scaled Value Changes over Time*

Date	Indicator Value	Maximum Value	Minimum Value	Scaled Value
2018/10/2 08:05	11	20	9	(11 - 9)/(20 - 9) * 100 = 18.18
2018/10/2 08:10	8	20	8	0
2018/10/2 08:15	25	25	8	100
2018/10/2 08:20	20	25	8	70.59
2018/10/2 08:25	27	27	8	100
2018/10/2 08:30	19	27	8	57.89

Thus, you can easily scale any indicator values to a single coordinate system and compare them with each other.

CHAPTER 3   ARCHITECTURAL SOLUTION PART 1: IDENTIFYING THE REQUIREMENTS

Summary

In this chapter, we went through the first stage of creating an architectural solution, namely, identifying requirements.

We identified the main entities of the system, as well as their relationships.

We decided to use optimization algorithms and also realized that the search for profitable strategies should be done in two stages.

We also discussed how our system should look in a production environment.

In the next chapter, we will pay more attention to the technical details. Let's discuss what subsystems and services should be in our system, as well as how they should interact with each other.

CHAPTER 4

Architectural Solution Part 2: Services and Subsystems

In the previous chapter, we described the logic of our system and compiled a list of requirements and entities. That is, we decided on what our system should do, and in this chapter we will talk about how it will do it. The goal of this chapter is to list the services and describe their functionality and dependencies.

I propose the following plan:

- We decide on the architecture. Before compiling a list of services, you need to decide what they will look like. Will it be one large application that can do everything or many small, conditionally independent services?

- We identify a list of subsystems. Any complex problem is easier and better solved by decomposing a large problem into smaller ones. This approach also works great when creating a system architecture. The first step is to identify a list of subsystems and a list of their functionality and dependencies.

CHAPTER 4   ARCHITECTURAL SOLUTION PART 2: SERVICES AND SUBSYSTEMS

- We identify a list of services. A subsystem is only an enlarged representation of the system. It does not contain information about the list of applications or their external contracts. That is, each subsystem must be divided into a list of services.

- We will create a short description for each service. You will get a detailed description of services in the following chapters. Here I want to focus only on describing the functionality, defining dependencies, and describing the general logic of work.

Microservice Architecture

To begin with, I will talk about ways to build systems (Figure 4-1). Figure 4-1 shows two types of application architecture.

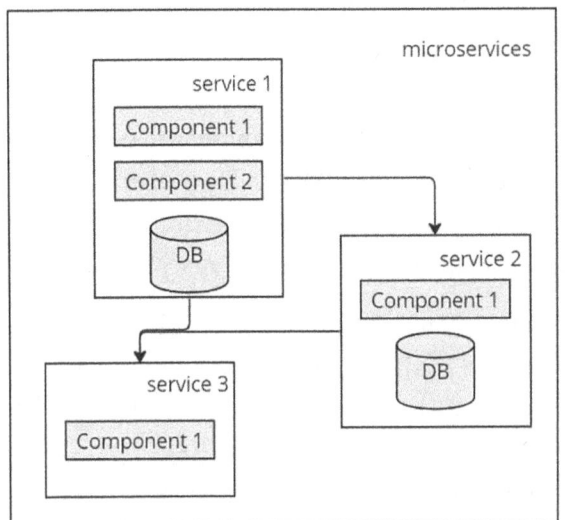
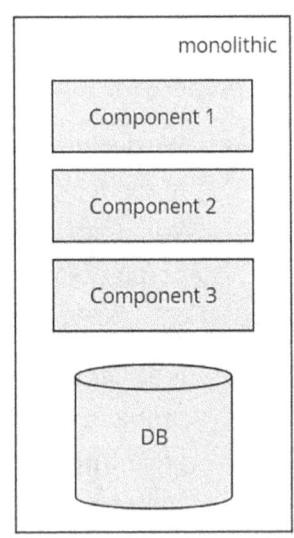

Figure 4-1. Two common methods: microsevices and monoliths

CHAPTER 4　ARCHITECTURAL SOLUTION PART 2: SERVICES AND SUBSYSTEMS

There are two common methods.

- A monolithic architecture is an architectural style based on one large application that is responsible for all the functionality of the system.

- Microservice application architecture is a design approach centered around the concept of microservices, which are small, independent, and loosely coupled software components. These microservices are self-contained and focused on specific business functionalities, making them highly modular and scalable. While individual microservices may not address user problems in isolation, they play a crucial role in collectively delivering complex functionalities within a larger system.

Some time ago, all systems were monolithic; this was primarily due to the lack of developed application life-cycle management mechanisms. Over time, these mechanisms have improved and become so simple that now almost all new systems are built on a microservice architecture.

Microservices have the following advantages:

- **Independence.** This is perhaps one of the main advantages of microservices. Each microservice can be updated independently of other services. First, this allows you to release releases more often, and second, you can localize errors faster.

    This is a very critical moment for our system. For example, if we talk about our system, it is unacceptable that the release of a new version of some component related to the search for profitable strategies will affect or even destroy the functionality of the real trading block.

CHAPTER 4   ARCHITECTURAL SOLUTION PART 2: SERVICES AND SUBSYSTEMS

- **Scaling.** Imagine that the number of users in the system has increased, but all of them use only one function of your application. If you used a monolithic architecture, then you would have to scale not only the services that implement the desired functionality but also all other services, and this is a waste of a lot of resources. This is also an important advantage for our system. It allows us to independently scale the obviously necessary blocks for finding strategies and real trading. Perhaps at first, only after the system has started, it makes sense to direct most of the resources to the search and optimization block, because a small number of profitable strategies will participate in real trading.

- **Contextual constraint.** Each microservice has its own strictly limited list of implemented functionality, which the microservice should not go beyond. This helps avoid tightly coupled services. Each service is essentially a separate program, with its own source code and interfaces. Thanks to this, you physically cannot use the internal classes of one service in the code of another service. All you have at your disposal are their interfaces; you don't need to know about the internal features.

- **Distributed architecture.** This has a valuable quality: your microservices can be deployed on different servers. For example, I use a cluster of several home computers to search and optimize strategies, and for real trading I rent servers because they guarantee uninterrupted operation. This approach allows me to save money, since home computers are cheaper and the requirement for uninterrupted operation is not so high.

CHAPTER 4 ARCHITECTURAL SOLUTION PART 2: SERVICES AND SUBSYSTEMS

Microservice architecture also has its disadvantages. The main one is the increasing complexity of system development. If in a monolithic architecture everything is synchronous and consistent, then in a microservices architecture this is not the case. It is necessary to start thinking asynchronously and about events. But this drawback for me was easily offset by the possibility of independent scaling and updating. For me, it is critically important to be able to quickly change the code of the components responsible for the search strategy and at the same time not break the strategies that work in real trading. It was also important that I could conduct testing on relatively cheap equipment at home and rent servers only for real trading. Then, to be honest, at first my real trading system worked on a separate computer at home. It was cheap, and I was also sure that if something went completely wrong, I could simply turn off the power to the computer.

Before we go any further, I would like to cover a few important concepts related to microservices so that there is no misunderstanding.

- A subsystem is a set of services related in meaning. For example, within our system I see two main large subsystems: the strategy search subsystem and the real trading subsystem.

- A service is what is called a microservice in a microservice architecture. This is an independent unit that serves one purpose and provides limited functionality.

- The application is what makes up the components of the service. Usually there are no more than two. One of them provides API functionality, and the other is responsible for executing possibly lengthy and resource-intensive asynchronous background tasks, such as periodically receiving or updating data from other systems or periodically taking a long time to calculate something.

CHAPTER 4   ARCHITECTURAL SOLUTION PART 2: SERVICES AND SUBSYSTEMS

- A library is a collection of software functions or classes intended for use in different applications. For example, it makes sense to use the same library for logging, rather than writing your own for each service.

Kubernetes

In this section, I'll talk about an important topic: Kubernetes. I'll tell you more about how to install it on a server, manage it, and deliver your applications to it in Chapter 9. But in this chapter I will cover a few important concepts so you can better understand some of my architectural decisions.

In the past few decades, a large number of approaches to software development have accumulated in the software field. Dozens of programming languages have become popular, each of which has its own compilation and execution mechanism. This means that in addition to the complexity of writing a program, there is also the complexity of running it on the server, because the system administrator has to understand the intricacies of how programs work in a particular language. Adding to this complexity is the different dependencies between applications. Often your program cannot run without other pre-installed applications. Sometimes when you create a service, it will fine on your personal computer, but when it is deployed to another server for testing, something goes wrong. It might be that your application requires one version of a pre-installed helper application, and the server has another installed. This problem was solved with the arrival of containers.

A container is a standardized and portable package that includes everything you need to run your application. This allows you to separate your application from the infrastructure, which includes the operating system and pre-installed applications.

CHAPTER 4   ARCHITECTURAL SOLUTION PART 2: SERVICES AND SUBSYSTEMS

It doesn't matter what environment your application will run in, what language it is written in, and what dependencies it has. The developer just needs to create a program and pack it into a container, and the administrator can work with the container, which is ready to run. Of course, you can launch it manually. If the developers have released a new version of the application, you will also have to update the entire system manually. You must not forget about the uninterrupted operation of the system, which means you first need to launch a new version, transfer the load to the environment with the new version, and only then stop the application on the old environment. Figure 4-2 shows how this process looks schematically.

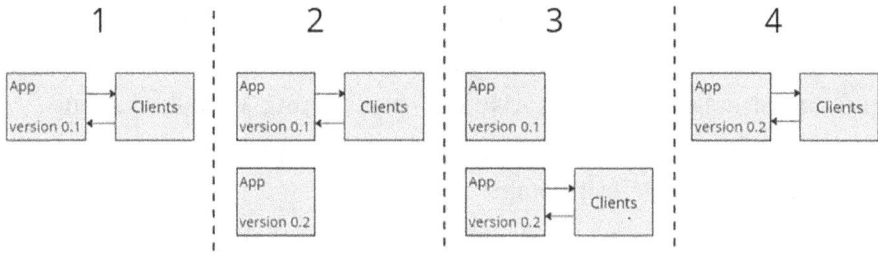

Figure 4-2. *Application update process*

There is a high chance of error in this entire procedure, which can be solved with orchestrators.

An orchestrator is a system that helps manage the launch and operation of containers. The most popular of them is Kubernetes. The orchestrator not only provides the functionality to deploy your containers but also allows you to easily scale, update, and monitor the performance of your entire system. In this chapter, it is important for me to tell you about scaling. One of the central concepts of Kubernetes is the pod. This is the basic building block of this orchestrator, and it is also the only object in Kubernetes that causes the container to run. Roughly speaking, a pod is a small computer on which your application runs. Kubernetes allows you to create multiple pods for one application. It is this feature that provides the

CHAPTER 4   ARCHITECTURAL SOLUTION PART 2: SERVICES AND SUBSYSTEMS

ability to horizontally scale your system. Since one application can have several pods, it is important when designing an application to remember that any of your applications may not be launched in a single copy. For example, if your application processes theories, it is important when designing it to consider that two different pods could start working in parallel on the same theory, which could lead to data corruption.

Now that you have the minimum knowledge required to design a system built on a microservices architecture, let's get started.

Subsystems

Let's first determine the list of subsystems and their functionality. I see only two subsystems in our system. This is a subsystem for searching for profitable strategies and a subsystem for real trading. We talked about them a lot in the previous chapter; I see no reason to complicate our system at the current design stage.

The task of the search subsystem is to find a profitable strategy and report this to the real trading subsystem. The real trading subsystem must start trading based on the found strategy and pass the strategy indicators to the search subsystem to optimize the strategy. As a result, the enlarged diagram of our system will look like Figure 4-3.

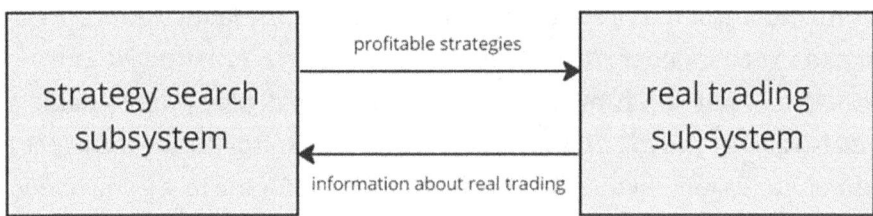

Figure 4-3. *Subsystem interaction diagram*

Strategy Search Subsystem

The purpose of the subsystem is to search for profitable strategies. Let me remind you that for this the user themselves or with the help of a generator must generate theories. This means that the search subsystem must provide the user with an interface that allows this to be done. This entails the creation of a separate front-end service.

Whenever it comes to users, it is very important to raise the issue of roles. What are the user roles in the system? How are these users authorized? Is there a need to store user actions? I decided not to add this functionality to my system. The main reason is that most likely the system will be used by a limited circle of people with the same full rights. I prefer to focus on the strategy search functionality and can add an authorization system and normal accounting of user actions later if necessary.

Since our system will not have users as entities, there is no need for a single API service to provide uniform functionality to the front end. It will be redundant and turn into a simple and nonfunctional layer. Therefore, at the current stage, the subsystem will look like diagram 2 in Figure 4-4.

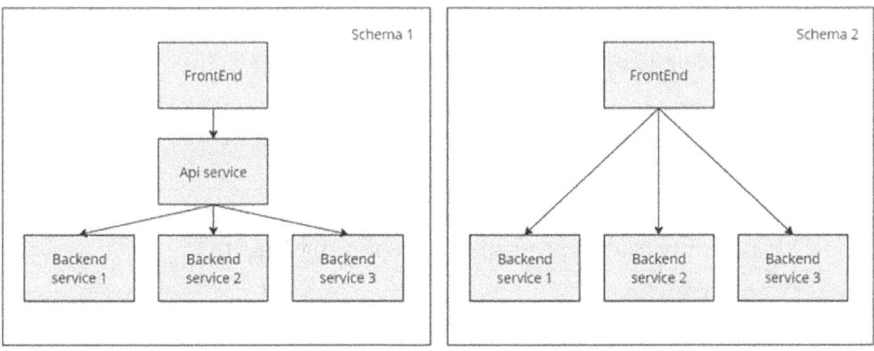

Figure 4-4. *Options for interaction with the front end*

CHAPTER 4   ARCHITECTURAL SOLUTION PART 2: SERVICES AND SUBSYSTEMS

Processing Generators

Let's go in order. The user, using our front-end service, should be able to control the generator to generate theories. So, the user went to the generator settings page, filled out the required fields, and clicked the generate button. The front end sends a request to the back end for generation, and theories are generated. They can be generated synchronously, when the user waits until the system generates all the theories, or asynchronously, when the user is notified that the process has started, and the result can be viewed in a special tab or in the same window.

I chose the asynchronous option for a number of reasons.

- Generating theories may take some time because there may be many of them. It's not a good idea to make the user wait all this time.

- It is not clear what to do if an error occurs during the generation process, when some of the theories have already been generated. Should I delete the old ones? Also, how do I understand which of them relate specifically to this request? It turns out that in the case of an error, the user will wait not only for the theories to be generated but also for them to be deleted.

- How will the user know the result if the session is suddenly interrupted such as when the Internet goes off?

Since the generation of theories will be asynchronous, it is necessary to somehow display information about the progress of the generator, as well as the generation status, on the front end. Since the generator has a state in the form of a status, it means it becomes an entity. That is, the user will be able to see a list of previously created generators with their statuses and settings.

CHAPTER 4 ARCHITECTURAL SOLUTION PART 2: SERVICES AND SUBSYSTEMS

There are several more arguments in favor of the generator as an entity.

- The generator as an entity allows the user to fill in only part of the required fields, save their work, and return to it later.

- The generator as an entity allows the user to create generators by copying. This means that if the user wants to change, for example, only the list of indicators, they will not have to enter the remaining fields again.

- The user will be able to see a summary of the generated theories in one place because they will be linked to a specific generator.

As a result, I see the generator settings page as shown in Figure 4-5.

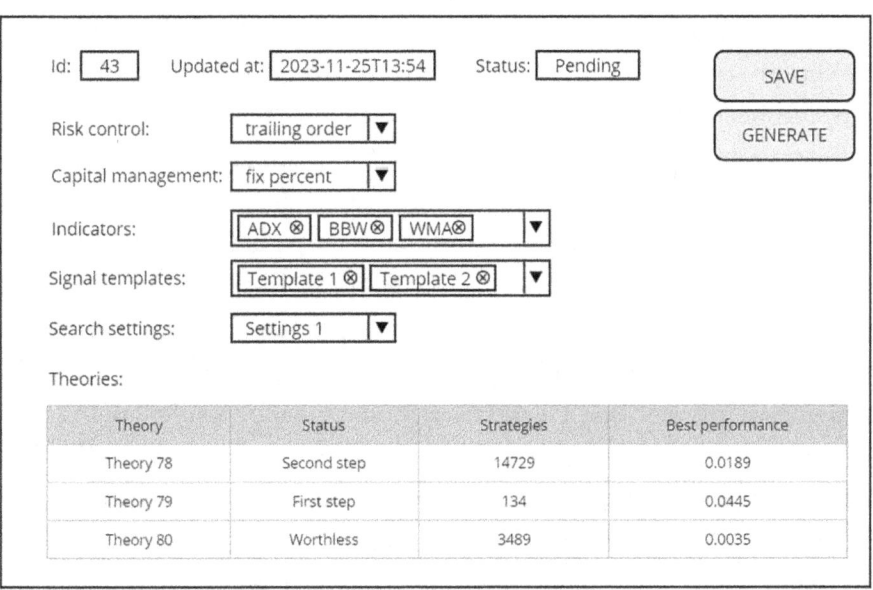

Figure 4-5. *Generator settings display option*

CHAPTER 4   ARCHITECTURAL SOLUTION PART 2: SERVICES AND SUBSYSTEMS

Let's move on. Here the user clicked the Generate button. The front end sent a signal to the back end to start generation. And we agreed that the generation of theories is an asynchronous process. This means the back end must somewhere note the fact that this generator needs to be processed and send a response to the front stating that the user's request has been processed.

Of course, the program must change the status of the generator to waiting. In principle, this status can be used as a flag for the generator processing process, and then some background job will pick up this generator and begin processing it. By background job, I mean a special process that runs on a schedule, for example once a minute, and does a specific job.

This solution has one big drawback: the degradation of the search speed for active generators. This happens because the total number of generators will grow, which means that a request to search for generators in a certain status will work slower and slower. An alternative to working with statuses is working with a queue. You can put a generator in a queue, and background jobs will see it, process it, and remove it from the queue. This way, only active generators will be stored in the queue and it will not grow. There are several options for implementing queues, for example based on a database. Many cloud platforms have great queuing and processing solutions. There are also several mechanisms for managing queues; one of the most popular is Kafka. However, cloud solutions does not suit me, because I want my system to be independent of the cloud platform so I can deploy it on my home computer. I also think that using Kafka to solve this issue is too cumbersome, because you need to understand it and also be able to administer it.

To make a decision about how this process will be implemented, it is necessary to take into account that the theory generators will be created by the user, which means that there will be few of them, and the degradation will be insignificant. Therefore, I propose taking the simplest route.

When calling the back-end method, the waiting status is set, which will serve as a flag that the generator needs to be processed. Then some job should hire him. What this job will do is run periodically, check if there are generators for processing, and, if any, process them. At this stage, it is important to discuss whether these jobs will run in the same application as the API or whether it will be a separate application.

I believe that this should be a separate application, and there is one important reason for this. The process of generating theories can be lengthy and costly. During this time, the user should be able to continue working without interruption or slowdown in performance. If an application is busy generating theories, then it will not be able to process user requests with the same efficiency as before. In addition, this approach will allow these two applications to scale independently of each other. After all, we understand that the API App load will most likely be lower than on the Background Jobs App. Therefore, at this stage, the strategy search service looks like Figure 4-6.

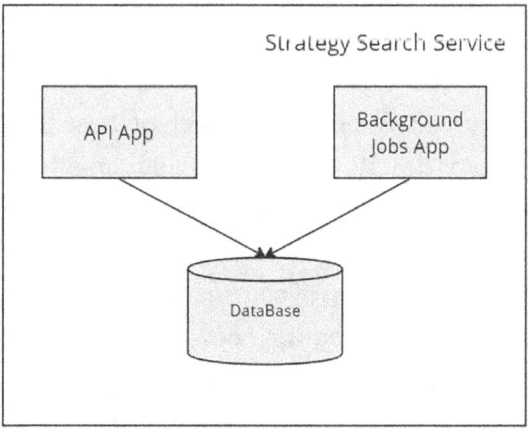

Figure 4-6. *Strategy Search Service application structure*

As a result, the process of automatic theory generation will look like this:

- The user enters the required data in the front-end service and clicks the Generate button.
- The API App of the Strategy Search Service accepts a request from the front end and sets the generator to Waiting status in the database.
- The Background Jobs App of the Strategy Search Service periodically queries the database table with generators, and if it finds a generator in the Waiting status, it begins to generate theories.
- After generating theories, Background Jobs App sets the generator status to Done and starts looking for the next generator in the Waiting status.

Queue

We have decided how theories will be generated. But after generation, the system must take these theories to work. Each of these theories must go through the three steps described in the previous chapter, and if the first step is unsuccessful, the process of searching for strategies according to this theory must be stopped.

To process theories, you can, of course, use statuses as in the case of generators, but I don't like this option because, unlike generators, there will be many theories, which means that the request to search for theories with the required status will degrade. There is also another problem that we will encounter: when two pods simultaneously take on the same theory. And this means only one thing: a queue is needed. I have already said that I do not want to use a queue built on the mechanisms of cloud platforms, since I do not want to tie my system to any solution provider, so we will build a queue at home.

CHAPTER 4   ARCHITECTURAL SOLUTION PART 2: SERVICES AND SUBSYSTEMS

I have several queue requirements.

- It should be preserved even if the pod is stopped.
- The ability to horizontally scale queue handlers is required.

There are several popular solutions for this task: RabitMQ, Kafka, or a Postgres-based queue.

I discard RabitMQ right away, since it does not guarantee message delivery, and for me this is an important point, because I do not want any of the theories to be processed.

Kafka is a great mechanism, but it requires quite a lot of server resources, so I will consider it as a growth point for my application. If it grows to such an extent that the Postgres-based mechanism becomes ineffective, then Kafka can be implemented.

The Postgres-based queue is perhaps not the most common solution, but it has one big advantage: it is cheap in terms of the resources required, and besides, our application will already use Postgres to store data.

So, our queue should provide the following functionality:

- Only those entities that need to be processed should be in the queue. This means that after processing, it is necessary to remove the processed entity from the queue.
- Ensure that entities are quickly added to the processing queue.
- Ensure that parallel processing of one entity by two pods is prohibited.

Let's immediately design the tables in the database that we will need to organize the queue. Of course, we will have a queue table with an entity_id column. It will contain entries with new theories. In order to prevent two pods from using the same theory, it is necessary to somehow mark the theories that are already being processed by the system.

Note Table locking in a database is a mechanism that allows you to lock an entire table or its individual records, for example, for reading or writing for another database user. I'll talk more about it in the next chapter, but for now the main thing to understand is that when a pod starts working on theories, it can lock a table or rows in it, and then a request from another pod will wait for the lock to end.

If we lock the queue table, then it will not be possible to add new records with theories to it. An additional table will help us get around this point, called active_queue, with an entity_id column. When the next pod wants to process the queue of theories, it will do the following:

- Lock the active_queue table
- Select an unoccupied theory, that is, a theory that is in the process_queue table and not in the active_queue table
- Record that it is active in the active_queue table
- Release the lock from active_queue

But what would you do if the pod started working on a theory and suddenly ceased to exist? How do other pods find out that no one is working with this theory anymore? To solve this problem, let's add a timestamp column to the active_queue table. When the next pod starts working, it will take over the theory even from the active queue if more than a certain amount of time has passed from the timestamp, for example several minutes. As a result, the tables providing the queue will look like Figure 4-7.

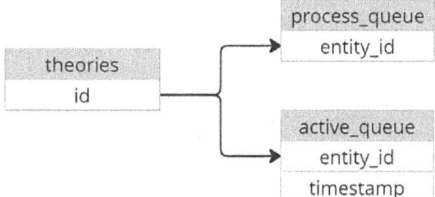

Figure 4-7. *Database table schema*

Let's also solve the scaling issue. There will be tasks for processing the launch queue of the BackgroundJobs application, which have already been generating theories, or it is worth moving them into a separate application, or a service.

I don't yet see any reason to move the theory processing process into a separate service, because this will add more work for us in the form of needing to transfer data about created theories to a new service. This is a large amount of data, and we will also have to solve the problem of transferring information about created indicators and methods and money management between the two services and ensure their consistency. Yes, perhaps our service is becoming like some kind of hybrid between a monolith and a microservice, but I am trying to strike a balance between the ability to quickly scale the system and the complexity of its development. If a team of developers, or even several teams, were working on it, then of course it would make sense to move work with theories into a separate service. But since I work alone and a temporary stop in processing the queue of active theories in the event of an unsuccessful update of the BackgroundJobs application is not critical for me, I believe that there is no need for a new service.

I propose solving the issue with easy horizontal scaling by increasing the number of applications for this service. Now there will be three of them with one common database, where the Theory Processing App will process the queue and guide the theories in three steps (see Figure 4-8).

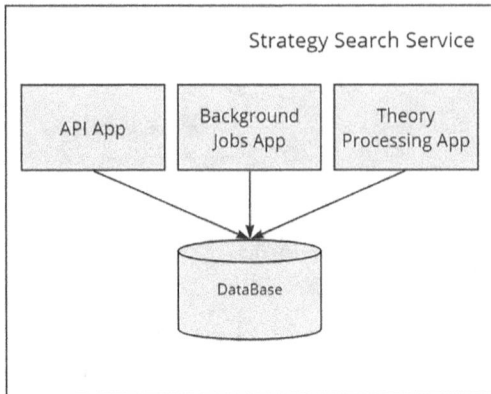

Figure 4-8. *Structure of Strategy Search Service with three applications*

Finite State Machine

We came up with a horizontally scalable solution for theory processing. But what will this processing look like? A simple movement from status to status does not suit us, if only because after the first step we can either recognize the theory as unsuitable or move on to the second step, which means that the process of processing the theory has branches. And when you are faced with the task of moving some entity through a business process, with branches, it makes sense to think about implementing a state machine. A state machine is one of the ways to process an entity according to a business process. The idea of a state machine or finite state machine is that your entity can be in only one state at any given time. The number of these states is finite, and the state machine also contains rules for transitions between states.

Transitions between states occur under the influence of external signals. For example, transitioning the state "Processing the first step" to "Checking the suitability of the theory" means calculating all strategies that were generated using the optimization algorithm. Figure 4-9 shows a simplified diagram of the movement of the theory through states.

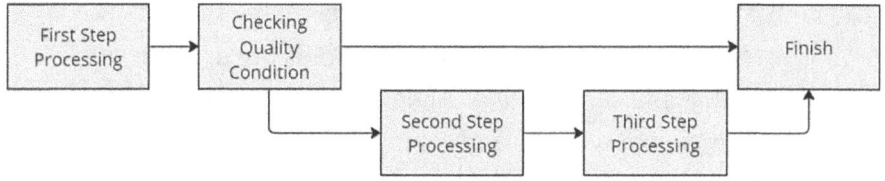

Figure 4-9. Enlarged theory processing process

Concept of Theory Processing Steps

At this stage, we decided how the theory would move through the process. Let's discuss how this process will occur. In the previous chapter we found out that the processing of the theory will be carried out in three steps.

- The first step is a quick test of the theory. In this step, a subtheory is created with a limited number of parameter variations by increasing the step of values for each of them. After this, an optimization algorithm configured in breadth is launched. Thanks to this, strategies are generated and calculated. This process is iterative because the optimization algorithm creates a new set of strategy parameters based on the performance of the strategies created in the previous iteration. After the optimization algorithm is completed, the strategies are checked against quality conditions. If at least one strategy meets these conditions, then the theory is considered to be of quality.

- If, as a result of the first step, the theory is recognized as qualitative, then the iterative creation of subtheories occurs with a decrease in the step of parameters and a narrowing of the range of their values. Next, all created strategies are checked for the second quality condition.

- In the third step, the suitable strategies of the second step are calculated again, but using tools not used in the first and second steps. After that, they are checked for final quality status and sent to the real trading subsystem.

When I described all three steps, the first thing I thought of was creating step entities because they have a lot in common. They take input settings in the form of an optimization algorithm and financial instruments, and as an output you get a set of strategies. See Figure 4-10.

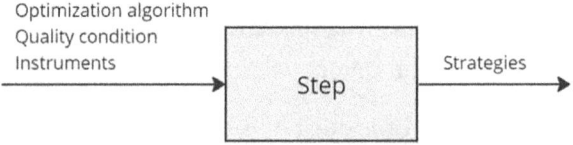

Figure 4-10. *Step entity*

But when I thought about what should happen in each step, I abandoned this idea because all three steps are significantly different from each other. In the first step, only one subtheory is created. There is absolutely no logic in narrowing the range of values and iterative search for strategies. In the third step, there is no work with the optimization algorithm; in this step, only the calculation of already created strategies and their selection occurs. As a result, I came to the conclusion that I would not be able to delegate the authority to create subtheories to another entity to facilitate the logic of passage through the theory process.

As a result, it turned out that the theory moves through the process within the first step, as shown on the state machine state map in Figure 4-11.

CHAPTER 4   ARCHITECTURAL SOLUTION PART 2: SERVICES AND SUBSYSTEMS

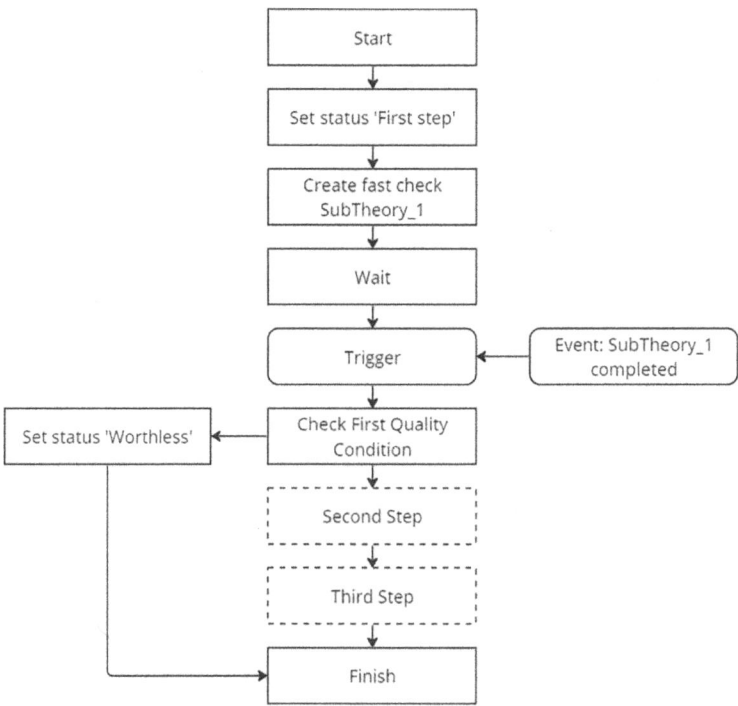

Figure 4-11. *Logic of the first step of the theory process*

In this process, special attention should be paid to the event of completion of subtheory calculations. Calculating a subtheory is an iterative process that can take a long time, and I may even decide to outsource this work to a separate application or service, which is why, instead of taking the "Calculation of a subtheory" step, I chose a scheme with asynchronous calculation. This means that the theory will wait and do nothing until a signal arrives that the subtheory has been completely calculated. I would also like to point out that in this diagram, the status is just a marking that will be needed to show the user the progress of work on the theory, nothing more. That is, this status has absolutely no effect on the process.

Figure 4-12 shows the second step of the processing process.

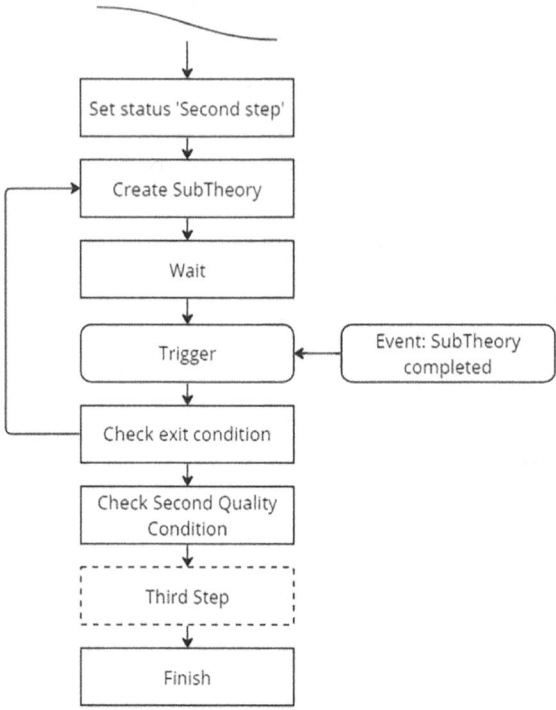

Figure 4-12. *Logic of the second step of the theory process*

In this diagram, it is worth paying attention to the fact that subtheories are created iteratively. Let me remind you that the calculation of parameters for a new subtheory is based on the calculation results of the previous subtheory, but the very first system will be created based on the settings of the theory.

Figure 4-13 shows the third step of the processing process.

CHAPTER 4   ARCHITECTURAL SOLUTION PART 2: SERVICES AND SUBSYSTEMS

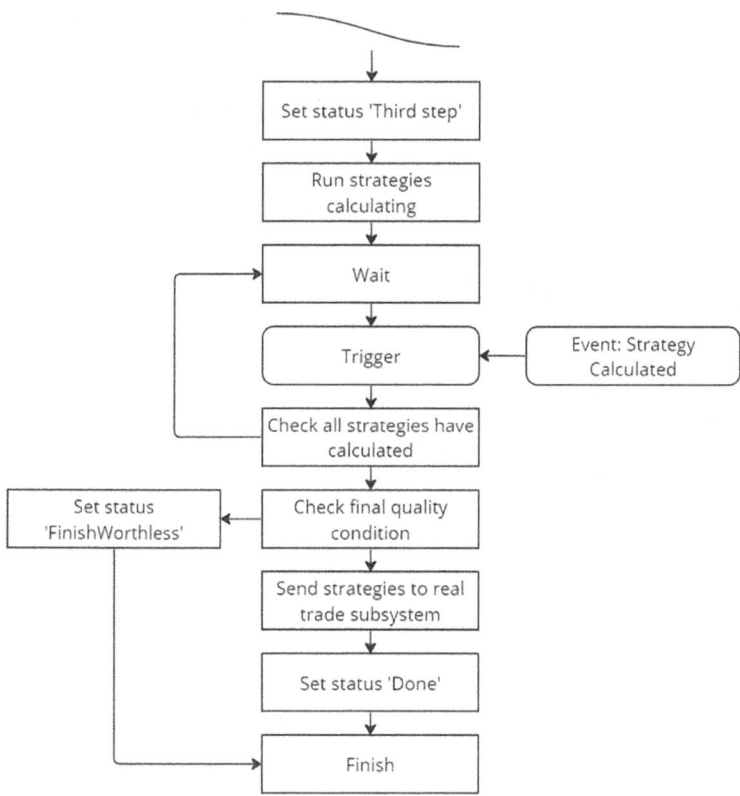

Figure 4-13. *Logic of the third step of the theory process*

There are several things that are notable about this scheme.

The first of them is the asynchronous calculation of strategies. We'll talk about this a little later, but I'll say right away that it will be parallel and horizontally scalable. The theory can move to the next state only after calculating all strategies, which means we need to check the fact that all strategies have been calculated every time we complete the calculation of the next strategy. It is also important that our state machine be able to work with the parallel arrival of events. Imagine a situation where the two last strategies were calculated at the same time. When checking, the service will "see" that there is another uncalculated strategy and will not change the state of the theory. As a result, the theory will forever remain at the "Wait" step.

Please also note that if the final check fails, I set the status to FinishWorthless, not Worthless. This is done so that the user can see the difference between a worthless theory after the first quick test and after the final one. It is quite possible that they will use ideas from this theory when generating the next batch of theories.

Calculation of Subtheories

Let's think about how the subtheory will work. Obviously, this has a certain process. At a minimum, it should have several statuses such as Created, In Progress, and Completed. The question is whether this process is complicated enough to start using a finite state machine. I see the subtheory process taking place as shown in Figure 4-14.

CHAPTER 4   ARCHITECTURAL SOLUTION PART 2: SERVICES AND SUBSYSTEMS

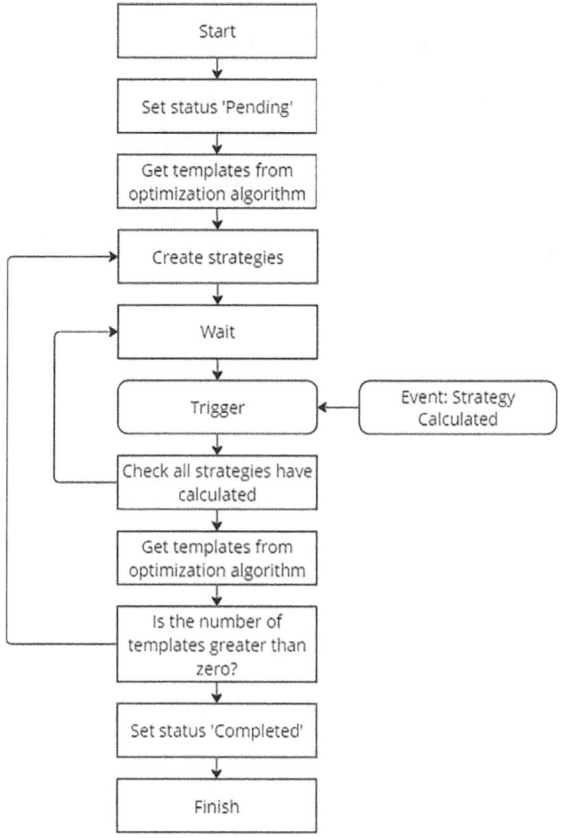

Figure 4-14. *Subtheory processing*

It's easy to imagine what this process would look like using a finite state machine. The main thing to remember is that a subtheory must have a separate state map.

Process Review for Generators

So at this stage we already have two entities that use the state machine. And you know what I really don't like at this stage in the system diagram? Generators have begun to deviate from the uniform pattern of entity processing. Even worse, the service will have a separate Background Jobs App exclusively for them. I suggest reconsidering this point.

CHAPTER 4   ARCHITECTURAL SOLUTION PART 2: SERVICES AND SUBSYSTEMS

> **Note** The fact that I periodically change my solution can be confusing, but let me remind you that creating an architectural solution is an iterative process. Revising architectural decisions is a normal phenomenon. It is better to reconsider your decisions now, before development begins, than to realize that something needs to be changed at a later time.

At this stage, the state map for the generators looks very simple (see Figure 4-15).

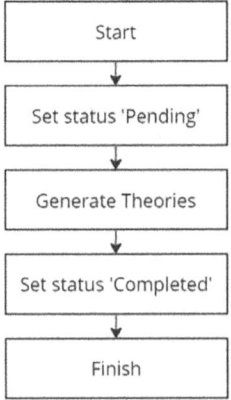

Figure 4-15. *State map for theory generation process*

The process of generating theories is iterative. Still, it's a slow process. Iteration will provide the user with the opportunity to interrupt the process of generating theories if the user understands that all the theories created in the previous iterations are worthless. Better yet, this check should be performed automatically, as shown in Figure 4-16.

CHAPTER 4   ARCHITECTURAL SOLUTION PART 2: SERVICES AND SUBSYSTEMS

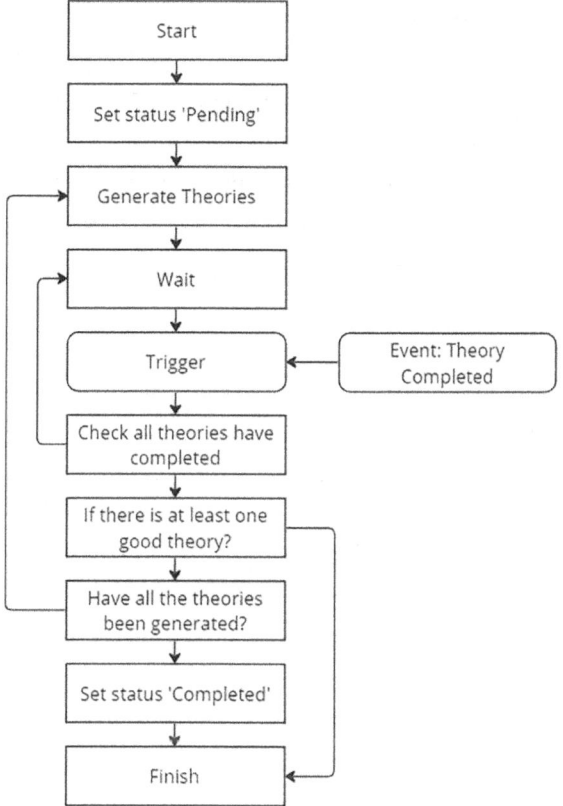

Figure 4-16. *Improved state map*

There is another option for the theory generation scenario: to implement it using an optimization algorithm. Once we have indicators of the theory's performance in the form of indicators of the effectiveness of its best strategies, then we can use this data to work with optimization algorithms. We will discuss this issue in more detail in Chapter 11.

Using a state machine to work with generators would be a proactive decision on our part. Although the requirements for the system did not explicitly indicate that the process of generating theories would be so complex, we will create a system that will make it quite easy to complicate this process.

CHAPTER 4   ARCHITECTURAL SOLUTION PART 2: SERVICES AND SUBSYSTEMS

That is, we will stop using Background Jobs to process generators and start using pods of the Theory Processing App for these purposes. This means that when the user clicks the Generate button, the API App will make a new entry in the processign_queue table.

Also, since the state machine will begin to process not only theories but also subtheories with generators, it makes sense to rename the Theory Processing App to the Processing App. I will talk in detail about the operation of my state machine in future chapters. Figure 4-17 shows the updated service diagram, without a separate application for background jobs.

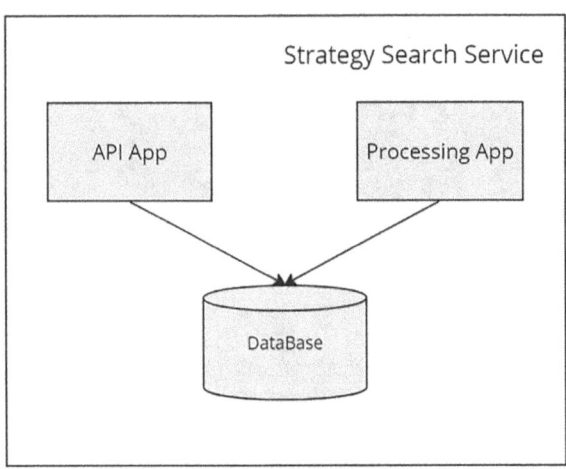

Figure 4-17. *Final Strategy Search Service application structure*

Optimization Algorithms

I would like to abstract the work with optimization algorithms into a separate module, which will have its own separate versions and which will not know anything about the fact that it works with strategies or subtheories. This is necessary to separate responsibilities between modules. Imagine that you want to make changes to the subtheory in such a way that the logic for generating variables for optimization algorithms will change. For example, you will add the ability to use not only indicator values in your signals but also their slope angles, or even switch to formulas instead of pure indicator values. If optimization algorithms are not abstracted and work directly with strategies, then you will have to change this block; otherwise, you will only need to change the class that is responsible for converting strategy data into a set of variables for the algorithm.

Moving optimization algorithms into a separate module provides another important advantage: you can test their work on much faster mathematical functions, such as the Kearfott or Rastigin function. I will discuss in detail how to test the optimization algorithm in Chapter 7. Now the main thing to understand is that complex optimization algorithms are not a constant, but a kind of constructor of methods and parameters. You can create an infinite number of variations of the genetic algorithm or other algorithms derived from it. Therefore, the functionality for quickly checking the operation of your algorithm is vital.

In Figure 4-18, I clearly demonstrated working with the future library of optimization algorithms.

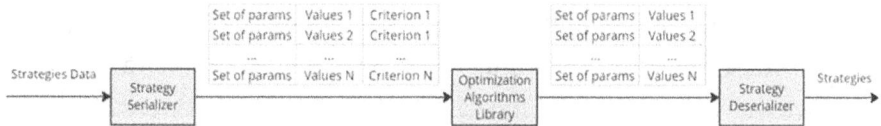

Figure 4-18. *An example of using the optimization algorithms module*

The fact that the user will have to independently create optimization algorithms based on some templates suggests that the optimization algorithm also becomes an entity.

CHAPTER 4   ARCHITECTURAL SOLUTION PART 2: SERVICES AND SUBSYSTEMS

Tasks

We have decided how strategies will be created. But how will they be calculated? To calculate a strategy, two components are required: the strategy itself and a certain period of historical data for the instrument.

I placed the historical data period into a simple entity called TestCandleInterval. This entity accumulates all the information necessary to obtain a set of candles.

Namely:

- Exchange Id. It is no secret that the same instrument can be traded on several exchanges, which means its prices can be different.

- Financial instrument Id.

- StartDate. All candles with an opening date greater than this value will be included in the selection for TestCandleInterval.

- StopDate. The second border is for the opening date of the candles.

In this book, I implement a relatively simple system. Therefore, the user will create the TestCandleInterval independently. But there is room for growth here. For example, you can create a TestCandleInterval while loading historical data. Remember in the previous chapter we talked about what tools should be used to launch a ready-made strategy. And one of the options was to separate them not by types of instruments but by types of charts. The new entity is perfect for both implementations because it contains a StartDate and a StopDate. This allows you to divide the historical data of one instrument into several test intervals.

In connection with the introduction of the new TestCandleInterval entity, it turns out that to calculate the strategy, only two components are needed: the strategy itself and TestCandleInterval. I combined these parameters into a separate entity and called it Task. It also makes sense to add a status to the task to understand whether it has been counted or is still being counted or maybe just waiting in queue for calculation. Tasks will not have a complex process. This is a small elementary unit that will have only four states with elementary logic for transitioning from each other: Created, Pending, Done, Error. There will be many tasks—hundreds of thousands. Putting them in the same queue as generators and theories is not a good idea. We will then lose flexibility in scaling the system. Therefore, I decided to put the tasks in a separate queue and even allocate a separate application for them.

This is how it will work:

- The subtheory will generate tasks and place them in a queue.

- A separate application with a large number of pods will take a task from the queue, mark it as active, and after calculation, remove it from the queue.

- If the user decides that the theory is bad even before completing all the steps, then when the theory calculation is cancelled, their subtheories will be cancelled, and their tasks will simply be removed from the queue.

Figure 4-19 shows the task queue processing process. It can receive tasks from several sources. For example, the user can create a task through the front end and set it to be calculated via the API App. Or the Processing App, while working on a subtheory, will set tasks for calculation.

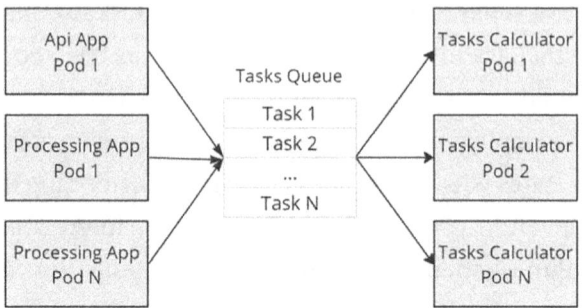

Figure 4-19. *Task queue processing process*

It is extremely important that the calculation of tasks is as fast as possible. This process needs to be optimized down to the millisecond. At this point, I ran into a problem. I must have a mechanism by which I can verify that my system is working correctly. To do this, I needed not only the final indicators of the effectiveness of the strategy but also the intermediate results, such as the calculated values of the indicators on each of the candles, as well as all created positions with system orders and deals. I would like to take a separate task and see how the strategy behaved, when, and why it opened positions. Obviously, to implement this functionality, it is necessary to save data on the progress of the strategy into a database, and this is not a quick procedure. I also knew that the automated parts of the system did not need this data; the final results were enough for it. In connection with all of this, I added three calculation modes to the task:

- **With only the final information about the calculation saved.** In this mode, the database will store information about the final results of the calculation, the minimum necessary for the operation of the automated parts of the system

- **With saving data on positions.** In this mode, in addition to the final results, the database stores information about open positions with status history, with all orders and transactions

- **With saving indicator values.** In this mode, not only all data from the previous two modes is saved, but also information about signal calculations, which includes the values of indicators and groups of conditions on each candle.

Core

In our entire scheme of dividing the system into two subsystems, I am confused by the fact that testing and verification of the trading strategy will take place in one subsystem, and the strategy will work in another. It is necessary to build the architecture in such a way that the system nodes responsible for making decisions about opening or closing positions, the logic of the system orders, and all the components of the strategy are common to the search and real trading subsystems.

This is reasonable, because we will test not only the strategies but also the code that implements them, which means this code should be the same. For this I created a separate library called Core. It is in Core that the logic of the strategy and all its components will be concentrated.

As input, Core will receive information about changes in the market, as well as signals about changes in the status of exchange orders, and as output, it will send signals about the need to place or close an order with a broker. See Figure 4-20.

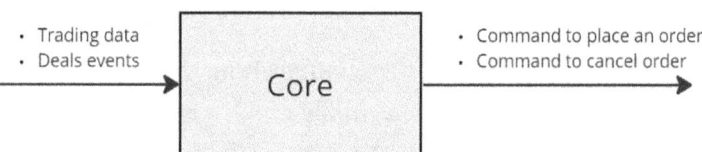

Figure 4-20. *Top-level view of the Core module*

Obviously, Core will store entities such as Strategy, Signal, Instrument, and so on. This means it must contain all the necessary components to work with the database. I thought about separating Core into a separate microservice but quickly abandoned this idea, mainly because when calculating tasks, a lot of time would be spent on network interaction between the task calculation service and Core, and we cannot afford this.

I would also like to include in Core the functionality for calculating indicators of the effectiveness of the strategies; it would be strange if the real trading system calculated indicators using one formula while the search subsystem used another.

Sandbox Exchange

At this stage, we need to know what will process signals and how we will process them. This means we will need to create a small Sandbox Exchange module that will store orders, respond to signals for placing or cancelling an order, and make a decision about closing an order as candles arrive.

As a result, I see the big-picture process of calculating the task as follows:

- We get candles by setting TestCandleInterval (all of it or in batches).
- In a loop we go through all the candles, doing the following:
    a. We notify Sandbox Exchange about the appearance of new candles.
    b. We notify Core about the appearance of new candles.

Such a system does not ideally correspond to what will happen in real trading because Sandbox Exchange in our version does not know anything about the order book. This means it will not be able to correctly simulate order execution because it doesn't know whether there were enough offers at that moment in time and at what prices they were offered.

But we still have no choice. There is no way we can wait several years until we collect the required amount of information, because it is almost impossible to find historical data with order books. Therefore, I will simply try to implement Sandbox Exchange as similar as possible to a real exchange.

Real Trading Subsystem

This subsystem has the following goals:

- Ensuring smooth operation of profitable strategies
- Ensuring the strategies work with the right types of financial instruments
- Constant determination of the type of financial instruments
- Providing the user with the ability to manage the trading process such as the ability to enable or disable a strategy

Again, since it's an interface, a separate front-end service is needed. As in the case of the search subsystem, I propose we abandon the system of roles and solving issues of access levels, because at the beginning the system will have a limited list of trusted users with the same full rights to all actions in the system.

CHAPTER 4   ARCHITECTURAL SOLUTION PART 2: SERVICES AND SUBSYSTEMS

Integration with Exchanges

In a real trading system, there is a big problem that we have to face: the large amount of information coming from exchanges. Imagine that the candle update information for an instrument such as the Bitcoin-Dollar pair could be received via websockets from the exchange at least once every 50 ms. And we will have many such financial instruments.

First, it is necessary to separate the work with exchanges from other services of the subsystem into a separate service that provides a single interface. I don't want other services to know anything about the internal implementation of integration with each of the exchanges. But is this enough? Imagine that you discovered a bug or decided to add integration with another exchange. If all the code for working with exchanges is located in one service, then when updating the code associated with one exchange, you will have to stop working with the others. This means that orders will not be placed and data on changes in candlesticks will not be received, which entails a loss of money. Therefore, it makes sense to make each of the adapters (the module responsible for converting specific information from the exchange into our single standard) a separate service.

Let's imagine a scenario where a certain service of our subsystem wants to place an order with a broker. To do this, the service will have to take the URL of the required adapter, which is responsible for integration with a specific broker. It turns out that each back-end service that needs to use adapters will have to contain the logic for determining this URL. What happens if the broker switches to a new version of the API and we have to change the adapter interfaces? This is the first problem. The second problem is that somewhere we need to store a mapping between our instrument names and the broker names. This means that we will need a database. And what? We have to create a separate database for each broker? To solve these problems, we can create a proxy service, an exchange gateway. This will take on the functionality of knowing

CHAPTER 4   ARCHITECTURAL SOLUTION PART 2: SERVICES AND SUBSYSTEMS

which of the adapters needs to be addressed, and it will also store name comparisons in its database and monitor the uniformity of adapter interfaces.

Figure 4-21 demonstrates both approaches.

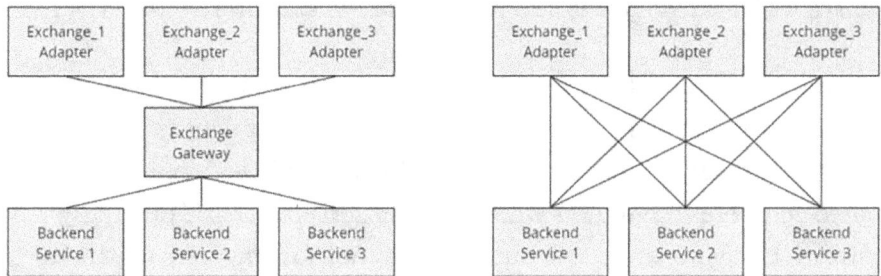

Figure 4-21. *Possible exchange gateway architectural solutions*

Now let's define the approximate functionality of the subsystem for working with exchanges. Since to work with exchanges it is necessary to create several services (and even this will be a relatively independent unit that can be used in other systems), I will separate it into a separate subsystem.

So, what functionality will be included in the subsystem for working with exchanges?

- Ability to place orders using a common interface for all exchanges.

- Possibility of order cancellation.

- Providing information on updating order statuses and completing deals.

- Providing trade data. In our case, this will only be data on updating candles, but in the future it can be expanded with information about changes in the order book.

153

Figure 4-22 shows what the first and second steps will look.

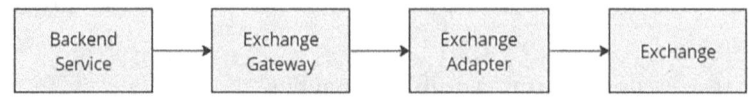

Figure 4-22. *Sequence of service calls when creating an order*

This looks bulky. Time will be wasted on networking, but I decided to compromise on this issue. I initially defined my system not as a system for scalping trading, since I understood that I most likely would not be able to compete with traders who rent their servers in close proximity to the exchange servers. I will purposefully look for strategies in which the average lifetime of open positions is measured in minutes or hours, not in seconds, and I believe it is worthwhile to compromise on ease of development and maintenance, at the expense of speed.

We have decided on placing and cancelling orders. Providing information about updating order statuses and trading data will be more difficult. Let's imagine that the exchange sent a message about a candle change. How will the information reach consumers? And there will be several of them, because it is normal for several strategies to work with one financial instrument, and both strategies should receive the same information. So, the adapter will have to know about all the strategies that need this information. That doesn't sound very good. In addition, the adapter may not have time to notify all information consumers before the arrival of a new message from the exchange.

I think there is only one solution that meets our needs to send messages to multiple consumers, even with high throughput: the use of message brokers. Message brokers were created to solve this problem. The source of information (in our case, the adapter) simply sends a message to the message broker, and that's it. That's where its work ends. It doesn't know anything about the number of consumers or whether they exist at all. Its task is simply to send the message to the message broker, and this is very fast operation. Then the broker ensures the transfer of data to all information consumers. So, the most suitable solution for the system is a solution based on the Kafka message queue system because we need high throughput and Kafka is capable of passing up to millions of messages per second. Of course, like any queue built not on pushing messages but on reading them by consumers, this does not guarantee real-time delivery of messages, especially if the consumer takes a long time to process the messages. But our architecture is based on distributing the load between pods, which will provide the ability to scale the system.

Note Kafka is a distributed message broker that works on a publisher-subscriber basis. Data in Kafka is represented as key-value pairs. Kafka guarantees that all messages will be ordered in the exact order in which they were received. Kafka stores read messages for a period of time.

The next question is, will the adapter itself send messages to the queue? Or will they also go through the exchange gateway? On the one hand, it makes sense for them to go through the exchange gateway; this way we will hide Kafka and leave working with it in one place. We also guarantee that Kafka topics will contain messages of the same type; that is, we will remove the problem when one adapter sends messages to the old version, and another to the new one.

On the other hand, the exchange gateway will become a bottleneck. If we need to update it or we find an error in it, it will affect information flows from all adapters.

As a result, I am more inclined to the second option, where we give the adapters some freedom and they themselves will write messages to the Kafka topic, because I am afraid that in the future there will be problems with the performance of the exchange gateway. Yes, perhaps here I am

CHAPTER 4 ARCHITECTURAL SOLUTION PART 2: SERVICES AND SUBSYSTEMS

breaking the encapsulation of the adapters, and they are starting to know too much; however, I will provide a library for sending messages to the topic, common to all adapters.

As a result, Figure 4-23 shows the process of obtaining data from exchanges.

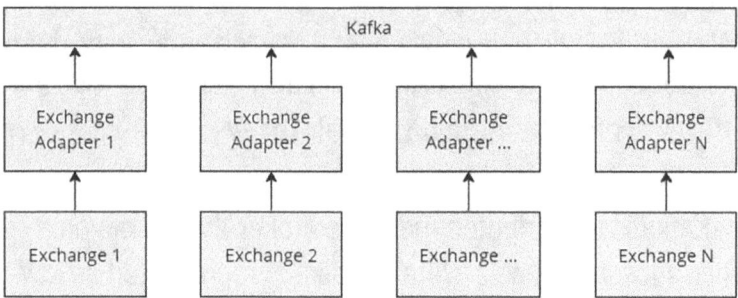

Figure 4-23. Adapter service architecture

Launch and Operation of Strategies

Let's get back to discussing how strategies work. A new strategy has entered our subsystem and needs to be launched, or maybe it's not a new strategy but simply a restart of the strategy after an update or failure. In any case, the startup process will look the same.

1. Store frequently used information in RAM, such as strategy identifier, exchange and financial instrument identifier, minimum lot size, number of decimal places in the price, and so on. There is not a lot of this information, but the strategy will use it often.

2. Correctly respond to messages about transactions that came from the exchange during downtime. If the strategy has not worked for a long time, then it may make sense to close all open positions.

CHAPTER 4   ARCHITECTURAL SOLUTION PART 2: SERVICES AND SUBSYSTEMS

3. It needs to subscribe to the desired trading information topic. For each exchange-instrument pair, a separate topic will be created in Kafka so that strategies can receive information only on the financial instrument they need.

4. After this, it needs to load historical trading data, because many indicators require information about previous candles to work correctly. This is especially important if we have to scale several indicators to the same scale.

5. Only after this can we consider that the strategy has begun to work.

The strategy operation block must be isolated so that data on the operation of one strategy does not affect the operation of another. The question is how do we do this? At what level should this insulation be ensured? In software, when a certain instance of a class is conditionally created for each strategy (which ensures the operation of the strategy, when will there be a separate pod in Kubernetes for each strategy-instrument pair? Or maybe some kind of hybrid solution, when, according to some logic, the number of working strategies on one pod will be set?

On the one hand, the strategies will work both in weakly volatile markets and in highly volatile ones. If changes in trading information occur rarely, then it may make sense to have one pod ensure the operation of several such strategies. On the other hand, such a small unit as a pod may not have time to process frequently received signals from highly volatile markets for several strategies. Therefore, it is important to maintain a balance.

There is one more important detail: a weakly volatile market can at some point become highly volatile, and then what? Redistribute strategies between pods? Provide yourself with periodic downtime at work? I don't like this option. I think that in this matter a good solution would be the logic of one pair of strategy/instrument and one pod. I also like this approach because we will know for sure that only one strategy works in this instance of the program, and we will certainly avoid trouble in the code associated with the influence of data from one strategy on another.

Enabling and Disabling Strategies

We have decided that each strategy will have a separate pod. But how will this work? Let's imagine that information came from the strategy search subsystem with a list of strategies with the types of instruments on which they can work. Let's first put them in the table with profitable strategies called profitable_strategies, where there will be two columns: strategy_id and instrument_type. But to launch a strategy, we need an instrument, not a type of it. It turns out that we need another instrument table where there is a type. At the start it will take an unoccupied strategy, so somehow we need to mark that it is already occupied and start working with it.

How will it understand that the strategy is not busy? It is possible, of course, for everyone to select a list of strategies from profitable_strategies, connect it with instruments, and then take an unused strategy-instrument pair to work. But what if we want to change this logic? For example, add an is_enabled checkbox for an instrument so that the user can independently enable or disable the instrument. Because the program code for determining working strategies will change, you will have to update it, which means you will have to restart the pods working with the strategies, which you would like to avoid. This means the logic for determining working strategies should be placed in a separate application with separate pods. That is, we will have one application (let's call it tasks), which will determine which strategies are working, and another application (let's call it worker), which launches these strategies and ensures their operation.

As a result, I see tables like these in the database, as shown in Figure 4-24.

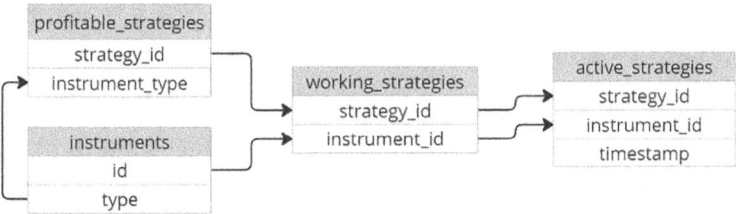

Figure 4-24. *Relationship between database tables*

This is how it will work:

1. The strategy search subsystem notifies the real trading subsystem about the emergence of new profitable strategies. They are written to the profitable_strategies table.

2. A special background job from the tasks application, which monitors the state of working strategies, "sees" that a new strategy has appeared that is not in the working_strategies table. It checks all required is_enabled conditions and makes an entry in working_strategies with the new strategy and the tools it can run on.

3. A free pod, on which a separate application for working worker strategies is running, "sees" that an entry has appeared in working_strategies, which is not in active_strategies, and takes it to work.

If the opposite situation occurs, when for some reason the user turns off a financial instrument or the type of the instrument changes, or maybe the strategy itself is turned off, then the job will delete records from the working_strategies table, and the worker under that works with it will detect this during the next check. This will delete the entry from active_ strategies and try to use the next free strategy.

There is one more important point to consider. There is a probability that a certain worker will suddenly cease to exist. What we get is that in active_strategies there is a record that the strategy-instrument pair is busy, but in fact it does not work. I solved this problem simply. Every time the worker pod checks the working strategies and nothing has changed, it updates the value in the timestamp column. If the date in this column lags behind the current one by a certain time interval, this will mean that the worker pod has stopped working with the strategy and it can be taken by another pod. At the current stage, I see the strategy service shown in Figure 4-25.

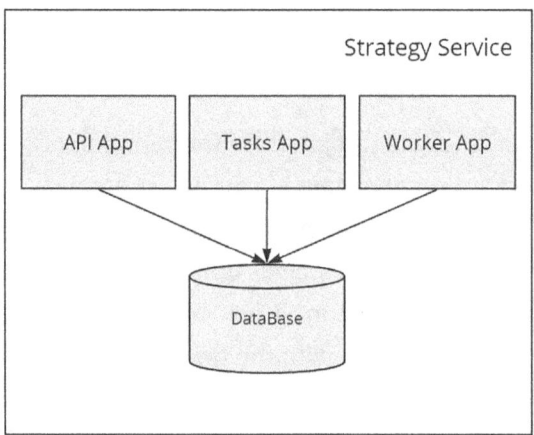

Figure 4-25. *Strategy Service structure*

Checking the Type of Financial Instrument

In the previous chapter, I mentioned the importance of determining the type of financial instrument. The type of instrument or chart greatly influences the profitability of the strategy. Often, a profitable strategy becomes unprofitable if it works on the wrong instrument. Perhaps the simplest way to determine the type of instrument is to use the logic already inherent in the signal. I think using a signal is a great option for these reasons:

- Often, determining the type of chart is based on indicator values. For example, a trend can be determined by analyzing the values of such indicators as Moving Average (MA), Moving Average Convergence Divergence (MACD), the Bollinger Band (BB), and Parabolic SAR. All conditions can be perfectly applied to the logic of the signal, and if the functionality is insufficient, it can be easily expanded by adding a specific indicator.

- The very purpose of the Signal entity helps us in solving the problem of determining the type of instrument. After all, the purpose of the signal is to provide us with a yes/no answer. That is, it helps us figure out whether the financial instrument corresponds to the type or not.

- This mechanism will already be implemented in the Core library, and we will not need to invent or create anything new.

It turns out that in the table with types of instruments, we will need a column with a signal, with the help of which the system will be able to determine the type of instrument in real time for the real trading subsystem and when loading historical data in the strategy search subsystem.

As is the case with ensuring the continuous operation of strategies, when determining the type of instrument, the system will need to analyze a large flow of trading data. Therefore, it makes sense, as in the case of strategy, to allocate its own pod for each instrument, which will be subscribed to the desired Kafka topic from which the trading data comes.

Why is that and not, for example, a pool of topics that process message queues? Well, to calculate most indicators, it is necessary to take into account candles in the previous n segments. And if the pod does not have

CHAPTER 4   ARCHITECTURAL SOLUTION PART 2: SERVICES AND SUBSYSTEMS

this information in its memory, then it will have to be taken, for example, from a database or directly from the exchange, and these requests are quite slow.

As a result, the strategy service has a fourth application: Instruments App. At this stage, I am starting to worry about the number of tasks that the strategy service is responsible for.

- API for the front end
- Background tasks such as managing the working_strategies table
- A separate application for ensuring the strategies work
- Separate application for determining the type of financial instruments

It looks like the strategy service needs to be divided into three independent services, with separate databases and applications.

- **Strategy Service.** This service will ensure the operation of strategies. It will have two applications: the API App for receiving a command to enable or disable a strategy-instrument pair and of course the Worker App, an application that will ensure the strategies work. It will have many pods, one for each strategy-instrument pair. I really like separating this logic into a separate service. It allows us to truly isolate the operation of strategies from other parts of the application.
- **Instruments Service.** This service will determine the types of financial instruments. It will also have two applications: the API App for information about changes in the instruments and a Worker App to define instrument types. There will be one pod for each instrument.

CHAPTER 4   ARCHITECTURAL SOLUTION PART 2: SERVICES AND SUBSYSTEMS

- **Strategy Manager Service.** Judging by the name, this service is a prime candidate for division into several smaller services because it will be responsible for solving several problems. However, since they are small, I don't see the point of making it too complicated for now. So, this service will also have two applications. The API App will provide the front end with the necessary methods. This application will also receive information from the search subsystem about the emergence of new strategies. You also need an application to manage the working_strategies table; let's call it the Tasks App.

As a result, at the current stage, the real trading subsystem looks like Figure 4-26.

CHAPTER 4 ARCHITECTURAL SOLUTION PART 2: SERVICES AND SUBSYSTEMS

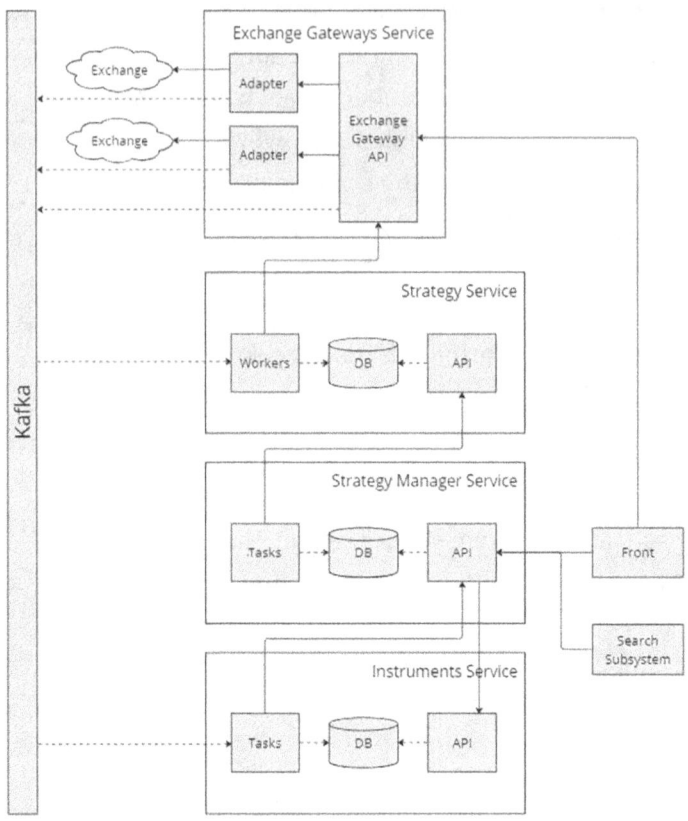

Figure 4-26. *General architectural diagram of the trading system*

Let's look at several scenarios for the real trading subsystem. Here is how new strategies arrive from the search subsystem:

1. Some service from the strategy search subsystem makes an HTTP request to the API App of the Strategy Manager Service, sending it information about profitable strategies and types of instruments.

2. The API App of the Strategy Manager Service records this information in the database without calculating anything.

3. The Tasks App of the Strategy Manager Service "sees" that new strategies have appeared and sends an HTTP request to the API App of the Strategy Service with a signal about the need to take on new strategies.

4. The API App of the Strategy Service writes to the database new working strategies.

5. One of the free Workers App pods of the Strategy Service "sees" that a new, unactivated strategy has appeared and takes it to work.

Here is how the Workers App of the Strategy Service works:

1. Every pod of the Workers App of the Strategy Service is subscribed to a specific Kafka topic, through which information about changes in candles for the financial instrument they need is broadcast. The Workers App responds to these changes, calculates signal values, and monitors the logic of system order execution. At some point, a signal to place an order with a broker may be triggered.

2. The Workers App of the Strategy Service sends an HTTP request to the API App of the Exchange Gateway Service to place an order with the broker.

3. The API App of the Exchange Gateway Service redirects the request to the desired Adapter App of the Exchange Gateway Service. The adapter places an order with the broker with which it is integrated.

4. After some time, the Adapter App of the Exchange Gateway Service "learns" that the status of this order has changed. The way to obtain order statuses can

CHAPTER 4   ARCHITECTURAL SOLUTION PART 2: SERVICES AND SUBSYSTEMS

be different; it all depends on the broker and its API. Maybe the adapter will periodically poll the broker about changes in information about orders, or maybe the broker provides a webSocket interface and itself will notify the adapter about these changes. It doesn't matter. The important thing is that the adapter somehow learned that the order status had changed.

5. The Adapter App sends messages about changes in order status to the desired Kafka topic.

6. The Workers App of the Strategy Service is subscribed to the topic from the previous step. This means it receives this message, and it acts according to the logic embedded within it.

This is how the Instrument Service works:

1. When creating a new financial instrument, the front end makes an HTTP request to the API App of the Strategy Manager Service, passing information about the new instrument to it.

2. The API App of the Strategy Manager Service makes an HTTP request to the API App of the Instruments Service with a message about the availability of a new financial instrument.

3. The API App of the Instruments Service writes information to the database.

4. A free one pod of the Tasks App of the Instruments Service "sees" that a new free tool has appeared, takes it to work, and subscribes to the desired Kafka topic with information about changing candles.

CHAPTER 4   ARCHITECTURAL SOLUTION PART 2: SERVICES AND SUBSYSTEMS

5. If the logic of changing the type of an instrument is triggered in the Tasks App of the Instruments Service, the application writes this information to the database and makes an HTTP request to the API App of the Strategy Manager Service with information about changing the type of the financial instrument.

6. The Strategy Manager Service Tasks App "sees" that the type of financial instrument has changed and gives the necessary commands to the Strategy Service to enable or disable strategies.

Master Data

I have one big question about this scheme. Which service is a source of reference information? Here a new signal is created, no matter whether it came from the search subsystem or the user. Where will it be created, and how will other services know that a new signal or strategy has appeared? Based on Figure 4-26, the central system for storing this information will be the Strategy Manager Service. It turns out that this service will have another task of storing reference information. I think this is too much. Typically, for such purposes, a separate Master Data Service is used, which stores general information used, for example, a list of signals, strategies, instruments, exchanges, etc.

Also, taking into account the fact that we have such a system, it may already make sense to add an API Service to hide information from the front end about which service it turns to for certain data.

With the advent of the Master Data Service, the real trading subsystem diagram will look like Figure 4-27.

167

CHAPTER 4   ARCHITECTURAL SOLUTION PART 2: SERVICES AND SUBSYSTEMS

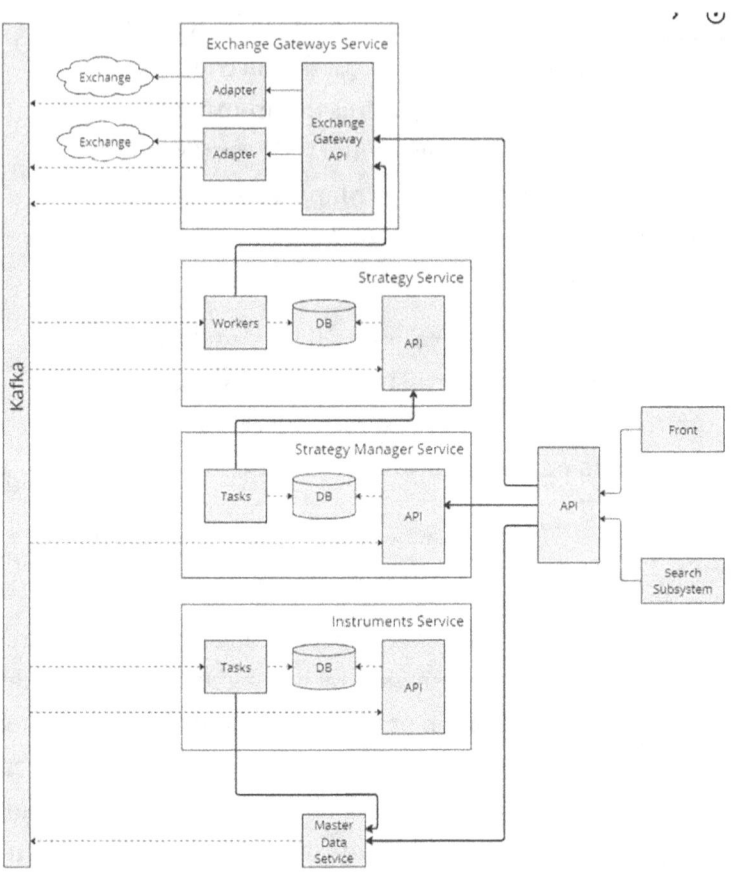

Figure 4-27. *General architectural diagram of the trading system with Master Data Service*

Figure 4-27 shows that all requests now go through the API Service, which decides which microservice to contact. The API Service will have only one application, which is the API App.

The script for creating reference information, such as a financial instrument, now looks like this:

1. The front end makes an HTTP request to the API Service to create a new tool.
2. The API Service makes an HTTP request to the Master Data Service.
3. The Master Data Service saves the new financial instrument in the database and sends a message to Kafka indicating that a new instrument has appeared.
4. All subscribers to this event will receive this message and save the information they need in their database.

Summary

This chapter did not describe everything that is necessary for a well-described architectural solution. In it, we only touched on tables in databases and did not touch upon signatures of API methods at all. Also, the functional diagrams were only superficially described. I plan to go deeper into these issues in future chapters dedicated to the subsystems.

In this chapter, I did the most important thing, which was to divide our system into independent parts, describe the tasks of each of them, and describe how they would solve them.

The scheme of the real trading subsystem turned out to be more complicated than the scheme of the strategy search subsystem, and it was also obvious that the architectures of these subsystems use different approaches. This is understandable, because in the strategy search subsystem, it was necessary to pay special attention to the speed of calculating strategies, which means that it is necessary to minimize

CHAPTER 4 ARCHITECTURAL SOLUTION PART 2: SERVICES AND SUBSYSTEMS

interservice interaction and, as a consequence, the number of services. On the other hand, in the real trading subsystem, it was necessary to pay more attention to independence. I consider the fact that it is possible to independently update and scale in this subsystem to be very critical. Therefore, it has more independent services.

Now we understand what our system will look like and the parts it will consist of.

CHAPTER 5

Technology Stack and Libraries

In previous chapters, we discussed the architectural solution of our system, learned what services it would consist of, and saw how they are connected to each other. In this chapter, we will discuss exactly how the services will be created, what technology stack we will use, what architecture we will use to build our services, and what logic we will use to create our classes and use them in the future. We will also discuss modern libraries for solving common problems, such as working with databases. Also in this chapter I will show how to implement the libraries that will be used in both subsystems, such as the state machine and the operation of background jobs.

Note that in this book we will pay more attention to the back end, and I will talk about the front end only in passing. This is because the front end of our system will not be complicated, so you can choose any framework to implement it. We will have no complex states or websocket connections. In fact, when creating the first version of my system, I did not create a front end for it at all. All I needed was a database tool such as pgAdmin or DataGrip to view and change my data, as well as Postman to run queries. Only much later, when the system began to generate income and trusted people joined me, did I implement the front end. Then, to build the front end, I used React, which I was familiar with, with a free library of components so as not to spend too much time on the part of the application that was not essential for me.

CHAPTER 5   TECHNOLOGY STACK AND LIBRARIES

Choosing a Framework

Let's start with choosing a language and framework. I think it makes sense to be pragmatic in this matter. This means I don't want to dive headfirst into learning a new technology and language just because it has some advantages over the languages I already know. My goal is not to learn a new technology but to build a trading system. For example, the leading language for developing serious trading robots right now is C++. But I don't know this well enough, and it's not as convenient as the C# I'm used to. Perhaps in the future, when I reach the C# ceiling in data processing speed, I will transfer some services to C++, but this definitely should not be done before the system is launched. It doesn't matter what language you write your first system in; the main thing is that you are comfortable and that your framework has reliable libraries for building an API, working with a database, and working with a distributed event streaming platform like Kafka.

At the time of writing this book, my stack, for example, included two popular frameworks: .NET.NET and NestJs. I wrote highly loaded systems on both, and both worked perfectly. But to build this system, I chose .NET. NET because it is much more convenient to work with arrays than in TypeScript. Also, .NET.NET works better with asynchronous code, unlike TypeScript, and is more productive. Also in .NET.NET it is much more convenient and easier to write autotests. And I will repeat once again that when choosing a framework, I advise you to be pragmatic and inclined to choose a framework that is familiar to you.

Application Architecture

Probably the first questions that any developer who creates a service from scratch asks is about naming and arranging your application projects. How many should there be? In what directories should they be located?

CHAPTER 5   TECHNOLOGY STACK AND LIBRARIES

How should classes be structured, and what should each be responsible for? If you look for the answer to these questions on the Internet, such designations as service layer, clean and onion architecture, DDD, CQRS, repositories, and much more pop up. Let's understand what types of architecture there are and what each of them has to offer. I will show how different approaches were created and evolved.

Spaghetti Code

Let's start with the very first approach to writing an application that is familiar to all developers: spaghetti code.

The following are distinctive features of this approach:

- **Lack of architecture.** Each developer writes code as they see fit.

- **Terrible connection.** Everything is connected to everything. If someone changes something in one part of the system, then something may break in another part of it.

- **Development time.** It takes a very long time for new developers to immerse themselves in the system code, because generally accepted patterns are not used.

When developers just started creating the first applications, most of the patterns had not yet been created and fixed. Therefore, programmers coped as best they could. They simply had no choice, because the developer community had not yet agreed on how applications would be built, and more modern approaches had not been developed.

But despite that spaghetti code, to put it mildly, is not suitable for writing applications in the modern world, it still continues to be used, and perhaps all of us have written and are still writing applications based on this approach. Spaghetti code is great for quickly writing code that will live in a matter of hours, or even minutes.

Chapter 5 Technology Stack and Libraries

Clean Architecture

Obviously, developers quickly realized that spaghetti code is not the best architecture for applications. Figure 5-1 shows what it looks like when we differentiate even slightly between levels in the code.

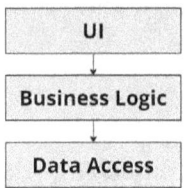

Figure 5-1. *Layers*

The code was still like spaghetti, but that spaghetti was strictly limited to the boundaries of its layer. The UI layer was responsible for representations, for example the data transfer objects (DTOs) for the API. The business logic layer in which the domain model, a certain layout of the real world, and all the logic associated with it are concentrated. The data access layer contains the logic for working with a database, for example. The code has definitely improved. Controllers and repositories appeared, which made the code much easier to understand.

But after the SOLID principles were formed, developers realized that the abstract domain code from the business logic layer depends on the implementation of the data access layer, which greatly violates these principles. Therefore, it was decided to expand the data access layer and make the business logic completely independent of the data access layer. The result was the so-called clean architecture, which is demonstrated in Figure 5-2.

CHAPTER 5   TECHNOLOGY STACK AND LIBRARIES

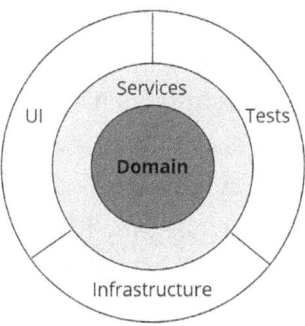

Figure 5-2. *Clean architecture*

I will briefly explain the SOLID principles here:

> **S – Single responsibility.** Your program unit should have only one responsibility. By unit I mean not only a class but also a library, part of your program or service.
>
> **O – Open/closed principle.** Software objects must be open for extension and closed for modification.
>
> **L – Liskov substitution principle.** The inheriting class should complement, not replace, the base class. In practice, this means that functions that use a base type should be able to use its subtypes without knowing it.
>
> **I – Interface segregation principle.** Interfaces that are too thick should be split into smaller ones so that clients of small interfaces are aware of the methods they need to do their work.
>
> **D – Dependency inversion principle.** Top-level modules should not depend on lower-level modules.

In a clean architecture, the domain layer, the former business logic layer, is placed at the center and accessed through services. Perhaps at the moment this is the most popular approach to building applications. This approach is justified until you start writing more complex applications, when you have many services. As a result, the map of their interaction becomes precisely the spaghetti they tried to get rid of. I know projects where you open a controller or service and there are dozens of imported classes and dependencies. I understand that such multitasking services need to be refactored and separated, but this did not solve the problem of strong connectivity of services.

That's when experts came onto the scene and proposed a different approach to building architecture. They showed that it might make sense to build applications based not on layers but on use cases. For this they suggested using the mediator pattern, namely, creating commands with handlers, as shown in Figure 5-3.

Figure 5-3. *Command handler*

Note A few words about the mediator pattern. This pattern belongs to a group of behavioral patterns. It helps reduce the interconnection of objects by moving these relationships into a separate mediator class. The mediator pattern causes classes to communicate not directly with each other but through an intermediary. Regarding commands, this means you will not issue commands to a specific handler or service but to an intermediary, who will decide who will process this command.

CHAPTER 5   TECHNOLOGY STACK AND LIBRARIES

In this approach, what is inside the handler becomes unimportant. Whether it's working with the domain model or maybe some legacy code that you isolate, it doesn't matter. The important thing is that now in your code you don't think about which service to place this or that function in or which layer is responsible for providing this or that functionality. Everything has become easier. You have a specific command and its handler. See Figure 5-4.

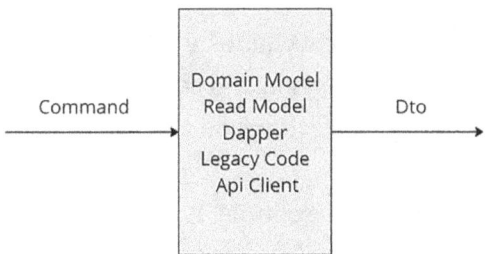

Figure 5-4. *Possible functionality of handlers*

Whether to use a service layer approach or use commands depends on the developer and their preferences. There is no universal solution. I prefer to use a mediator and commands. Then it's easier for me to divide the application into independent parts and understand how it all works.

Domain-Driven Design vs. Anemic Model

Another question that periodically arises when creating systems is what type of model to use.

Domain-driven design (DDD) tells us to build a rich domain layer with a thin service layer when data structure and behavior are combined. In fact, this means that the classes that implement your domain model will be large, and they will contain most of the logic responsible for the behavior.

In the anemic model, everything is different. Data structure and behavior are divided between classes such as entity and service.

177

Some people think that the anemic model is an anti-pattern. And if a developer uses this approach, it means they have a poor understanding of the subject area and, because of this, are unable to competently build a domain model.

But if you look at many projects on GitHub, you will see that most of them are built on an anemic model. Why? It's because building an application based on DDD is not just expensive, but very expensive. When designing a system with a rich domain model, it is necessary not only that the developers have excellent knowledge of the domain but that the domain itself is well-established and consistent. Unfortunately, this is often not the case, especially when you are writing a completely new application.

If we take our system as an example, I'm not sure that I identified the entities correctly, which means I'm not at all sure that my rich domain model will be correct. Therefore, I propose to take the evolutionary path. In other words, first build applications using the anemic model, and then gradually migrate the established code to the domain model.

Object Relational Mapper

Let's talk about what object relational mapper (ORM) we will use. What is an ORM? It is a library that helps us work with the database. There are several popular ORMs in .NET, and the most commonly used one is, of course, the Entity Framework (EF). But I propose we consider another popular ORM, or rather a mini-ORM: Dapper. And there is one reason for this, namely, speed.

If you look at the speed reports on the official Dapper page (`https://github.com/DapperLib/Dapper`), Dapper is the most productive ORM. This is understandable. It simply does not have a lot of functionality that EF has. There is practically nothing in it except mapping.

It turns out that I will have to independently implement some of the functionality available in EF. But am I willing to sacrifice my development time for the sake of productivity? Of course! We built the entire system, trying to make it the fastest and most productive.

Since most developers use EF, I would like to pay a little attention to the functionality of Dapper here so that later in the book we can focus on more interesting things. I will do this using the example of creating one of our entities: ExchangeOrder.

How to Use Dapper

First, you need to create the entity classes ExchangeOrder and ExchangeDeal. ExchangeDeal is not an entity in the general sense of the word, but we agreed that first we will make the system cheaper, which means we use an anemic model. I could put the models that we work with in the business logic layer into separate classes and make my own classes for the ORM, but then I would have to write a lot of code to map these classes into each other, and this is a long and not very interesting task. Perhaps when the system becomes more complex, it will be possible to switch to rich models, but now we are not doing this. Therefore, ExchangeDeal is an entity and also a class that maps a database table.

Listing 5-1 I shows what my classes look like.

Listing 5-1. Implementation of Entity Classes

```
[Table("\"ExchangeOrders\"")]
public class ExchangeOrder
{
    public int id { get; set; }
    public int ExchangeId { get; set; }
    public int InstrumentId { get; set; }
    public decimal Amount { get; set; }
```

```
    public IEnumerable<ExchangeDeal> Deals;
}

[Table("\"ExchangeDeals\"")]
public class ExchangeDeal
{
    public int ExchangeOrderId { get; set; }
    public decimal Amount { get; set; }
    public decimal Price { get; set; }
}
```

I use PostgreSql in my projects because it is free, well-supported, popular, and used in many projects. I will also use this to build a trading system.

Pay attention to the `Table` attributes. They use double quotes to indicate the table name. The fact is that in PostgreSql, if the names of columns or tables are not in snake_case, then in queries they must be framed in double quotes. I could follow the PostgreSql conversion and name columns and tables in snake_case, but I won't, because according to the C# conversion, public fields and classes should be named in PascalCase.

As I said earlier, `ExchangeDeal` is not an entity, because deals cannot exist without orders, so `ExchangeDeal` does not have an id column or property.

After we have written our entities, we need to implement a repository. But first I would like to implement a special class that is responsible for working with connections to the database. In EF, working with connections is hidden from us. Many developers don't even think about the fact that their number of connections and how exactly they are created and destroyed. Since Dapper is not such a high-level library, we will have to create connections ourselves. Listing 5-2 presents a rudimentary implementation of the class that is responsible for working with them.

Listing 5-2. DbConnector Implementation

```
public class DbConnector
{
    private NpgsqlConnection dbConnection =>
        new (Environment
            .GetEnvironmentVariable("POSTGRES_CONNECTION_
            STRING"));

    public async Task<T> PerformDbActionAsync<T>(
        Func<DbConnection,
        Task<T>> dbAction)
    {
        try
        {
            await using var connection = dbConnection;
            await connection.OpenAsync();

            await using var dbTransaction =
                await connection.BeginTransactionAsync();
            try
            {
                T actionResult = await dbAction.
                Invoke(connection);
                await dbTransaction.CommitAsync();
                return actionResult;
            }
            catch (Exception)
            {
                await dbTransaction.RollbackAsync();
                throw;
            }
        }
```

```
            finally
            {
                dbConnection.Dispose();
            }
        }
    }
```

Several things are notable about Listing 5-2. First, for each action with the database, its own connection will be created. Of course, this logic can be implemented in a more complex way, but at this stage I believe that this is enough. The second is that the actions will occur in one isolated transaction, we will need this when saving entities that use several tables in the database.

Now it's time to implement the repository. Listing 5-3 shows the interface of this repository, which has the minimum required functionality.

Listing 5-3. IExchangeOrderRepository Interface

```
public interface IExchangeOrderRepository
{
    Task<int> InsertOrderAsync(ExchangeOrder exchangeOrder);
    Task InsertExchangeDealAsync(ExchangeDeal exchangeDeal);
    Task<ExchangeOrder> GetOrderAsync(int id);
}
```

Of course, all methods are asynchronous. Also note that although deals are part of the order, the method for saving it is separate. This is done because deals for orders will arrive separately, which means they can be saved separately from the order.

The implementation of the order creation method is very simple, thanks to the Dapper.Contrib package. In a pure Dapper package, we would have to write the Insert SQL code ourselves, but it's enough to use the InsertAsync function.

CHAPTER 5　TECHNOLOGY STACK AND LIBRARIES

Listing 5-4. InsertOrderAsync Function

```
public Task<int> InsertOrderAsync(ExchangeOrder exchangeOrder)
    {
        return _dbConnector.PerformDbActionAsync(connection =>
        connection.InsertAsync(exchangeOrder));
    }
```

The code for receiving an order is interesting. In it we need to execute two queries to the database. They queries receive orders and deal with data. See Listing 5-5.

Listing 5-5. GetOrderAsync Function

```
public Task<ExchangeOrder> GetOrderAsync(int id)
    {
        string sqlOrders = "select * from \"ExchangeOrders\"
        where id = @id";
        string sqlDeals = "select * from \"ExchangeDeals\"
        where \"ExchangeOrderId\" = @id";

        return _dbConnector.PerformDbActionAsync(async
        connection =>
        {
            var multipleResult = await connection.QueryMultiple
            Async($"{sqlOrders};{sqlDeals}", new {id});
            ExchangeOrder exchangeOrder = await multipleResult.
            ReadFirstOrDefaultAsync<ExchangeOrder>();
            if (exchangeOrder == null)
                return null;

            IEnumerable<ExchangeDeal> deals = await
            multipleResult.ReadAsync<ExchangeDeal>();
            exchangeOrder.Deals = deals;
```

183

```
            return exchangeOrder;
        });
}
```

Migrations

Another point worth covering when working with Dapper is migrations. One of the most common libraries for these purposes is FluentMigrator. It's very easy to work with and well-documented. Perhaps its biggest inconvenience is the need to write migrations yourself, but I understood what I was getting into when I agreed to use a micro ORM. Listing 5-6 shows an example migration for our two tables.

Listing 5-6. Migration

```
[Migration(202312171002)]
public class Migration_202312171002: Migration
{
    public override void Up()
    {
        Create.Table("ExchangeOrders")
            .WithColumn("id").AsInt32().PrimaryKey().Identity()
            .WithColumn("ExchangeId").AsInt32().NotNullable()
            .WithColumn("InstrumentId").AsInt32().NotNullable()
            .WithColumn("Amount").AsDecimal(20, 10).
            NotNullable();

        Create.Table("ExchangeDeals")
            .WithColumn("ExchangeOrderId").AsInt32().
            NotNullable()
            .WithColumn("Amount").AsDecimal(20, 10).
            NotNullable()
```

```
            .WithColumn("Price").AsDecimal(20, 10).
            NotNullable();
    }

    public override void Down()
    {
        Delete.Table("ExchangeOrders");
        Delete.Table("ExchangeDeals");
    }
}
```

Listing 5-6 demonstrates the implementation of the migration class, which is used to create tables in the database. In this I create two tables, Table("ExchangeOrders") and Table("ExchangeDeals"), and then create columns of the types I need in them.

I have covered the minimum required to start working with Dapper. If you want to dive deeper into it, there is a lot of useful information on the Internet.

Finite State Machine

In the previous chapter, we talked about what a finite state machine is and briefly discussed the principle of its operation. In this chapter, let's dive deeper and talk about its implementation.

I have seen all sorts of options for the implementation of finite state machines. On GitHub you can find many options for ready-made solutions built on various technologies. Let's look at one of the simplest ones, which we used in one of the online stores where I once worked.

Before we begin, let me first remind you of the main points related to the finite state machine. A finite state machine is a way for an entity to move through a process.

CHAPTER 5   TECHNOLOGY STACK AND LIBRARIES

Here are the basic principles:

- An entity can be in only one state at any given time.
- The number of these states is finite.
- There are precise rules for transitions between states.

Principle

The center of the state machine that we will implement is ProcessMap. There can be only ProcessMap for the entire application, and it contains entity transition rules between process map nodes. All entities move along it from top to bottom. The system also provides events that "rip" an entity from the current node, and it immediately "falls" onto the node that reacts to the event.

There are five types of nodes:

- **Act.** This node performs some action. For example, send a letter to a user or calculate something and write the result to a database.
- **Waiting.** Such nodes are necessary to wait for some event that will "rip" the entity from this node. When creating a node of this type, be sure to specify a timeout. If the entity has waited on this node for the specified time, then it will move to the next node.
- **Terminal node.** It means that the entity must be removed from the process queue and stop processing.
- **Trigger.** The node on which the entity will fall when an event with the type specified in the node settings arrives.
- **Description.** Nothing happens in nodes of this type. But they are necessary as reference points for moving from other nodes.

CHAPTER 5 TECHNOLOGY STACK AND LIBRARIES

Let me give an example of how this works, using the example of processing theory. We'll take a small part of the process, because now my goal is to explain to you how it works. Figure 5-5 shows part of the theory processing flow in the second step.

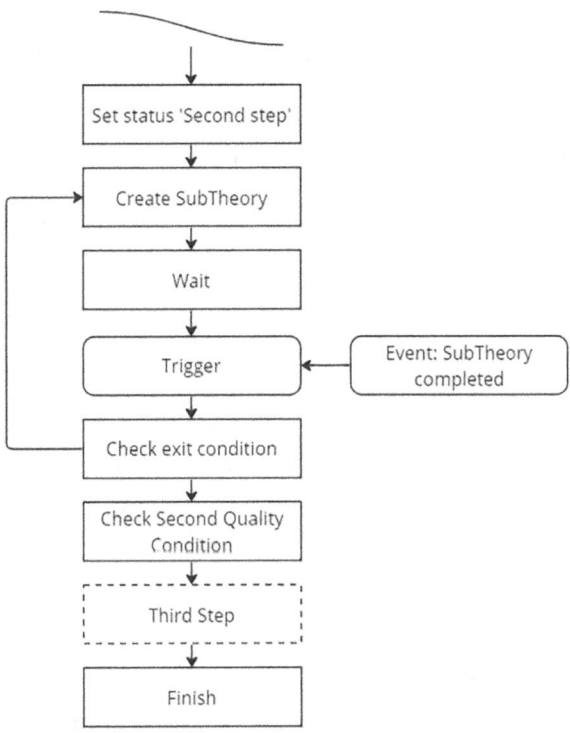

Figure 5-5. *Second step of theory flow*

Let's transfer this process to the process map of our state machine, as shown in Table 5-1.

CHAPTER 5   TECHNOLOGY STACK AND LIBRARIES

Table 5-1. List of Nodes

N	Node Name	Node Type	Params
1	Set status 'Second step'	Act	Status Id
2	Create SubTheory	Act	
3	Wait	Waiting	1 day
4	Stop and report		
5	SubTheory completed event	Trigger	Event id
6	Check exit condition	Act	Node id = 2
7	...		
8	Finish	Terminal	

Node 1. Set status 'Second step'. This is a node of type Act, which sets the status of a theory somewhere in the database. I have specified the status ID that we want to set in the parameters of this node. This will help us write code to set the status only once and use Act with this type when we go to set the status Worthless, for example. That's why I wrote down the Status Id in the Params column of Table 5-1.

Node 2. Create SubTheory. At this step, some kind of SubTheory is generated and launched. There is probably nothing more to say about this step. It is unique and cannot be reused in any way, so the parameters are empty.

Node 3. Wait. Our theory will be at this step, the period specified in the parameter is 1 day. And if during this time the "SubTheory completed" event does not occur, then the entity will move on to Node 4.

Node 4. Stop and report. Obviously, if a subtheory has not been considered within a reasonable time, then something needs to be done with it. Alternatively, stay on this node and periodically write in the logs that something went wrong, in the hope that the user will notice it and somehow solve the situation.

CHAPTER 5   TECHNOLOGY STACK AND LIBRARIES

Node 5. SubTheory completed event. This is the trigger node; it is where the theory will "fall" if the "SubTheory completed" event arrives. Of course, in the parameters of this node, you must specify the identifier of the event to which this trigger will react.

Node 6. Check exit condition. This is an act, but not a simple one. It specifies the identifier of the node to which the theory will move if the check of the condition from the "Check exit condition" is unsuccessful.

This is how we implemented the loop. If the "Check exit condition" fails, then the theory returns to node 2; otherwise, it moves to the node located below, that is, 7.

Hosted Service

So, the basic principle is more or less clear. Let's implement such a straight machine using .NET. First, our application must be of the ASP.NET type because we must not forget that our service will be run as a microservice, which means that the orchestrator must periodically check that our application continues to work. For this purpose, Kubernetes uses a liveness probe. That is, Kubernetes periodically executes an HTTP request to a special endpoint, waiting for a successful response.

So we have an ASP.NET.NET application. To run background tasks based on it, Microsoft provided us with a hosted services mechanism. Adding a new service is very simple; it is done with just one line of code.

```
services.AddHostedService<ProcessBotHostedService>();
```

But is this reasonable? Should we tie our bot process (a task that moves entities along the ProcessMap) to one specific application? Yes, when you can make it as a library and use it in many applications. After all, in a bot's process, it doesn't matter at all what kind of entity moves through the process. The main thing is that it has a unique identifier. But how do we solve the problem that Act nodes will contain unique, application-specific logic? Interfaces will help us with this. The process bot library will provide

189

CHAPTER 5   TECHNOLOGY STACK AND LIBRARIES

the IProcessingAct interface, and the implementation of each such action will be located in the application that uses the library. Of course, when initializing the process bot, we also need a factory that will create the Act node we need based on its identifier.

To register the processing bot to the application, we will create an extension for IServiceCollection, as shown in Listing 5-7.

Listing 5-7. IServiceCollection

```
public static IServiceCollection AddProcessBot(
        this IServiceCollection services,
        Action<ProcessBotOptions> setupAction,
        Type actFactoryType,
        params Assembly[] actAssemblies)
    {
        services.AddOptions();
        services.Configure(setupAction);

        services.AddSingleton<ProcessBot>();
        services.AddSingleton(typeof(IProcessActFactory),
        actFactoryType);
        AddTasksImplementations(services, actAssemblies);
        services.AddHostedService<ProcessBotHostedService>();

        return services;
    }
```

You have no idea how much I love .NET! Listing 5-7 embodies a lot of what I love about it. First, we implemented the extension, and we did it simply and beautifully. Pay attention to the first parameter of the function `this IServiceCollection services`; it will contain an instance of the class whose function we are calling. Thanks to the extension, it is now very easy to register the process bot.

`services.AddProcessBot().`

What's even more interesting is that in the next Action<ProcessBotOptions> setupAction parameter, the user of our library will have to pass a procedure that will build an instance of the options class, which will be available for connection in any class constructor used in the IServiceCollection instance. For now, only the database connection string will be stored in the options.

The next parameter type, actFactoryType, passes the type of the class that implements the IProcessActFactory interface. The idea is that the process bot should not depend on the specific implementation of the act creation factory. The interface is enough for this.

And the very last parameter is params Assembly[] actAssemblies, in which the user must pass assemblies that contain all implementations of the IProcessAct interface. And again, in the process bot we do not need the actual implementation of the acts. It is enough to know that they have all the methods we need. We will just add all these implementations to the collection of services for their easy accessibility. I understand that now you may not understand much, but wait a little, and everything will fall into place.

Pay attention to the line services.AddHostedService<ProcessBotHostedService>(); in fact, it will be the exact launcher of the process bot. As required by the AddHostedService function, our ProcessBotHostedService class must be an implementation of the IHostedService interface, which has two methods: StartAsync and StopAsync. And it is in StartAsync that I will make an infinite loop, in which I will periodically launch the entities handler. Listing 5-8 shows how I implemented this.

Listing 5-8. StartAsync Function

```
public async Task StartAsync(CancellationToken
cancellationToken)
    {
        _logger.LogInformation("ProcessBot start");
        _stop = false;

        Stopwatch stopwatch = Stopwatch.StartNew();
        while (!_stop && !cancellationToken.
        IsCancellationRequested)
        {
            try
            {
                stopwatch.Restart();

                await _processBot.RunAsync(cancellationToken);

                stopwatch.Stop();

                var sleepTime = 1000 - (int)stopwatch.
                ElapsedMilliseconds;
                if (sleepTime > 0 && !_stop)
                    await Task.Delay(sleepTime,
                        cancellationToken);
            }
            catch (Exception e)
            {
                _logger.LogError(e, "unknown error");
                await Task.Delay(5000, cancellationToken);
            }
        }

        _logger.LogInformation("ProcessBot stop");
    }
```

There are a few notable things about this code. The first is the condition for stopping the while loop (!_stop && !cancellationToken. IsCancellationRequested). Of course, here I use the cancellationToken passed to the function, as well as the private variable _stop, which I set to false when calling the StopAsync method.

Second, I use stopwatch. I need it so that the bot does not start too often. Imagine that there will be no entity in the queue for processing. Then the bot can work in tens of milliseconds, and if you do not set a delay, it will start immediately after processing is completed. Third, I also set a delay in the catch section; it is necessary so that the bot does not try to start working immediately after an exception occurs.

Of course, all these magic numbers could be included in the options, or it would be better to abandon the infinite loop altogether and use some more interesting external mechanism, but I remind you that this is one of the simplest implementations that will withstand relatively heavy loads. And this is just an example; of course you can create your own implementation or use one of the existing ones.

So, we started running our bot periodically. But what will it do? Of course, process the processing queue. In one of the previous chapters we discussed this mechanism and even started designing database tables for it. Let me update this information. We discussed that to support the processing queue, two tables would be created in the database: ProcessingQueue and ActiveQueue, as shown in Figure 5-6.

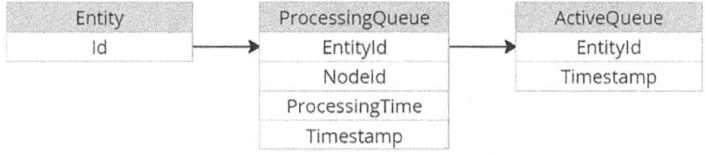

Figure 5-6. *Database table schema*

The `ProcessingQueue` table will contain all entities that need to be moved through the process. If the entity is not in this table, then it will not be processed. In addition to the `EntityId` column, this table also has a `NodeId` column. When the robot walks along the process map, it will note in this column what state it is in or, in the terminology of our state machine, what node the entity is currently on. The `ProcessingTime` column is necessary for nodes with the `Waiting` type. When the robot searches for a free entity, it will take only the entity with a `ProcessingTime` less than the current date, and the `Waiting` node, in turn, will set the date value in this column as the current date plus the number of seconds specified in parameter to the node. `Timestamp` column is informational. It displays the time at which the entity string was last modified.

The `ActiveQueue` table is necessary so that two application pods cannot simultaneously work on the same entity. Before taking on an entity, the bot will lock the `ActiveQueue` table, then select an unoccupied entity, mark it as busy writing to the `ActiveQueue` table, and then release the lock.

As a result, I got the RunAsync function, as shown in Listing 5-9.

Listing 5-9. RunAsync Function

```
public async Task RunAsync(CancellationToken cancellationToken)
    {
        List<ProcessingQueueElement> queueElements = await _
        processingQueueRepository.GetAndLockEntitiesAsync
        (_maxEntitiesCount);
        if (!queueElements.Any())
            return;

        IEnumerable<Node> nodes = await _nodeRepository.
        GetAllAsync();
        ProcessMap processMap = new ProcessMap(nodes);
        await HandleEntitiesAsync(processMap, queueElements);
```

```
        await _processingQueueRepository.UnlockEntitiesAsync
        (queueElements.ConvertAll(e => e.EntityId));
}
```

What's interesting about this code is that I decided to process not one entity per robot pass but several at once. This is because when getting a process map, getting and blocking an entity are not free procedures. I expect each step of the process map to be a lightweight operation that is completed quickly, so I don't see the point in spending so many resources to perform a small step on just one entity.

Also pay attention to the `GetAndLockEntitiesAsync` function. Yes, it violates the SOLID principle, because the logic about which entities can be taken into work has moved from the business logic layer to the repository layer. How could one get out of this situation? Get a separate database transaction, call the `ActiveQueue` table locking method, get the necessary data from the repositories, write the necessary data using the repository methods, and commit the transaction. I understand this, but I won't do this for now, because I will have to create classes for creating transactions and split `IProcessingQueueRepository` into two repositories `IProcessingQueueRepository` and `IActiveQueueRepository`, and all this for the sake of one place in the code. Am I right? I don't know. But we live in the real world where it is possible to move away from patterns if your code is ultimately clearer. After all, in the end, patterns were created precisely for a simpler understanding of the code.

Next in this code, I want to pay attention to the `ProcessMap` class, which will be responsible for such functionality as whether we move further along the process map. If we had a rich model, then `ProcessMap` would definitely be an entity, but now it is just a class that is close to services. Perhaps we could even rename it `ProcessMapService`.

Listing 5-10 shows an implementation of the `HandleEntitiesAsync` function.

CHAPTER 5 TECHNOLOGY STACK AND LIBRARIES

Listing 5-10. HandleEntitiesAsync Function

```
private async Task HandleEntitiesAsync(ProcessMap processMap,
List<ProcessingQueueElement> queueElements)
    {
        await HandleEventsAsync(processMap, queueElements);
        await HandleProcessingQueueAsync(processMap,
        queueElements);
    }
```

Please note that first the bot "rips" the entity from the node using events and only after that processes the nodes.

Listing 5-11 shows the implementation of the HandleEventsAsync function.

Listing 5-11. HandleEventsAsync Function

```
private async Task HandleEventsAsync(ProcessMap processMap,
List<ProcessingQueueElement> queueElements)
    {
        List<string> entitiesIds = queueElements.ConvertAll
        (e => e.EntityId);
        List<Event> unprocessedEvents =
            (await _eventRepository.GetUnprocessedAsync
            (entitiesIds))
            .ToList();
        foreach (ProcessingQueueElement queueElement in
        queueElements)
        {
            var entityEvents =
                unprocessedEvents
                    .Where(e => e.EntityId == queueElement.
                    EntityId)
```

```
            .OrderBy(e => e.CreatedAt);
    foreach (Event entityEvent in entityEvents)
    {
        int? nextNodeId = processMap
            .GetNextNodeId(queueElement.NodeId,
            entityEvent.Type);
        if (!nextNodeId.HasValue)
            continue;

        await _eventRepository
            .MarkAsProcessedAsync(entityEvent.Id);
        await _processingQueueRepository
            .UpsertAsync(queueElement.EntityId,
            nextNodeId.Value);
    }
  }
}
```

Please note that the entity identifier is a string value. Why not a long? It's simple—we will have several entity types in our system such as generator, subtheory, and theory. If they all have a long ID, then how can we understand which entity ID 1457 belongs to? Therefore, the id will be a universally unique identifier.

Note A universally unique identifier (uuid) is a standard identifier, usually of the form 0453bf87-68d4-4568-8f0b-c642154f579c. It gives sufficient confidence that where and when the uuid was not generated, it most likely will not match any previously created uuid.

This code also takes into account that there can be several events. The bot will process them in the order in which events enter the system.

CHAPTER 5 TECHNOLOGY STACK AND LIBRARIES

Another important point is that the bot processes only those events whose triggers are located lower than the current position of the entity on the process map. This is done on purpose because, logically, some events may no longer be relevant when the entity has reached a certain state.

Listing 5-12 shows an implementation of the HandleProcessingQueueAsync function.

Listing 5-12. HandleProcessingQueueAsync Function

```
private async Task HandleProcessingQueueAsync(
    ProcessMap processMap,
    List<ProcessingQueueElement> queueElements)
{
    IEnumerable<ProcessEntityData> entitiesData =
        await _processEntityDataQueries
            .GetDataAsync(queueElements.ConvertAll
            (e => e.EntityId));
    List<ProcessEntityData> entitiesDataList = entitiesData.ToList();
    foreach (ProcessingQueueElement queueElement in queueElements)
    {
        try
        {
            int? nextNodeId = processMap.GetNextNodeId(queueElement.NodeId);
            if (nextNodeId == null)
                throw new Exception("next node is empty");
            var entityData = entitiesDataList.First(d => d.Id == queueElement.EntityId);
            await MoveAsync(
                processMap,
```

```
            nextNodeId,
            entityData,
            queueElement);
    }
    catch (Exception e)
    {
        _logger.LogError(e, $"processing entity error.
        Entity id '${queueElement.EntityId}'");
    }
  }
}
```

There are a few interesting things about this feature. First, it refers to the class that implements the IProcessEntityDataQueries interface. This class should be provided by the application that connects the library. The idea is that the application will create a class derived from ProcessEntityData, which contains the minimum necessary information about the entity. Why is all this needed? It's need to not to receive this data when processing each step, and there may be several of them in one robot pass. Imagine a situation where on each node you use the same information that will not change, for example, some constant data about the entity. So as not to get it from the database every time, I added ProcessEntityData. This class will contain immutable and easily obtainable information about the entity. For subtheories, for example, this could be the theory identifier or something else.

Before moving on to implementing the MoveAsync function, I'd like to demonstrate the fields of Node because it depends on the node parameters how the Entity will be processed.

Listing 5-13. Node Class

```
public class Node
{
    public int Id;
    public int Code;
    public string Name;
    public bool IsParent;
    public int ParentId;
    public NodeType? Type;
    public bool Fast;
    public string Params;
    public int WaitingSeconds;
    public int ActId;
    public int EventTypeId;
    public bool Deleted;
}
```

It is worth explaining why each of the fields is needed.

- **Id.** Each node has its own identifier, which is needed for nodes with conditions, for example: "If the quality condition is completed, then go to the node with id 1783."
- **The Code field.** This is required to sort nodes on the process map. The robot needs to somehow understand in what sequence to process the steps of the map.
- **Name.** This is exclusively a UI field.
- **IsParent and ParentId.** These are important fields. Our application can process entities of different types, and each of them can have its own process map, but how can we separate them from each other? The easiest way is to group. It was for grouping purposes that I entered these two fields.

CHAPTER 5 TECHNOLOGY STACK AND LIBRARIES

- **Type.** This is a field that stores the node type. It is from this that the program will understand how to process this node.

- **Fast.** This is perhaps one of the most interesting node fields. I added this field to indicate that the robot should perform several steps in one pass. If a node has the value of this field equal to true, then the robot will process it and then process the next step, and so on until the next node has the value of this field false. This field can be used to regulate the load, set fast and low-cost nodes to fast, or when you want to perform a series of steps without the risk of your entity being ripped by a trigger in the middle of processing.

- **Params.** This is a string with node execution parameters that will be passed to the class that implements the specific action.

- **WaitingSeconds.** This is an option for nodes with the Waiting type. It shows the number of seconds the entity must wait on this node.

- **ActId.** This is the value that will be passed to IProcessActFactory to obtain an implementation of the IProcessAct interface.

- **EventTypeId.** This parameter will store the event type identifier. Events will be stored in a separate table, and, of course, each of them will have its own type, because events are different. The robot will understand which trigger to disrupt the entity precisely thanks to this parameter.

- **Deleted.** This field is required for the soft delete feature of a node. In fact, if a node has a value of this field that is true, this means the process map will not see it.

201

Let's move on to the very heart of our bot, namely, the MoveAsync function.

Listing 5-14. MoveAsync Function

```
private async Task MoveAsync(
    ProcessMap processMap,
    int? nodeId,
    ProcessEntityData entityData,
    ProcessingQueueElement queueElement)
{
    if (!nodeId.HasValue)
        return;

    Node node = processMap.GetNode(nodeId.Value);
    (bool move, int? nextNodeId) = node.Type switch
    {
        NodeType.Act=> await MakeActAsync(processMap, node,
        entityData),
        NodeType.Waiting => await MakeWaiting(processMap, node,
        entityData, queueElement),
        NodeType.Terminal => await
        MakeTerminalAsync(processMap, node, entityData),
        NodeType.Trigger => MakeNextStep(processMap, node),
        NodeType.Description => MakeNextStep(processMap, node),
        null when node.ItsParent =>
        MakeNextStep(processMap, node),
        _ => throw new Exception($"unknown node type
        {node.Type}")
    };

    if (nextNodeId.HasValue)
```

CHAPTER 5   TECHNOLOGY STACK AND LIBRARIES

```
        await _processingQueueRepository.
        UpsertAsync(entityData.Id, nextNodeId.Value);

    move = move && node.Fast;
    if (move)
        await MoveAsync(processMap, nextNodeId, entityData,
        queueElement);
}
```

The first thing you need to pay attention to is that the MoveAsync function is recursive. That is, it calls itself. Typically, recursion is used when it is not clear how many iterations need to be performed. We don't know this in advance, because we don't know what types of nodes we will encounter when processing an entity and whether they will all be fast (with the field value fast = true). Another notable point in this code is the move variable. Why not stop only based on the node.Fast condition? Why did it have to be complicated? It's simple: we will have nodes like "Stop and report," which must perform some action, which means it will be a node with the Act type, but after its execution, the bot should not move further.

Listing 5-15 shows the code that implements the remaining processing functions for each type of step.

Listing 5-15. MakeActAsync Function

```
private async Task<(bool move, int? nextNodeId)> MakeActAsync(
    ProcessMap processMap,
    Node node,
    ProcessEntityData entityData)
{
    try
    {
        IProcessAct? act = _processActFactory.
        GetAct(node.ActId);
```

```csharp
            if (act == null)
                throw new Exception($"unknown act with id {node.
                ActId}");

            (bool move, int? nextNodeId) =
                await act.MakeAsync(node.Params, entityData);
            if (move && !nextNodeId.HasValue)
                return MakeNextStep(processMap, node);

            return (move, nextNodeId);
        }
        catch (Exception e)
        {
            _logger.LogError(
                e,
                $"unknown error processing error entityId
                {entityData.Id} nodeId {node.Id}");
            return (false, null);
        }
    }

    private async Task<(bool move, int? nextNodeId)> MakeWaiting(
        ProcessMap processMap,
        Node node,
        ProcessEntityData entityData,
        ProcessingQueueElement queueElement)
    {
        if (queueElement.NodeId == node.Id)
            return MakeNextStep(processMap, node);

        DateTime processingTime = DateTime.UtcNow
        .AddSeconds(node.WaitingSeconds);
            await _processingQueueRepository
```

```
        .UpsertAsync(entityData.Id, node.Id, processingTime);
    return (false, null);
}

private async Task<(bool move, int? nextNodeId)>
MakeTerminalAsync(
    ProcessMap processMap,
    Node node,
    ProcessEntityData entityData)
{
    await _processingQueueRepository.RemoveAsync(entityData.Id,
        node.Id);
return (false, null);
}

private (bool move, int? nextNodeId) MakeNextStep(
    ProcessMap processMap,
    Node node)
{
    int? nextNodeId = processMap.GetNextNodeId(node.Id);
    return (true, nextNodeId);
}
```

Perhaps the only noteworthy thing about this code is that the MakeAsync() function of the IProcessAct interface returns (bool move, int? nextNodeId). I explained why I needed the move variable earlier, but why did I need the nextNodeId value? It is necessary for acts with conditions, where when a certain condition is met, it is necessary to move the entity not to the node immediately after the act but to some completely different place on the process map.

CHAPTER 5 TECHNOLOGY STACK AND LIBRARIES

Listing 5-16 shows the methods implemented in the ProcessMap class.

Listing 5-16. GetNextNodeId Function

```
public int? GetNextNodeId(int nodeId, int eventType)
{
    Node currentNode = GetNode(nodeId);
    Node? nextNode =
        _nodes
            .Where(n =>
                n.Deleted == false
                && n.ParentId == currentNode.ParentId
                && n.Type == NodeType.Trigger
                && n.EventTypeId == eventType
                && n.Code <= currentNode.Code)
            .MinBy(n => n.Code);

    return nextNode?.Id;
}

public int? GetNextNodeId(int nodeId)
{
    Node currentNode = GetNode(nodeId);
    Node? nextNode =
        _nodes
            .Where(n =>
                n.Deleted == false
                && n.ParentId == currentNode.ParentId
                && n.Code <= currentNode.Code)
            .MinBy(n => n.Code);

    return nextNode?.Id;
}
```

CHAPTER 5   TECHNOLOGY STACK AND LIBRARIES

Listing 5-16 shows that nodes are sorted by code. It is also taken into account that an event can have several triggers, in which case the entity will fall to the trigger node closest to its current position.

I hope that I showed a fairly clear and easy-to-use straight machine. Now, based on this example, you can implement your own or use an existing one, but I hope the basic principle of operation is clear to you.

Backworker

There is one more general mechanism whose operation I will reveal. This is a mechanism for running background tasks on a schedule. We will need such a mechanism, for example, in the real trading subsystem in the Strategy Manager Service. Its Tasks application will periodically check the types of financial instruments and the list of working strategies to instruct the Strategy Service to enable or disable instrument-strategy pairs. Also, this mechanism will most likely be needed to receive data from exchanges, because not all exchanges implement a web socket interface for all of their functionality. You can take one of the implemented libraries or write your own. Here I will demonstrate one of the simplest implementations of this mechanism.

The idea of how it works is similar to how the state machine was implemented. Each application pod will run an infinite loop, which will periodically take on a task. As with the state machine, of course we will encounter the problem of having several pods for the application and solve it in the same way. I ended up with the list of tables in the database that is shown in Figure 5-7.

CHAPTER 5   TECHNOLOGY STACK AND LIBRARIES

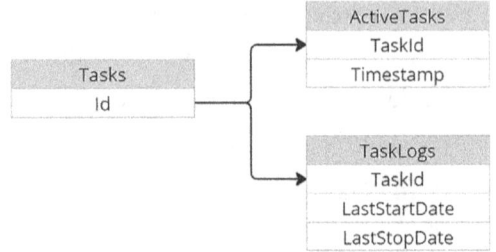

Figure 5-7. *Database table schema*

As in the example with the state machine, we need a table to store active tasks so that other pods do not take them to work. We also need a table to store information with the date of the last start and stop of task processing. This information will be needed to determine whether it is time to run the task or not. But everything is in order. First, we need to implement an extension for ISeviceCollection, where we will add all the necessary dependencies, including the hosted service.

Listing 5-17. AddBackworker Function

```
public static IServiceCollection AddBackworker(
    this IServiceCollection services,
    Action<BackworkerOptions> setupAction,
    Type actFactoryType,
    params Assembly[] assemblies)
{
    services.AddOptions();
    services.Configure(setupAction);

    services.AddSingleton<BackworkerManager>();
    services.AddSingleton(typeof(IBackworkerTaskFactory),
    actFactoryType);
```

CHAPTER 5 TECHNOLOGY STACK AND LIBRARIES

```
    AddTasksImplementations(services, assemblies);
    services.AddHostedService<BackworkerHostedService>();

    return services;
}
```

Listing 5-17 shows the implementation of the Add Dependency feature for the Backworker mechanism. You probably noticed that this code is very similar to the code implemented in Listing 5-7, where we connected dependencies for ProcessBot. And that's great! A consistent code style is very important. I love .NET and programs developed on it for this quality, uniformity, and a single code style.

I won't bore you with the implementation of the BackworkerHostedService class because it is similar to the ProcessBotHostedService class. Let's jump straight into the BackworkerManager. Listing 5-18 shows an implementation of the RunAsync method, which is run periodically by ProcessBotHostedService.

Listing 5-18. RunAsync Function

```
public async Task RunAsync(CancellationToken cancellationToken)
{
    BackworkerTask? backworkerTask =
        await _backworkerTaskRepository.
        GetAndLockStartBackworkerTaskAsync();

    if (backworkerTask == null)
        return;

    try
    {
        await _backworkerTaskLogRepository
            .UpsertStartAsync(backworkerTask.Id);
```

```
        IBackworkerTaskAct? task =
            _backworkerTaskFactory.
            GetTask(backworkerTask.Type);
        await task.RunAsync(backworkerTask.MagicString,
        cancellationToken);

        await _backworkerTaskLogRepository
            .UpsertStopAsync(backworkerTask.Id);
    }
    catch (Exception e)
    {
        _logger.LogError(e,
            $"Unknown error run backworker task
            {backworkerTask}");
    }

    await _backworkerTaskRepository
        .UnlockBackworkerTask(backworkerTask.Id);
}
```

As in the case of ProcessBot, this function calls the repository function GetAndLockStartBackworkerTaskAsync, which contains the logic for selecting the task that should run. Please note that the TaskLog table is written twice, before the task starts and after.

Listing 5-19 shows an implementation of the BackworkerTask class.

Listing 5-19. BackworkerTask Class

```
public class BackworkerTask
{
    public int Id;
    public string Name;
    public int Type;
    public bool Active;
```

CHAPTER 5 TECHNOLOGY STACK AND LIBRARIES

```csharp
public string MagicString;

public int RepeatPeriodMs;
public int RestartDelayMs;
public int CrashRestartDelayMs;

public bool NeedsToStart(
    DateTime now,
    DateTime? lastStart,
    DateTime? lastStop,
    DateTime? lockTime)
{
    return Active
            && TimeToStart(
                now,
                lastStart ?? DateTime.MinValue,
                lastStop ?? DateTime.MinValue,
                lockTime);
}

private bool TimeToStart(
    DateTime now,
    DateTime lastStart,
    DateTime lastStop,
    DateTime? lockTime)
{
    bool scheduleStartTime =
        (now - lastStart).TotalMilliseconds >=
        RepeatPeriodMs
        && (now - lastStop).TotalMilliseconds >=
        RestartDelayMs;

    bool restartCrash =
```

```
            lockTime.HasValue
            && (now - lockTime.Value).TotalMilliseconds >=
            CrashRestartDelayMs;

        return scheduleStartTime || restartCrash;
    }
}
```

the meaning of most fields is clear from their names, but I will still explain them so that there is no misunderstanding.

- **Id.** This is the task identifier. This is the only unique field in the table.
- **Name.** This is a field that has no logical load but is necessary for the user.
- **Type.** It is by this field that the class that implements the IBackworkerTaskFactory interface will create classes that implement the IBackworkerTaskAct logic. The Tasks table can contain several tasks with the same type and different launch parameters. This is necessary for handlers of the same type.
- **Active.** This flag is responsible for enabling/disabling the task. Essentially this is a soft delete.
- **MagicString.** This is a line with the parameters for launching the handler. This could contain anything, including JSON with a complex parameters object.
- **RepeatPeriodMs.** This parameter displays how often the task should run in milliseconds.
- **RestartDelayMs.** Imagine a situation where RepeatPeriodMs = 10 seconds and your task completed in 20 seconds. Should it start again immediately, or

should it wait a while? This parameter was introduced precisely so that some tasks would not be launched immediately after execution but after some time had passed.

- **CrashRestartDelayMs.** When a pod starts a task, it makes an entry in the ActiveTasks table and notes in it the time when it started working on this task. After this, the pod may cease to exist, but the entry in ActiveTasks will remain. This means that another pod needs to take over this task, but how will it understand that this can be done? After all, ActiveTasks has a record that this task is already in operation. It is for this case that CrashRestartDelayMs was introduced. If more than CrashRestartDelayMs milliseconds have passed since the blocking time marked in ActiveTasks, then another pod can take over this task.

Summary

In this chapter, I highlighted the main approach that I will use in developing system applications, namely, the use of commands instead of services. It also highlighted the main advantages of this approach.

I also showed the simplest implementations of a state machine and a backworker, which we will use in our services.

As a result, I hope you have accumulated enough information to start implementing application services.

CHAPTER 6

Optimization Algorithms

One of the key modules of our system is the optimization algorithm module, which searches for and optimizes strategies in the strategy search subsystem.

Our task of finding a profitable strategy has several features such as nonlinearity, multiextremality, complete absence of analytical expression, high dimension of the search space, and high computational complexity of the optimized function. All of these features explain why there is no universal algorithm for solving the optimization problem and finding a profitable strategy. This means that the optimization module must implement a number of different optimization algorithms.

To solve the global optimization problem, several classes of optimization algorithms have been developed, one of which is the population algorithms class.

In population algorithms, simultaneous work is carried out on several options when solving an optimization problem, in contrast to classical algorithms, in which only one candidate evolves.

Population algorithms have a number of advantages that make them perfect for solving our problem.

- They have proven themselves to be excellent in solving problems of high dimensionality, multimodality, and low formalization.

- They are not algorithms with a strictly defined order of steps. They rather have a set of standard operations and rules with which you can create a large number of your own variations of optimization algorithms.

- They are most effective in finding a suboptimal, that is, close to optimal, solution. To find a profitable strategy, a suboptimal solution is often enough.

In this chapter, I will cover the minimum necessary theory that will allow you to dive into the world of population algorithms and implement an optimization module.

Formulation of the Problem

In optimization theory, there are two types of optimization problems: deterministic and stochastic. In the first case, the target function is deterministic. That is, it does not contain random parameters. The stochastic function contains it. Our target function, namely, the function for calculating the performance strategy on a section of historical data, is deterministic. The general formulation of a deterministic optimization problem is as follows:

$$\max_{|X|} f(X) = f(X^*) = f^*$$

$|X|$: The dimension of the vector of variable parameters $X = x1, x1, ..., x|X|$.

$f(X)$: The objective function or optimality criterion.

X^*: The he required optimal solution.

CHAPTER 6 OPTIMIZATION ALGORITHMS

f*: The esired optimal value.

D = G(X) : The set of admissible vector values X, where G(X) is the vector bounding function consisting of components $g_1(X), g_2(X), ..., g_{|G|}(X)$.

The determinism of the task means that the objective function $f(X)$ and the limiting function G(X) do not contain random parameters.

If $|X| > 1$, then the problem is called *multiparameter*.

An objective function may have points at which it reaches its largest or smallest value. These points are called *extrema*. If the objective function has several such points, then this function is said to be *multi-extremal*.

A test is an operation of one-time calculation of the target and limiting functions. In our case, calculating the objective function is an expensive operation that requires a lot of computing resources, so the main requirement for optimization algorithms is to find the optimal value of the objective function in the least number of tests.

Population Algorithms

The problem of finding the optimal solution is now clear, so let's start solving it using population algorithms.

The main idea of these algorithms is based on working on several solutions at once. One solution option, in population algorithms, is called an *agent*. The set of agents generated at the iterative step is called a *population*.

The general scheme for solving an optimization problem using population algorithms includes the following steps:

1. **Initialization of the population.** Using some algorithm, a first approximation of the solution to the optimization problem is generated. That is, the first set of agents will be generated.

2. **Migration.** According to a certain scenario or set of operations, agents are migrated in such a way as to ultimately approach the desired extremum. That is, the next generation of agents will be created.

3. **Checking the search termination condition.** The conditions for the end of iterations are checked. If these conditions are not met, then return to step 2.

When initializing a population, both deterministic and random algorithms can be used. If the initial population is formed near the global extremum, that is, the maximum or minimum value of the function throughout the entire definition domain, this will significantly speed up the search for the optimal solution. But in the general case, we do not have a priori information about the location of the global extremum, so often the agents of the first population are distributed evenly throughout the entire search area.

There are two popular search termination conditions. The first is by the number of iterations, when the search stops after creating a given number of generations. The second is according to the stagnation condition, when the best achieved value of the objective function does not change for a given number of generations.

It is clear that population algorithms have a highly modular structure. This means that by varying operations and migration algorithms, you can get a large variety of your own unique optimization algorithms.

In most cases, population agents have the following properties:

- **Autonomy.** Agents move in the search space conditionally independently of each other.
- **Stochasticity.** The process of migration or generation of new agents contains a random parameter.
- **Limited representation.** All agents have information only about part of the search area they are investigating.

In some algorithms, agents "share" information with each other, but in most algorithms this is not the case.

- **Decentralization.** There is no hierarchy among agents.
- **Communication skills.** Agents, to varying degrees, can exchange information with each other.

One of the problems in designing population algorithms is the problem of maintaining a balance between search intensity and search breadth. Intensity refers to the rate of convergence, or the speed at which the algorithm finds a solution. And the problem of search breadth is understood as diversifying this, that is, ensuring a sufficient variety of agents to increase the likelihood of finding a global extremum.

Intensification of the search requires rapid convergence, which entails a requirement for a rapid reduction in the diversity of agents. Diversification, on the contrary, is designed to provide a broader overview of the space under study, which entails the requirement to maintain a large number of agents.

A popular approach to maintaining a balance between the intensity and breadth of search is the so-called adaptation and self-adaptation mechanisms. When these mechanisms are applied, the free parameters of the algorithms gradually change so as to gradually move from diversification to intensification.

Since population algorithms are stochastic, their efficiency strongly depends on the values of random variables, which means they can achieve different results even while maintaining the same values of free parameters. For this reason, multiple runs are used to evaluate the effectiveness of algorithms. When the same algorithm is used to solve the same problem, this approach is called the *multistart method*.

CHAPTER 6   OPTIMIZATION ALGORITHMS

Genetic Algorithms

Genetic algorithms are a popular type of algorithm belonging to the population class. These are the ones I will use in the search for the optimal strategy.

Genetic algorithms became known to the world after the publication of the book *Adaptation in Natural and Artificial Systems* (J. Holland, 1975). This class of algorithms was based on the ideas of Darwin's theory of natural selection.

Darwin showed that the evolutionary development of the earth's flora and fauna is based on the following principles:

- **Heredity.** Some traits of parents are passed onto offspring.

- **Variability.** It is difficult to find two identical individuals.

- **Natural selection.** Only the fittest individuals survive.

Everyone knows that the substance that determines hereditary processes is deoxyribonucleic acid (DNA). It is the molecular biological processes of heredity that form the basis of genetic algorithms.

The structure containing DNA is called a **chromosome**. A gene is a specific part of a chromosome in which innate personality qualities are encoded (eye color, skin color, height, etc.). A **locus** is the location of a gene on a chromosome. An **allele** is the functional significance of each gene. A **genotype** is the totality of genes of a particular individual. The set of personality characteristics is called a **phenotype**.

To give an analogy with our system, a chromosome is a set of strategy parameter values. A gene is the value of one of the parameters, for example LookbackPeriod for the average directional index (ADX) indicator.

During the sexual reproduction of living beings, the fusion of two sex cells occurs in which the DNA of the parents interact with each other and the result is the DNA of the descendant. This procedure is called **crossing**.

Because of many factors, genes in the DNA of the parents' germ cells can change. This process is called **mutation**. Mutated genes are passed on to the offspring and give it properties not found in either parent. If unique properties turn out to be useful, then they are likely to be retained in the population.

The diagram of a typical genetic algorithm is as follows::

1. According to some algorithm, a set of individuals (agents) is created.

2. Individuals are evaluated using an objective function. This means that for each individual, we calculate the objective function.

3. The selection stage is carried out. That is, based on adaptability (the value of the objective function), we select individuals for crossing.

4. We apply mutation and crossing operators to selected individuals. As a result, we get a new generation (population) of individuals.

5. We check the algorithm stopping condition. If the condition is not met, then return to step 2.

The essence of genetic algorithms is that each new generation, on average, is more fit than the previous one.

CHAPTER 6 OPTIMIZATION ALGORITHMS

Mutation Operators

The essence of the mutation operator is to replace gene x_i with gene x_i'. That is, in the general case, any mutation operator consists of two stages.

1. Selecting genes to be replaced
2. Replacing these genes

Let's take a closer look at a few operators.

Random Operator

The method is to assign to gene x_i a random number from the interval $\left[x_i^-; x_i^+\right]$.

The algorithm for the random mutation operator is as follows:

1. We generate η random integer nonmatching numbers whose values are in the interval from 1 to |X|. These numbers will be equal to the numbers of genes that will be subject to mutation. η is a free parameter of the operator, which is responsible for the number of genes to be mutated.

2. We generate a random number in the interval from x_i^- to x_i^+ and equate this value to the gene numbered i of the descendant.

3. Using the same scheme, we mutate the remaining genes selected for mutation.

4. The descendant takes the remaining genes from the original individual without changes.

The simplest implementation of this operator can be considered the implementation of the boundary mutation operator, in which the gene x_i is assigned the value x_i^- or x_i^+ with equal probability. See Figure 6-1.

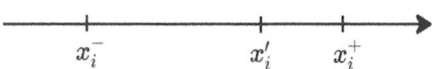

Figure 6-1. *Interval of acceptable mutant gene values: example 1*

Arithmetic Real Number Creep Operator

The algorithm for this operator looks exactly like the random operator algorithm. But the formula in step 2 takes the following form:

$$x'_i = x_i + \xi(2\psi - 1)$$

ξ: This is another free parameter.

ψ: This is a random number that ranges from 0 to 1.

As a result, the value x'_i will take values on the interval $[x_i - \xi; x_i + \xi]$. See Figure 6-2.

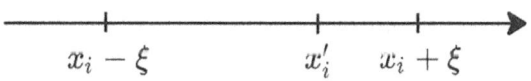

Figure 6-2. *Interval of acceptable mutant gene values: example 2*

Gauss Operator

According to the algorithm of this operator, the new value x'_i must deviate from the parent value x_i by an amount calculated by the Gaussian function.

$$x'_i = x_i + \Phi(\mu, \sigma)$$

μ: This is a free operator parameter, which is the mathematical expectation or an average value. It is usually equal to 0.

σ: This is a free operator parameter. The standard deviation is responsible for how much the final value of the function will differ from the value of the mathematical expectation. See Figure 6-3.

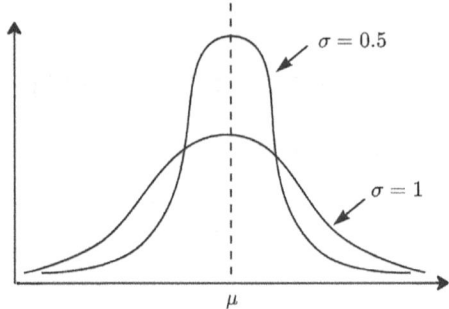

Figure 6-3. Graph of the probability of assigning a value μ to a gene

Crossover Operators

The purpose of these operators is to obtain, from two parent individuals, one or more offspring individuals. Or, to put it in formulas, it creates child chromosomes $X'_1, X'_2, \ldots, X'_n$ based on two parent chromosomes, X_1 and X_2.

Let's look at a few operators.

Flat Crossover

In this operator, the gene x'_i of the child is a random number located in the interval from x_i^{min} to x_i^{max}, where x_i^{min} is the minimum of the parent gene values, and x_i^{max} is the maximum of them. See Figure 6-4.

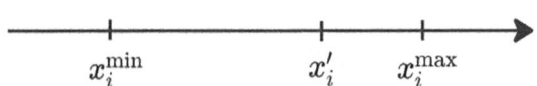

Figure 6-4. Range of acceptable values

Blend Crossover

In this operator, the gene x'_i of the child is a random number located in the interval from $x_i^{min} - \lambda\sigma$ to $x_i^{max} + \lambda\sigma$.

$$\sigma_i = x_i^{max} - x_i^{min}$$

λ is a free operator parameter. Obviously, the larger it is, the more the gene of the descendant will differ from the genes of the parents. You can build your algorithm in such a way that the parameter value will be different for each gene. See Figure 6-5.

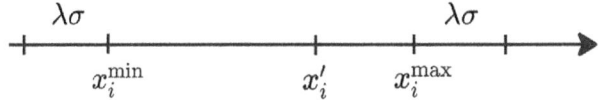

Figure 6-5. *Range of acceptable values*

Arithmetical Crossover

According to this operator, the chromosomes of the descendants are created according to the following formula:

$$x'_{1,k} = \lambda x_{1,k} + (1-\lambda)x_{2,i}$$

$$x'_{2,k} = \lambda x_{2,k} + (1-\lambda)x_{1,i}$$

λ: This is a random number ranging from 0 to 1.

Heuristic Crossover

In this operator, the gene x'_i of the descendant is calculated using the following formula:

$$x'_i = \lambda(x_{1,i} - x_{2,i}) + \lambda x_{1,i}$$

CHAPTER 6   OPTIMIZATION ALGORITHMS

In this formula, it is assumed that the first individual is more fit than the second.

λ: This is a random number that can range from 0 to 1.

Linear Crossover

According to this operator, three descendants will be created according to the following formulas:

$$x'_{1,i} = 0.5x_{1,i} + 0.5x_{2,i}$$

$$x'_{2,i} = 1.5x_{1,i} - 0.5x_{2,i}$$

$$x'_{3,i} = -0.5x_{1,i} + 1.5x_{2,i}$$

See Figure 6-6.

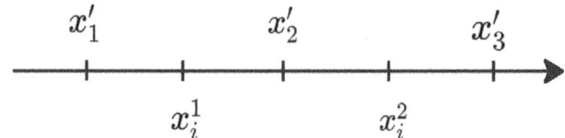

Figure 6-6. *Range of acceptable values*

Fuzzy Crossover

When you use this operator, you will end up with two children. The probability that the gene x'_i of a daughter individual is described by a triangular probability density function designated as $F(x'_i)$. So for x'_i, the left corner of the triangle will be located at the value $x'_i - \lambda\sigma$, and the right corner will be located at $x'_i + \lambda\sigma$.

λ is the operator parameter; the most commonly used value is 0.5. See Figure 6-7.

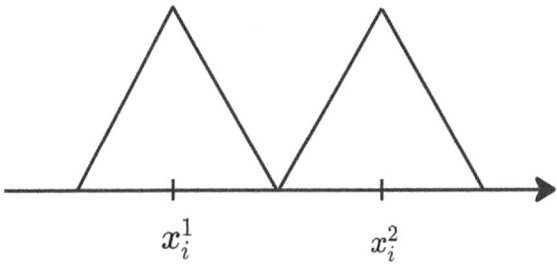

Figure 6-7. *Graph of the probability of assigning values to genes*

Simulated Binary Crossover (SBX)

According to this operator, two descendants are created; the value of gene i is calculated by the following formula:

$$x'_{1,i} = 0.5\left((1-u)x_{1,i} + (1+u)x_{2,i}\right)$$

$$x'_{2,i} = 0.5\left((1-u)x_{2,i} + (1+u)x_{1,i}\right)$$

u is a number whose probability density is calculated using the following formula:

$$\beta(u) = \begin{cases} (2u)^{\frac{1}{n+1}}, u(0,1) \geq 0,5 \\ \left(\frac{1}{2(1-u)}\right)^{\frac{1}{n+1}}, u(0,1) < 0,5 \end{cases}$$

n is a free parameter of the operator, a number taking values from 2 to 5. An increase in the number n entails an increase in the probability that the value of the child gene will be generated in the vicinity of the value of the parent gene. See Figure 6-8.

CHAPTER 6 OPTIMIZATION ALGORITHMS

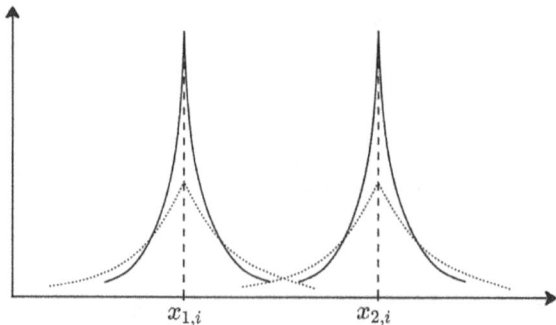

Figure 6-8. *Graph of the probability of assigning values to genes*

Filtering Operators

This group of operators helps to form a new population by adding the most suitable individuals to it.

Roulette Method (Proportional Sampling)

The roulette method is based on representing the population in the form of a roulette wheel, where each individual has its own sector, the size of which is proportional to the value of its objective function. See Figure 6-9.

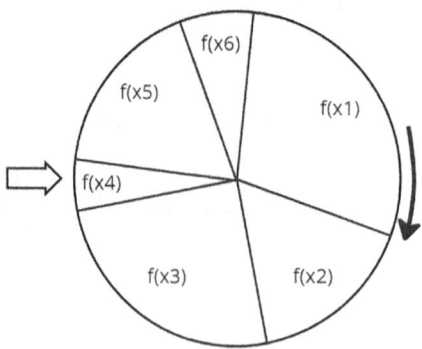

Figure 6-9. *Roulette of probabilities*

The filtering algorithm using the roulette method is as follows:

1. For each individual s_i, we calculate the probability of its selection using the formula $p_i = \dfrac{f_i}{\sum_{i=1}^{|S|} f_i}$.

2. Divide the interval from 0 to 1 by |S| subintervals in proportion to the values calculated in the previous step.

3. We spin the roulette. We generate a random number from 0 to 1, depending on which sector this number falls into, and that individual will be selected.

4. We repeat step 3 until the required number of individuals is selected.

It is clear from the formula that the higher the subinterval allocated for an individual, or, in other words, the value of the objective function, the higher the probability that it will be selected.

The disadvantage of this method is that individuals with low adaptability will be very quickly excluded from the population, which will lead to premature stagnation of the algorithm. Another disadvantage of the method is that individuals with high adaptability will not always be selected. As a result, the new population may lose promising search directions.

Proportional Sampling Method

This method is considered a development of the roulette method. It is built on the following formula:

$$\mu = \frac{f(s_i)}{f(S)}$$

$\overline{f(S)}$ is the average value of adaptability of individuals of generation S.

The integer part of μ will indicate how many times an individual needs to be recorded in the intermediate population, and the fractional part shows its probability of getting there again.

Stochastic Universal Method

This is another variation of the proportional filtering method. But the selection is carried out in two stages.

1. The n fittest individuals will be included in the new population. n is a free operator parameter.

2. The remaining required number of individuals is selected using the roulette method.

As a result of this method, individuals with high adaptability can enter a new population more than once, which means they are more likely to interbreed with more than one individual.

Tournament Method

The method involves the formation of groups of n individuals each based on the population. In each group, an individual with the greatest adaptability is selected and will be included in the intermediate population.

n is a free operator parameter called *tournament size*. Obviously, if it is equal to 1, then the tournament filtering method will degenerate into the random filtering method. Typically the value of this parameter is 2 or 3.

The tournament filtering algorithm is as follows:

1. In any way we divide the population into groups of n individuals in each.

2. In each group, for each individual, we calculate its adaptability and select the most adapted individual. We include this in the intermediate population.

3. Repeat steps 1 and 2 as many times as necessary. The final intermediate population will be the result of this method.

Rank-Based Method

The rank method is similar to the roulette method, only instead of the selection probability depending on the value of the individual's objective function, this method uses the selection probability depending on the rank.

The rank is equal to the number of the individual in the list of individuals in the population, sorted by increasing the value of the objective function.

The rank filtering algorithm is as follows:

1. We calculate the objective function for all individuals in the population.

2. We sort the individuals in ascending order of the objective function.

3. We number this list and assign each individual this number, which is called a *rank*.

4. We match the rank to the value of the selection probability function. As a function, you can use a simple linear function of the form $\mu(r) = ar + b$, $a < 0$. Where r - is a rank, a and b - are free operator parameters.

5. Using the roulette method and using the probabilities from the previous step, we select the required number of individuals.

The main advantage of rank selection is the elimination of early stagnation of the genetic algorithm, since the method helps preserve population diversity.

Elitism-Based Method

This method is based on two steps. At the first step, the required number of best individuals is guaranteed to be selected. At the second stage, the missing quantity of copies is selected using any of the mentioned filtering methods. There are modifications of this algorithm when the second step does not select individuals from the remaining ones but generates new ones based on one of the initialization algorithms for the initial population.

The intermediate population may include, for example, 10% of the best individuals, and the remaining 90% are selected using the roulette method.

The main advantage of this method is that it guarantees the preservation of one or more of the fittest individuals.

Clipping Method

The clipping method is a type of filtering method based on elitism. It sets the threshold for the value of the objective function φ. We sort the population individuals in descending order of their objective function value. We randomly select an individual whose fitness is greater than the threshold value φ. We repeat the operation the required number of times.

Of course, this method can be modified, and individuals can be selected not by a random method but, for example, by the roulette method.

The main disadvantage of this method is the fact that there is a high probability that individuals with the highest adaptability will not end up in the intermediate population.

Crowding Method

The crowding method is based on the removal of close individuals from a population. For these purposes, the value of the function that determines the measure of proximity of individuals is used. For example, for these purposes, you can use the Euclidean norm.

$$\psi(s_1, s_2) = \sqrt{\sum_i (x_{1,i} - x_{2,i})^2}$$

The algorithm of this method is as follows:

1. For a population, we form a matrix of distances between individuals of the population with the values of the proximity measure $\psi(s_1, s_2)$.

2. We select a cell in this matrix with the minimum value of the proximity measure and, with equal probability, exclude individual s_1 or s_2 from the new population.

3. We continue to repeat step 2 until the required number of individuals remains in the population.

This method can be modified. For example, we could use tournament selection, where groups are formed not randomly but based on the values of proximity measures.

In addition to the considered methods of forming a population in two stages, like this:

$$S(t) \rightarrow S'(t) \rightarrow S(t+1)$$

CHAPTER 6　OPTIMIZATION ALGORITHMS

it makes sense to consider the possibility of forming a population in three stages, like this:

$$S(t) \to S'(t) \to S''(t) \to S(t+1)$$

$S'(t)$ is an auxiliary population created, for example, using some mutation operator. Or maybe it makes sense to use different filtering methods both times.

Selection Operators

The purpose of these operators is to select from a population pair of individuals to be crossed. The basic principle of selection operators is that the probability of selecting the fittest individuals increases with the increasing population number.

The vast majority of selection operators are based on an assessment of the fitness of individuals. Figure 6-10 shows examples of the dependence of the probability of selection on the fitness value of an individual.

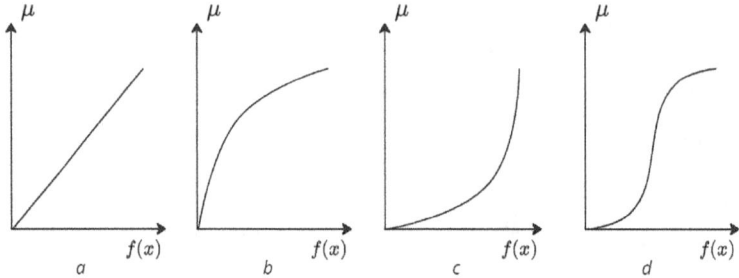

Figure 6-10. *Examples of the dependence of the probability of selection on the fitness value of an individual*

The sampling function in Figure 6-10a corresponds to proportional sampling.

CHAPTER 6   OPTIMIZATION ALGORITHMS

In the case of the function in Figure 6-10b, individuals with average fitness scores have an equal chance of being selected as individuals with high fitness scores. Selection operators of this type slow down the convergence of the algorithm or the improvement in the average fitness of the population in favor of a more complete exploration of the search space. That is, the balance between intensity and breadth is shifted in favor of breadth.

Figure 6-10c shows the opposite situation: individuals with average fitness have a significantly lower probability of selection compared to individuals with high fitness, which increases the convergence of the algorithm but reduces the diversity of the population.

The nature of the function presented in Figure 6-10d allows the advantages of the two previous operator implementations to be combined.

In most cases, two individuals are used for crossing. To select them, you can use filtering operators, with a given target number of individuals equal to 2. But there are also several specific selection operators.

Panmixia Method

The essence of the method is a random, equally probable selection of parental individuals. The main feature of the method is that one individual can end up in several parental pairs. The method is simple to implement and quite effective. A well-known disadvantage of this method is its degradation with increasing population size. As the population size increases, the effectiveness of this method and the algorithm as a whole decreases.

The method algorithm looks like this:

1. We assign each individual of the population a probability of $\mu = \frac{1}{|S|}$.
2. Using the roulette method, we select the first individual for the parent pair.

3. We select the second individual in the same way. If the second individual matches the first, then try again.

Selective Selection Method

This method is based on two conditions.

- Only those individuals whose fitness is higher than or equal to the average fitness of individuals in the population become parents.
- All individuals satisfying the first condition can form pairs with equal probability.

The method algorithm is as follows:

1. For each individual in the population, we calculate the value of the objective function.
2. We calculate the average fitness value of the population: $\underline{f}$.
3. We select individuals from the population whose fitness is not lower than the average value calculated in the previous step.
4. We assign each individual a probability: $\mu = \frac{1}{|S|}$.
5. Using the roulette method, we select a pair of parent individuals.

Because of the limitation of individuals who can participate in crossing, this method has high convergence, which can lead to early termination of the algorithm in the local minimum zone.

Inbreeding

This selection method is based on two stages. In the first stage, the first parent is selected randomly. In the second stage, the selection of the parental pair is carried out on the basis of probability, depending on the value of the measure of proximity to the first individual. The closer the individual is, the more likely it is that it will be chosen as the second parent in the pair. The Euclidean norm can be used as a measure of proximity.

$$\psi(s_1, s_2) = \sqrt{\sum_i (x_{1,i} - x_{2,i})^2}$$

The algorithm of this method is as follows:

1. Using the panmixia method, we select the first parental individual from the population.
2. For all remaining individuals, we calculate the measure of closeness to the first parent.
3. We assign to each individual a probability value proportional to the value of the proximity measure: $\mu = \dfrac{\psi(s_i)}{\underline{\psi}}$.
4. Using the roulette method, we select the second parent individual based on the values of the probability function calculated in the previous step.

This method provides high search intensity by quickly dividing the population into separate groups of individuals close to each other.

Outbreeding

This selection method is based on two stages. In the first stage, the first parent is selected using the panmixia method. In the second stage, the parental pair is selected based on the probability depending on the value of the measure of proximity to the first individual. The further away the individual is, the more likely it is that it will be chosen as the second parent in the pair. The scheme of the outbreeding method practically coincides with the scheme of the inbreeding method, with the difference that for each individual we assign a probability value inversely proportional to the value of the proximity measure.

$$\mu = \frac{1/\psi(s_i)}{\sum_{j=1}^{|S|} 1/\psi_j}$$

The outbreeding method, as opposed to the inbreeding method, prevents early convergence of the algorithm in favor of population diversity and, as a consequence, high diversification of the search.

The inbreeding and outbreeding methods can be modified by using other filtering operators, such as selective selection, to select the first individual. You can also try different formulas for measuring the proximity measure, which will also affect the operation of the algorithm. It is obvious you can build your own variation of the genetic algorithm based on a combination of several selective selection methods.

Restrictions

Many of the previously discussed mutation and crossover operators use a random variable to create a new individual. This gives rise to the possibility that the chromosome of a new individual will go beyond the permissible D values.

Let me remind you of formula D, which we used when setting up the optimization problem.

$D = \{X \mid G(X) \geq 0\}$ is the set of admissible values of the vector X, where G(X) is the function limiting the vector, consisting of components $g_1(X)$, $g_2(X)$, ..., $g_{|G|}(X)$.

CHAPTER 6   OPTIMIZATION ALGORITHMS

There are several options to solve this problem.

- Use operators that generate only valid individuals.
- Use algorithms for reducing conditional optimization problems to unconstrained optimization problems.
- Use special methods developed for evolutionary algorithms.

Algorithms for reducing a conditional optimization problem to unconstrained optimization include the following:

- Penalty method
- Sliding tolerance method

Special methods include the following:

- Death penalty
- Static penalties
- Dynamic penalties
- Segregated genetic algorithm
- Reduction method
- Behavioral memory method

Sliding Tolerance Method

The essence of this method is that the condition $G(X) \geq 0$ is satisfied with some accuracy. The value X is considered valid if $0 < \kappa(X) < v$ and invalid if $\kappa(X) > v$.

> $v = v(t)$: This is the sliding tolerance criterion depending on the iteration number.
>
> $\kappa(X)$: This is the functional defined over all limiting functions.

The sliding tolerance criterion should decrease with an increasing number of iterations t. As the value v decreases, the boundaries of region D at which the value is considered acceptable also narrows. As a result, with a sufficiently high number of iterations, only valid values will be accepted for consideration.

The functional $\kappa(X)$ must be created in such a way that when X belongs to the range of acceptable values D, $\kappa(X) = 0$. And also the value $\kappa(X)$ increased as the value of X moved away from the nearest boundary of the range of acceptable values.

The method algorithm looks like this:

1. Using a set of operators, the next generation of agents is created without taking into account the conditions of D. Next, each of them is tested. If $\kappa(X) \leq v$, that is, the value is admissible, we assume that the agent is admissible and leave it in the population.

2. If $\kappa(X) > v$, that is, the value is unacceptable, then we look for point $X´$, which lies closer to the boundary of the region of acceptable values D. To do this, it is necessary to solve the problem of local unconditional optimization. We will talk about these algorithms as little later in this chapter)
$\min \kappa(Y) = \kappa(X")$ with the termination condition
being the expression $\kappa(X´) \leq v$.

3. When all agents become valid, we move on to the next iteration of the optimization algorithm.

The main advantage of this algorithm is that the permissible range of values narrows gradually as it approaches the solution of the optimization problem. In other words, in the first iterations the restrictions are much softer compared to the restrictions in the last iterations. This allows you to reduce computational resources in the first iterations of searching for the optimal solution.

Penalty Method

The essence of this method is to transform the conditional optimization problem.

$$\max_{|X|} f(X) = f(X^*) = f^*$$

On the unconstrained optimization problem, we have this:

$$\max_{|X|} \psi(X) = \max_{|X|}(f(X) + \phi(X, \alpha))$$

$\phi(X, \alpha)$ is a penalty function whose value increases as X approaches the range of permissible values D.

α is the value of the penalty function parameter. The higher it is, the faster the value of the penalty function increases. See Figure 6-11.

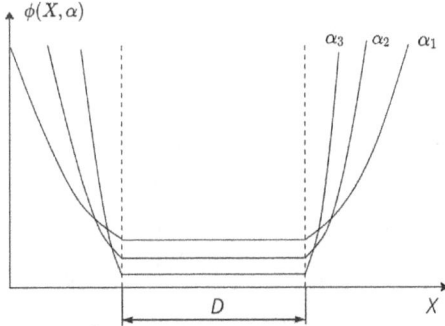

Figure 6-11. Examples of penalty function graphs

Figure 6-11 shows examples of penalty function graphs. It shows $\alpha_3 > \alpha_2 > \alpha_1$.

CHAPTER 6   OPTIMIZATION ALGORITHMS

The penalty function $\phi(X, \alpha)$ is chosen in such a way that when the value of X is in the range of acceptable values, the value of the function $\psi(X)$ differs very little from the value of the objective function f(X). This difference grows as X moves away from the range of acceptable values. It is worth noting that, despite the penalty functions, the values of X can still go beyond the range of acceptable values and be even more optimal than the values that satisfy the conditions of D.

In the general case, the penalty function formula has the following form:

$$\phi(X,\alpha) = \alpha \sum_{i=1}^{|G|} \rho_i L_i(g_i(X))$$

α: This is a vector of penalty function parameters.

ρ: This is a vector of coefficients that allows you to change the influence of an individual component X on the final value of the penalty function.

$L_i(g_i(X))$: This is a functional over the limiting function. Typically the formula for this functionality looks like this:

$$\begin{cases} L(g(X)) = 0 & G(X) \geq 0 \\ L(g(X)) > 0 & G(X) < 0 \end{cases}$$

This formula shows that if X is in the region of acceptable values, then the value of the penalty function is equal to zero. As soon as X leaves this region, then the value of the functional begins to become greater than zero.

It would be logical to use the distance from point X to the nearest boundary of the region of permissible values D to calculate L. But often calculating this distance is a difficult task. Therefore, the other functionality is used more often.

$$L_j(g_j(X)) = (e_j(X))^2$$
$$e_j(X) = \begin{cases} 0 & G(X) \geq 0 \\ g_j(X) & G(X) < 0 \end{cases}$$

CHAPTER 6   OPTIMIZATION ALGORITHMS

As a result, the algorithm of the penalty function method looks like this:

1. We create an initial population X^0 and set the initial values of the parameters of the penalty function α, ρ.
2. Using a set of operators, we generate a new set of individuals X^τ.
3. We calculate the values of the unconditional optimization function for it.
4. Using a set of operators, we again generate a new set of individuals $X^{\tau+1}$.
5. We check the conditions of restrictions. If the conditions are met and the condition for ending the search is met, then we consider that we have found the optimal solution and stop searching. Otherwise, according to some rule, we increase the values of the parameters (those genes that went beyond the permissible values) and again proceed to step 4.

The criterion for ending the search for an unconstrained optimization problem is most often the criterion for ending the search for conditional optimization.

The main disadvantage of this method is the significant complication of the function being optimized, which is the price to pay for eliminating restrictions.

Death Penalty

This method is based on simply discarding invalid individuals.
   The algorithm for this method is as follows:

1. The operator is executed, resulting in a new individual s'.
2. The new individual is checked for admissibility; that is, a check is made to check the restrictions $G(X) \geq 0$.
3. If the individual successfully passes the test, then it remains in the new population. If not, then it is discarded and goes to step 1.

In this approach, there is a high risk that this algorithm will go in cycles; that is, each newly generated individual at the first step will not be within the range of acceptable values.

When the set of admissible values of the objective function is a multidimensional parallelepiped, then the check at step 2 is reduced to checking each gene of the individual s' separately using the formula $x_i^{min} \leq x_i' \leq x_i^{max}$. If we are talking about an operator that changes only certain genes, then it is enough to discard the invalid gene and repeat the calculations of the operator again.

The disadvantage of this method is the need to repeatedly apply the operator, although perhaps not to all genes, but to some of them.

Static Penalties

The peculiarity of this method is that it takes into account not how strongly the restrictions were violated but how many of them were violated.
   The penalty function for this method is as follows:

$$\phi(X) = b - \sum_{i=1}^{n} \frac{b}{|G|}$$

b is the free method parameter. It is a large positive number.

The value of the modified objective function in this case is calculated using the following formula:

$$\psi(X) = \begin{cases} f(X) + \phi(X) & X \in D \\ \phi(X) & \text{not } X \in D \end{cases}$$

The free parameter b must be chosen in such a way that the value of the objective function for values outside the acceptable range is significantly less than for acceptable values.

The main disadvantage of this method is that it does not take into account how many boundaries of permissible values were violated but takes into account the total number of their violations.

Dynamic Penalties

The penalty function for this method is as follows:

$$\phi(X) = -(at)^b \sum_{i-1}^{|G|} L_i(g_i(X))$$

a, b, c: These are free method parameters:
$L_i(g_i(X))$: This function is calculated by the following formula:

$$L(g(X)) = \begin{cases} 0 & g(X) \geq 0 \\ |g(X)| & g(X) < 0 \end{cases}$$

A special feature of the dynamic penalty method is that the penalty increases with the number of generations t. Recommended values for free parameters a, b, c are a = -0.5, b = 2.0, c = 2.0.

Segregated Genetic Algorithm

This algorithm uses not one but two penalty functions: $\phi_1(X)$, $\phi_2(X)$. The goal of this algorithm is to try to avoid penalty functions that are too large or too small.

CHAPTER 6   OPTIMIZATION ALGORITHMS

The sequence of steps of this algorithm is as follows:

1. For each individual s of the population, we calculate the values of both penalty functions: $\phi_1(X)$, $\phi_2(X)$.

2. We sort each of the values $\phi_1(X)$, $\phi_2(X)$ in ascending order.

3. We combine these lists into one sorted array of length $2|S|$ and remove the last $|S|$ terms so that the length of the remaining part becomes equal to $|S|$. The remaining members will correspond to the individuals that violated the limits of acceptable values to the least extent.

4. We apply genetic operators to the resulting population to obtain a new population, S^{t+1}.

The problem with this method is the lack of clear recommendations on the choice of penalty functions: $\phi_1(X)$, $\phi_2(X)$.

Reduction Method

The reduction method is based on the use of the reducing function r(X), with the help of a transformation of an unacceptable individual s^- to an admissible s'. The individual s' obtained in this way is called *restored*.

There are a large number of different reducing functions. Let's look at the mutation operator as an example. Suppose that as a result of applying this operator to a valid individual, the parent s has mutated some of the genes so that the descendant s^- is invalid.

$\underline{s} = \left(h_1, \ldots, h_i, \underline{h_i}, h_{i+1}, \ldots, h_k, \underline{h_k}, h_{k+1}, \ldots, h_j \right)$, where the overline of a gene is a symbol of its mutation.

Then the reduction can be done as follows:

1. Sequentially for j = 1, 2, ..., n we return to the gene $\underline{h}_i$ its previous value h_i, and at each step we check the individual for entry into the range of acceptable values. If at any of these iterations an admissible individual is obtained, then we stop the calculations. Otherwise, we move on to the next step.

2. We successively return the pair of genes $\underline{h}_k, \underline{h}_j$, which is randomly selected from the set of genes, to their previous values. If at any of these iterations an admissible individual is obtained, then we stop the calculations. Otherwise, we move on to the next step.

3. We perform actions similar to step 2, but for three genes.

4. We perform actions for four genes and so on untIl an acceptable individual is obtained.

If the region of permissible values is a multidimensional parallelepiped, then the operator of projecting a point onto a multidimensional parallelepiped can be proposed as a reducing function, so that $X' = L(X^-)$, as shown in Figure 6-12 for a two-dimensional vector X.

CHAPTER 6   OPTIMIZATION ALGORITHMS

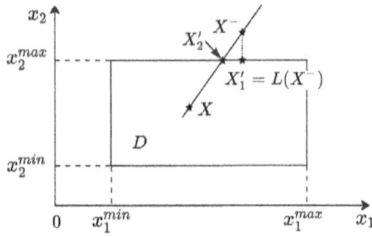

Figure 6-12. *The operator of projecting a point onto a multidimensional parallelepiped*

Please note that the reconstructed individual s' can be taken both from point X_1' and from point X_2'.

Behavioral Memory Method

The idea of this method is to gradually connect restrictions. That is, the more iterations completed or the more populations created, the more restrictions are connected.

The algorithm for this method is as follows:

1. When a certain number of iterations is reached, we add the first constraint.

2. Using one of the already discussed methods of taking into account restrictions, we ensure that the majority of individuals in the population are acceptable.

3. After a certain number of iterations, we activate the second constraint.

4. Again, using one of the methods of taking into account restrictions, we ensure that the majority of individuals in the current population are acceptable under two conditions.

5. And so on until all the conditions of the restrictions are taken into account.

Local Unconstrained Optimization Algorithms

The goal of these algorithms is to quickly search for a local extremum of the objective function.

This is necessary at the last stage of optimization to improve the best individuals. When the parameter values of these agents serve as starting points for local search algorithms, this allows you to achieve even better results from the genetic algorithm.

These methods are also used in some constraint accounting algorithms. We looked at one of these methods: sliding tolerance method.

There are three classes of stochastic local search algorithms: single-point/one-step, multistep algorithms, and multipoint algorithms.

One-Step Algorithms

In general, the formula for the one-step *random search (RS)* algorithm is as follows:

$$X^{k+1} = X^k + \lambda^k D^k$$

k is a positive number meaning the step size in the random direction D^k.

In its simplest form, the sequence of actions in a one-step local search algorithm looks like this:

CHAPTER 6 OPTIMIZATION ALGORITHMS

1. We randomly or otherwise select a starting point in the range of acceptable values.

2. Randomly select direction D^k.

3. We step toward this direction by the amount λ^k.

4. If the condition $f(X^{k+1}) > f(X^k)$ is met, then we accept a new point and repeat all steps, but with the exact X^{k+1}; otherwise, we return to point 1, using point X^k.

Of course, in the general case, the determination function X^{k+1} is not such a simple linear function but rather represents a more complex deterministic or stochastic function of the following form:

$$X^{k+1} = \Phi\left(X^k, D^k\right)$$

Selecting the Search Direction

The **random line search (RLS) algorithm** was proposed by H. J. Bremermann in 1970. The components of the direction vector D^k according to this algorithm are determined by the following formula:

$$d_k = \pm U(0;1)$$

That is, each component of the vector can be equally distributed between three numbers: -1, 0, and +1.

The step size according to the RLS algorithm is determined by the following formula:

$$\lambda^k = \alpha \, max\left(x_k^{max} - x_k^{min}\right)$$

x_k^{min} и x_k^{max} : This creates the boundaries of the range of permissible values.

α: This is the free parameter of the algorithm. It takes values from 0 to 1.

The idea of the **single-dimension perturbation search (SDPS) algorithm** is to split the direction selection step into several steps, in which the vector D^k takes the following form:

$$D_i^k = \left(0,\ldots,0,U(-1,1),0,\ldots,0\right)$$

That is, at each sub step i of the direction selection, only the i-th component of the direction vector is nonzero. Of course, this approach at each substep i ensures that the direction is searched only along the i-th coordinate direction. That is why the method is called *single-dimension*.

$U(-1, 1)$ is a function that determines the value of the nonzero component of the direction vector. This function can be a uniform probability distribution function or a normal distribution function $N(0, \sigma)$, in which the mathematical expectation is zero and the standard deviation is a free parameter of the algorithm.

Rules for Choosing Step Size

If the step size remains unchanged throughout all iterations, then the algorithm is called **fixed step size random search** (FSSRS), but if step size λ varies from iteration to iteration, then the algorithm is called **adaptive step size random search** (ASSRS).

There are a large number of algorithms for changing step λ in ASSRS algorithms. For example, in the local unimodal sampling algorithm, this value is calculated using a geometric progression. That is, if the condition $f(X^{k+1}) > f(X^k)$ is not met, then the step size is reduced according to the following formula:

$$\lambda = \eta \lambda$$

η: This is a free algorithm parameter whose value ranges from 0 to 1.

CHAPTER 6 OPTIMIZATION ALGORITHMS

In the SDPS algorithm, the step is reduced according to the following formula:

$$\lambda = \lambda_0 \frac{k^{max} - k}{k^{max}}$$

λ_0: This is the initial step size; it is a free parameter.
k^{max}: This is the maximum number of iterations.
k: This is the current iteration number.

Obviously, according to this method, the step will decrease as it approaches the optimal value of the objective function

According to the **adaptive maxing random search** (AMRS) algorithm, step size λ should be calculated in two stages. At the first stage, the maximum permissible value λ_{max} is determined, which ensures the admissibility of all points of the form $X^{k+1} = X^k + \lambda_{max} D$.

At the second stage, the step is calculated as a random variable located in the area $U(0, \lambda_{max})$. In this method, as in SDPS, the step decreases as the optimal value of the objective function is approached.

One of the classic algorithms that demonstrates the operation of one-step algorithms is the **return algorithm when a step fails**.

To obtain a new approximation, it uses a standard formula of the following form:

$$X^{k+1} = X^k + \lambda^k D^k$$

The algorithm diagram looks like this:

1. We set the starting point X^0, as well as the initial values of the free parameters: λ^0, which is the initial step length; β, which is the maximum number of unsuccessful attempts (it is recommended to set this value equal to $|X|$); and η, which is a step λ reduction factor.

2. Set the initial value of the counter of failed attempts as j=1.

3. Using some algorithm, we calculate the vector D^k. Find the current value of X^k and the value of the objective function $f(X^k)$.

4. If the condition $f(X^{k+1}) > f(X^k)$ is satisfied, then go to step 2. If not, then go to the next step.

5. If $j \leq \beta$, then j = j+1, and go to step 2. If not, then go to the next step.

6. We check the search end condition. If the condition is met, then we stop the calculations; if not, then we set $\lambda = \eta\lambda$ and go to step 2.

Figure 6-13 illustrates how this algorithm works.

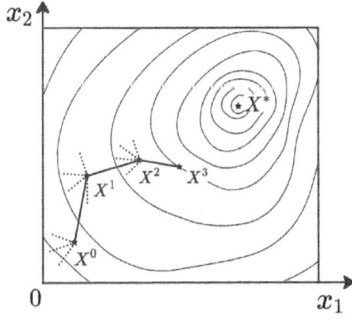

Figure 6-13. *Extremum search trajectory*

CHAPTER 6 OPTIMIZATION ALGORITHMS

Multistep Algorithms

In general, the formula for a multistep algorithm looks like this:

$$X^{k+1} = \sum_{j=0}^{j-1} \alpha_j X^{k-j} + \lambda^k D^k$$

j is a free parameter. It specifies the number of steps in a multistep algorithm.

α_j is the set of free parameters. These are the weights of the previous search steps.

λ^k is the step size in the random direction D^k.

As in the case of a one-step algorithm, the new value X^{k+1} will be accepted if the condition $f(X^{k+1}) > f(X^k)$ is met. If the condition is not accepted, then according to some rule the step and direction are changed.

As an example, consider the following algorithm:

1. Set the starting point X^0 and the number of maximum attempts.

2. Using some one-step algorithm, we calculate points X^1 and X^2.

3. We calculate the direction vector D^k as the average search direction of X^1 and X^2.

4. Using the formula $X^{k+1} = X^k + \lambda^k D^k$, we calculate the following approximation: X^{k+1}.

5. If the condition $f(X^{k+1}) > f(X^k)$ is satisfied and the condition for ending iterations is met, then we stop the calculations. If the condition $f(X^{k+1}) > f(X^k)$ is met and the condition for ending iterations is not met, then increase the step length and go to step 2.

6. If the condition $f(X^{k+1}) > f(X^k)$ is not met, then we make j attempts to increase the value of the objective function by changing the search direction; if this does not lead to a result, then we reduce the step length and go to step 2.

Figure 6-14 shows the operation of this algorithm.

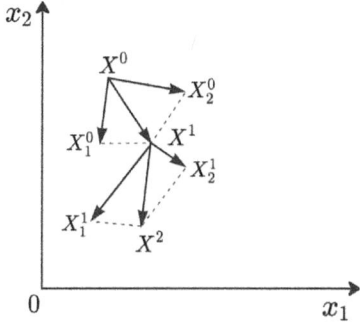

Figure 6-14. Representations of how the algorithm works

Multipoint Algorithms

The idea of this group of algorithms is to use not one point, but several, to find the optimal value of the objective function.

Simplex or Complex Algorithm

Complex is a polyhedron with n>(|X|+1) vertices.
In its enlarged form, the algorithm is constructed from several steps.

1. Generation of the complex
2. Reflection of the top of the complex
3. Compression of the complex

CHAPTER 6 OPTIMIZATION ALGORITHMS

Generation of the complex

This operation must be carried out using any one-step local optimization algorithm.

1. Choose a starting point.

2. We generate the required number of vertices of the complex using the formula $X^i = X^0 + \lambda \dfrac{D}{\|D\|} = X^0 + \lambda \underline{D}$. In this formula $\|D\|$ is the norm of the vector D, which means that the construction $\dfrac{D}{\|D\|}$ has unit length and parameter $\underline{D}$ serves as a direction indicator.

Figure 6-15 demonstrates the complex generation process.

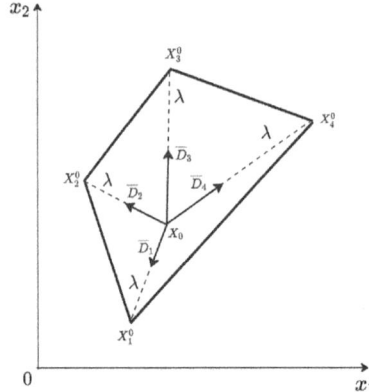

Figure 6-15. *Complex generation*

Reflection of the top of the complex

The purpose of this step is to reflect the vertex X^i of complex C through the center of gravity. Usually they reflect the vertex with the worst value of the objective function. In the resulting complex C', all vertices, the edge of

CHAPTER 6 OPTIMIZATION ALGORITHMS

the i-th, coincide with the corresponding vertices of the original complex C. The i-th vertex is on a straight line passing through vertex X^i and the center of gravity of complex C.

The formula for calculating the reflected vertex is as follows:

$$X = X_c + \lambda \left(X_c - X^i \right)$$

λ is the coefficient of stretching of the complex. It is a free algorithm parameter. Of course, this parameter can be adaptive. So, for example, you can decrease the value of this as the number of iterations increases. Or you can increase it if there is no significant increase in the value of the objective function.

The center of gravity can be determined by the following formula:

$$X_c = \frac{1}{n} \sum_{i=1}^{n} X_i$$

According to this formula, the center of mass of the complex is the arithmetic mean of all vertices of the complex. The logic for determining the center of mass can be complicated by introducing significance coefficients for the vertices, depending on the values of the objective function. Thus, if some of the vertices have values of the objective function that are much better than the values of the remaining vertices of the complex, then the center of mass will be shifted toward them.

It is worth noting that this procedure is carried out several times.

Figure 6-16 shows an example of how vertex flipping works.

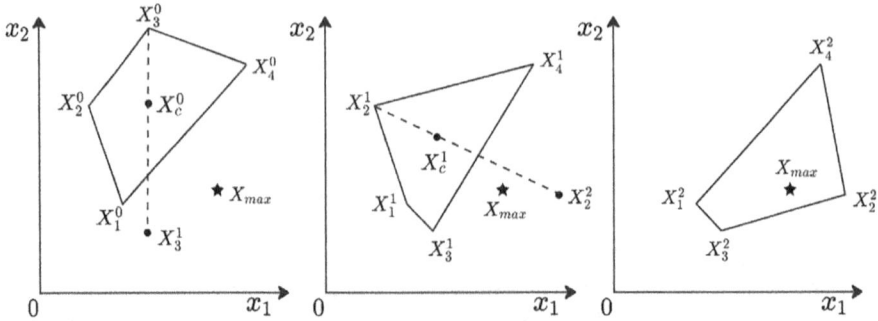

***Figure 6-16.** Trajectory of change of the complex*

Compression of the complex

This step is similar to the complex stretching step. It also involves reflection of the vertex X^i of complex C through the center of gravity. But in this case, the formula for obtaining a new vertex is as follows:

$$X = X_c + \beta(X_c - X^i)$$

β is the free parameter of the algorithm. This is the so-called compression ratio. It must be less than 1.

A simplified algorithm of the method complex looks like this:

1. We generate the initial complex C^0 from the initial point X^0. To do this, we generate the vertices of the complex using one or another algorithm.

2. We calculate the values of the objective function at each vertex.

3. We reflect the vertex X^i that has the worst value of the objective function and obtain a new vertex X_*^i and a new complex C'. We calculate the value of the objective function at the new vertex.

CHAPTER 6   OPTIMIZATION ALGORITHMS

4. If the value of the objective function at the new vertex has improved compared to the old vertex, then we compress the complex and proceed to step 2.

5. We check the search end condition. If it is satisfied, then we stop the calculations. Otherwise, go to step 2.

You can use the following conditions as search end conditions:

- The maximum length of a complex edge does not exceed the specified solution accuracy.

- The maximum difference between the values of the objective function at the vertices of the edges of the complex does not exceed the required accuracy of the solution.

Hypersphere Algorithm

The idea of the hypersphere algorithm is to generate random points evenly distributed over the surface of the hypersphere.

The algorithm looks like this:

1. We set the initial point X^0, the initial radius of the hypersphere R^0, and the number of points on the hypersphere n.

2. We generate n random points X_i^t, uniformly distributed over the surface of a hypersphere of radius R^t with a center at point X^t.

3. We calculate the value of the objective function at all points obtained and find the point at which this value is the best.

4. Using any of the single-point optimization algorithms, we find the maximum of the objective function in the direction $(X_i^t - X^t)$ using the formula $X^{t+1} = max\left(X^t + \lambda\left(X_i^t - X^t\right)\right)$.

5. We check the search end condition. If it is satisfied, then we stop the calculations. Otherwise, we set the point X^{t+1} as the center of the sphere and go to step 2.

As with any optimization algorithm, there are many variations for this one. For example, you can change the radius of the hypersphere as it approaches the optimal value. You can also not search for the minimum of the objective function in the direction $(X_i^t - X^t)$ but perform a step with a given length. Some generate points on the hypersphere not uniformly, but randomly in a certain sector.

The radius of the hypersphere can be used as a criterion for ending the search; it should not be less than the specified accuracy of the solution.

Random Search Algorithms

This group of algorithms makes significant use of random variables to find a local extremum. This group of algorithms can also be used to find the global optimal value of the objective function and generate the first generation of genetic algorithm.

Monte Carlo Algorithm

This algorithm can rightfully be considered the ancestor of all other random search algorithms. It is often used to generate starting points for other more complex algorithms.

It consists of several steps.

1. Set the final number of iterations n and set t=1.

2. Using any random number generator, we generate the point X^{t+1} and calculate the value of the objective function at it. Increase t by one t=t+1.

3. If the number of iterations t exceeds the maximum number of iterations n, then we stop the calculations. Otherwise, repeat step 2.

Simulated Annealing Algorithm

One of the oldest algorithms that has proven its effectiveness in solving many problems. The idea of the algorithm was based on a mechanism for correcting defects in the crystal lattice of metals.

Defects in the crystal lattice of a metal are often caused by the fact that some of the atoms occupy incorrect (nonoptimal) positions. At normal temperature, they do not have enough kinetic energy to overcome the potential barrier and take the correct position; that is, the crystal lattice is in a state of local energy minimum. To overcome the barrier and bring the system from a local minimum to a global one, the system is heated. In this case, atoms occupying the wrong position acquire energy and can take the correct places. In this case, as the metal cools, the atoms lose energy, and the system again stabilizes in a state of local minimum.

If this analogy is applied to optimization theory, then each local minimum can be considered as a defective crystal lattice. Improvement of the solution occurs due to periodic changes in the found solution, the intensity of which decreases as it approaches the optimal solution.

The main difference between this algorithm and others is that it allows periodic deterioration of the solution to the optimization problem.

CHAPTER 6 OPTIMIZATION ALGORITHMS

The algorithm diagram looks like this:

1. We set the starting point X^0, and ξ - is a positive threshold, which will decrease as the iterations of the algorithm increase. It represents a random variable with a mathematical expectation. This gives meaning to the temperature of the annealed metal.

2. We randomly generate a new value in the vicinity of the current approximation $X^{t+1} = \omega(X^t)$.

3. The solution X^{t+1} becomes a new approximation with a probability determined by the formula

$$\theta(f) = \begin{cases} 1 & f^{t+1} \leq f^t \\ exp(-\frac{f^{t+1}-f^t}{\xi}) & f^{t+1} > f^t \end{cases}$$

Random Restarts Algorithm

Random search algorithms have one big drawback: they require a large number of tests. This algorithm belongs to the class of two-phase random search algorithms. Such algorithms include two search phases: global phase and local phase. The goal of the first phase is to generate a certain number of random points. The second phase consists of using local search algorithms, where the starting point is the point formed in the first stage.

The general scheme of this algorithm is as follows:

1. Set the total number of starting points n.

2. Generate coordinates of point X^t.

3. Using point X^t as the initial point, we find the local extremum using one of the previously presented local search algorithms.

4. If the number of starting points is less than n, then we return to step 2; otherwise, we complete the calculations.

The danger of this approach is that some local solutions may be found many times, while others may not be found at all.

Iterated Local Search

The idea of this algorithm is to use perturbation of the previous solution found instead of generating starting points randomly. The problem with this approach is that it is necessary to overcome the local extremum zone. Otherwise, the local search algorithm will return to this extremum again. Therefore, on the one hand, perturbation should be strong enough, but it should not be too strong. Otherwise, this algorithm will differ little from the random restarts algorithm.

The sequence of actions of the iterated local search algorithm is as follows:

1. We generate a random initial value X^0 belonging to the range of acceptable values.
2. I use point X^t as the starting point; using any local search algorithm we find the solution X_*^t.
3. Perturbate point X_*^t and get point X^{t+1}.
4. If the condition for ending the search is met, then we stop the calculations; otherwise, we return to step 2.

Perturbation

The perturbation procedure can be built on the basis of any population algorithm. Often a genetic algorithm is used for these purposes. There are also a large variety of perturbation implementation options based on algorithms using random variables.

CHAPTER 6   OPTIMIZATION ALGORITHMS

The main thing is that perturbation meets the following requirements:

- It must be strong enough to overcome the area of attraction of the current local extremum.
- It doesn't have to be completely random.
- It can use the history of solutions found.

Summary

In this chapter, you learned the basics of population algorithms, in particular the genetic algorithm. I showed the logic of a number of operators of this algorithm, which will help create the first version of a library of optimization algorithms.

It is worth noting that the genetic algorithm is far from the only algorithm from the population class.

Also, to solve the problem of searching and optimizing profitable strategies, algorithms such as the particle swarm optimization algorithm, the artificial immune systems algorithm, and many others are of interest. The implementation of these algorithms, as well as an increase in the number of operators used, can be considered a growth point for our system.

CHAPTER 7

Implementation of Optimization Algorithms

In the previous chapter, I covered the theory of constructing optimization algorithms. We looked at what genetic algorithms are and from which operators they can be constructed. In this chapter, the time has come to put this information together to create a library that will become one of the important modules of the system for searching for profitable strategies.

As with building any module or service, creating this will consist of several steps.

1. Write a description of use cases. This step is necessary to understand what functionality will be included in the new library and how it will be used.

2. Make a list of the required functionality.

3. Implement it.

In this chapter, I plan to first talk to you about my expectations of the optimization algorithms module and describe my general vision.

After this, we will implement the simplest optimization algorithm, namely, the brute-force algorithm. Since it is simple, when implementing

CHAPTER 7   IMPLEMENTATION OF OPTIMIZATION ALGORITHMS

it, most of our effort will be on creating the foundation of the module. Implementing a mechanism that includes new optimization algorithms will not affect library users.

Once the foundation is ready, we will begin implementing the genetic algorithm.

I am using a framework to implement .NET, but that does not mean this chapter will be useful only to those who already know or are interested in .NET. I could have used any other popular language and framework with equal success. The ideas discussed in this chapter will be useful to any person who has decided to create their own trading system, regardless of the chosen programming language.

I hope that after reading this chapter you will have enough information and ideas to create your own library of optimization algorithms.

General View

In the previous chapter, much attention was paid to the fact that optimization algorithms are not a list of clearly defined rules but rather ideas for constructing your own algorithms. If we take the genetic algorithm as an example, many operators have been developed for it, on the basis of which you can implement a large number of your own variations of the genetic algorithm.

And since the list of optimization algorithms is not limited and each of them is unique and has its own list of settings and parameters, this means that the optimization algorithm in the service for finding a profitable strategy will be an entity.

I see the scenario for creating an optimization algorithm as follows:

1. The user opens a special form for creating an optimization algorithm in the UI part of the application.

2. The user possibly enters the name of the new algorithm.

3. The user selects the type. In this chapter, we implement only two types of algorithms: brute-force algorithm and genetic algorithm.

4. The user configures operator types or other options.

5. The user sets the values of free parameters.

6. The user saves the result.

What does the module of optimization algorithms have to do with this? After all, it will not contain a UI or even a database. But pay attention to steps 3, 4, and 5. Where will the application get the list of available algorithm types? What about the types of operators and the list of free parameters for them? All this information will have to be provided by the optimization algorithms module.

Here we have highlighted the first functionality that the module must implement.

Functional requirement: Return all necessary information for creating and configuring variations of optimization algorithms.

Let's say the user created a new optimization algorithm or changed an existing one. How will he understand that his algorithm is efficient enough? Of course, it makes sense to perform a preliminary check by testing it on some simple subtheory with a small number of optimized parameters and on a not too large period of historical data, but is this enough? In addition, even such testing will take time and may not reveal all the advantages or disadvantages of the new optimization algorithm.

All this leads to the need to create a different way to test the effectiveness of algorithms. And there is such a way. It is based on training algorithms on special mathematical functions. Of course, this method does not give an absolute result. As was correctly noted in the previous chapter, the problem of finding optimal parameter values is completely unformalized. That is, it does not have any mathematical model. This means it is impossible to find a training mathematical function that is remotely similar to this.

But we know that it is multi-extremal and has a range of permissible values, which is a multidimensional parallelepiped. This knowledge allows us to test the performance of the algorithm on multi-extremal mathematical functions with or without the addition of a range of acceptable values.

Functionality requirement: Provide functionality that allows you to test the created algorithm on training mathematical functions.

From the fact that using the module it is possible to optimize not only strategies, but also mathematical functions, another requirement follows.

Functional requirement: The module must be independent of the context in which it is used.

This means that for the algorithms embedded in the module, there should be no difference between the optimization of the candle interval (1 min, 5 min, 1 h, and so on) for calculating the indicator of one of the conditions of the signal to buy the strategy and the value of one of the components of the vector X of the three-dimensional function of Hartman.

So, using the optimization algorithms module, the user was able to create a new algorithm and test its operation on mathematical functions, after which he selected the new algorithm in the settings of the theory generator and clicked the generate button. Next, the theory is generated, and on its basis a subtheory is created, which uses this algorithm to create and test strategies.

Let's imagine that the user has chosen a brute-force algorithm, and according to the subtheory settings, there are several thousand variants of strategies, each of which needs to be tested. Should the algorithm immediately return several thousand variants of parameter values? Of course not. First, saving and queuing thousands of strategies at once is not a good idea, because something can go wrong in the middle of this process.

CHAPTER 7   IMPLEMENTATION OF OPTIMIZATION ALGORITHMS

Second, there is a possibility that the user may change his mind and stop the calculation. Then it will turn out that a large number of strategies and tasks will be created in vain and will only waste space in the database. This means that it makes sense for the module to provide variations in parameter values in portions.

The iterative nature of most optimization algorithms also speaks in favor of chunkiness. If we take, for example, a genetic algorithm, then it has the concept of generations, which are also generated sequentially.

Functional requirement: Generating sets of values for calculating the objective function (calculating strategy indicators) must be an iterative process.

As a result, the operation of the module can be represented as a loop, as shown in Figure 7-1.

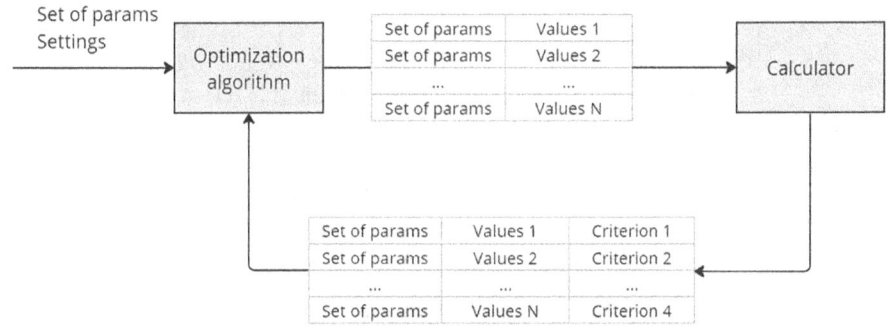

Figure 7-1. *Operation of the optimization module*

Let's fix the final list of functionality that is required from the library.

1. Provide all the necessary information to create and configure variations of optimization algorithms.

2. A module must be independent of the context in which it is used.

CHAPTER 7 IMPLEMENTATION OF OPTIMIZATION ALGORITHMS

3. Generating sets of values for calculating the objective function should be an iterative process.

4. Provide functionality that allows you to test the created algorithm on training mathematical functions.

Brute-Force Algorithm

The essence of this method is to enumerate all the possible options for parameter values. Let's start with the first requirement: provide information about the algorithm settings. First, let's discuss how the library classes will be used.

I see it this way:

1. The connection will of course be made using IServiceCollection. Dependency injection (DI) facilitates testing by allowing dependencies to be replaced with mock implementations. It also reduces coupling between modules and promotes better separation of responsibilities in code. This is a generally accepted practice that should not be abandoned, even if at first glance it seems that DI is not needed.

2. Of course, enum or its equivalent will be used to store the list of available algorithm types if we need more advanced functionality in the future.

3. All functionality will be embedded in classes that implement the IOptimizationAlgorithm interface. One class will be created for each type of optimization algorithm.

CHAPTER 7   IMPLEMENTATION OF OPTIMIZATION ALGORITHMS

4. To obtain an instance of a class that implements an algorithm, you need to contact the factory, which will match the type of the algorithm with the desired class and generate its instance.

Let's get started. Listing 7-1 shows an implementation of an extension to IServiceCollection. Here I use functionality that was implemented in the latest version of .NET 8 Keyed Services. The idea is to be able to add a named implementation of an interface. I use one of the enum elements as the key.

Listing 7-1. Adding Dependencies

```
public static IServiceCollection AddOptimizationAlgorithms(this
IServiceCollection services)
{
    services.AddSingleton<AlgorithmFactory>();

    services
        .AddKeyedTransient<IOptimizationAlgorithm,
        BruteForceAlgorithm>(
            AlgorithmTypes.BruteForce);

    return services;
}
```

I connect the factory as a singleton because this class is stateless, so I don't see the need to generate a new instance every time I get an instance from the collection. But IOptimizationAlgorithm will be Transient, because it will store the necessary settings for calculating the next portion of parameter values.

Listing 7-2 shows the implementation of the function that gets an instance of an algorithm in the AlgorithmFactory class.

Listing 7-2. GetOptimizationAlgorithm Function

```
public IOptimizationAlgorithm GetOptimizationAlgorithm(
    AlgorithmTypes type)
{
    return _serviceProvider
        .GetRequiredKeyedService<IOptimizationAlgorithm>(type);
}
```

Getting Info

Let's take a look at IOptimizationAlgorithm in Listing 7-3, since the first step was to implement the functionality of obtaining information about the algorithm. Now it contains only one function.

Listing 7-3. IOptimizationAlgorithm Interface

```
public interface IOptimizationAlgorithm
{
    public AlgorithmTypeInfo GetTypeInfo();
}
```

The brute-force algorithm has only one free parameter: the number of returned sets of values at each iteration. So, the AlgorithmTypeInfo class looks simple (Listing 7-4), but when we start implementing a genetic algorithm, it becomes much more complex.

Listing 7-4. AlgorithmTypeInfo Record

```
public record AlgorithmTypeInfo(AlgorithmTypes Type)
{
    public List<AlgorithmTypeInfo_Param> Params { get; }
    = new();
}
```

```
public record AlgorithmTypeInfo_Param(
ParamTypes Type,
decimal DefaultValue);
```

The information generation function for `BruteForceAlgorithm` will look like that shown in Listing 7-5.

Listing 7-5. GetTypeInfo for Brute-Force Algorithm

```
public AlgorithmTypeInfo GetTypeInfo()
{
    var info = new AlgorithmTypeInfo(AlgorithmTypes.
    BruteForce);
    info.Params
        .Add(new AlgorithmTypeInfo_Param(ParamTypes.
        PointsCount, 100));

    return info;
}
```

I've added the `PointsCount` parameter, so now let's pass it to the class that implements the algorithm. To do this, I created an `AlgorithmInfo` class, which is very similar to `AlgorithmTypeInfo`, but instead of `defaultValue`, you need to fill in the `value` field.

You also need to add the `Init()` function to the `IOptimizationAlgorithm` interface and call it in the factory. Listing 7-6 shows the modified code in the `AlgorithmFactory` class. I made both factory methods public. One creates an algorithm for the purpose of calculation, and the other creates the necessary information.

Listing 7-6. GetOptimizationAlgorithm Function

```
public IOptimizationAlgorithm GetOptimizationAlgorithm(
    AlgorithmInfo info,
    List<FunctionVariable> functionVariables)
{
    IOptimizationAlgorithm optimizationAlgorithm =
        GetOptimizationAlgorithm(info.Type);

    optimizationAlgorithm.Init(info, functionVariables);

    return optimizationAlgorithm;
}
public IOptimizationAlgorithm GetOptimizationAlgorithm(
    AlgorithmTypes type)
{
    return _serviceProvider
        .GetRequiredKeyedService<IOptimizationAlgorithm>(type);
}
```

Listing 7-7 demonstrates the implementation of the Init function of the BruteForceAlgorithm class.

Listing 7-7. Init Function

```
public void Init(AlgorithmInfo info, List<FunctionVariable>
functionVariables)
{
    _pointsCount =
        (int)info.Params
            .First(p => p.Type == ParamTypes.
            PointsCount).Value;
    _functionVariables = functionVariables;
}
```

CHAPTER 7 IMPLEMENTATION OF OPTIMIZATION ALGORITHMS

Let's take a look at the `FunctionVariable` type, which is a representation for a function parameter. It is the set of these parameters that the optimization module must optimize. Listing 7-8 shows my implementation of this class.

Listing 7-8. FunctionVariable Record

```
public record FunctionVariable
{
    public IVariableId Id { get; }

    public decimal? MinValue { get; }
    public decimal? MaxValue { get; }
    public decimal? Step { get; }

    public List<decimal>? Values { get; }

    public FunctionVariable(
        IVariableId id,
        decimal minValue,
        decimal maxValue,
        decimal step)
    {
        Id = id;
        MinValue = minValue;
        MaxValue = maxValue;
        Step = step;
    }

    public FunctionVariable(IVariableId id, List<decimal>? values)
    {
```

```
        Id = id;
        Values = values;
    }
}
```

First, pay attention to the type of the Id field. Imagine a scenario where an application works with a library. The service for searching for optimal strategies based on subtheory must generate an array of these parameters. Then the library returns sets of these parameters with values. How will the application understand which signal, condition, and indicator this parameter belongs to? It would be possible to make this field as a string in which the application encoded the necessary information, for example, in JSON format. But what if some algorithm needs to sort these identifiers or some other action is needed? It's just that the string most likely will not be able to provide us with a sufficient level of functionality.

At this point, the IVariableId interface looks pretty simple.

`interface IVariableId: IEquatable<IVariableId>`

I immediately added IEquatable<IVariableId> because implementations of this interface will probably have to be compared with each other.

Please note that I have significantly simplified the range of acceptable values of the objective function, leaving only min, max parameters or a list of values, because this library is created to find profitable strategies, so I believe that I cannot implement more complex scenarios of limiting functions in it. Pay attention to the two constructors; they ensure data integrity. In one case, the list of values will be filled, and in the other, the boundaries of possible values will be filled. This mechanism could be implemented by using inheritance, where one type would implement a variable with restrictions and another with a list of values.

CHAPTER 7   IMPLEMENTATION OF OPTIMIZATION ALGORITHMS

Getting a Set of Values

It's time to implement a method for getting sets of values. Listing 7-9 shows my implementation of this function.

Listing 7-9. GetNextPoints Function

```
public IEnumerable<AlgorithmPoint> GetNextPoints(
    List<ObjectiveFunctionResult>? previousResults)
{
    List<AlgorithmPoint> allPoints = GetPoints();
    IEnumerable<AlgorithmPoint> nextPoints = allPoints
        .Where(allPoint =>
            previousResults == null
            || !previousResults.Exists(r => r.Point ==
            allPoint))
        .Take(_pointsCount);
    return nextPoints;
}
```

There is nothing complicated about the function itself. Of interest is the AlgorithmPoint class and the comparison operator r.Point == allPoint. Listing 7-10 shows an implementation of this class.

Listing 7-10. AlgorithmPoint Class

```
public class AlgorithmPoint
{
    public List<FunctionVariableValue> Values { get; } = new();

    public static bool operator ==(AlgorithmPoint? a,
    AlgorithmPoint? b)
    {
        if (ReferenceEquals(a, b))
            return true;
```

277

```
        if(a is null || b is null)
            return false;

        if(a.Values.Count != b.Values.Count)
            return false;

        return a.Values
            .OrderBy(v => v.Id)
            .SequenceEqual(b.Values.OrderBy(v => v.Id));
    }
    public static bool operator !=(AlgorithmPoint a,
    AlgorithmPoint b)
    {
        return !(a == b);
    }
}
```

Let's take a closer look at this code. First, I ask you to pay attention to the fact that it uses the OrderBy function by identifier, which is an implementation of the IVariableId interface. This means the class that implements this interface must also implement IComparable, because the OrderBy implementation calls the CompareTo function.

Let's return to the GetNextPoints function. It left undisclosed the implementation of the GetPoints function. The purpose of this is to return all possible variations of sets of variable values. The difficulty of this algorithm is that we do not know how many variables the target function contains. I built a solution based on templates.

Imagine that the set of variables has the form in Table 7-1.

Table 7-1. Variables Example

Id	Min	max	step
1	1	2	1
2	10	20	10
3	100	200	100

Then the algorithm will look like this:

1. Take all possible values of variable 1. Obviously, this has only two possible values: 1 and 2. Create a template from these two values. Get an array of two templates.

2. Take the first template [1, ...] and "expand" it to the values of the second variable. Get the patterns: [1, 10, ...] and [1, 20, ...].

3. Take the pattern [1, 10, ...] and expand it to the values of the third variable. Get possible sets of values: [1, 10, 100] and [1, 10, 200].

4. Repeat steps 2 and 3 until all unfilled templates are exhausted.

The idea of recursion is that steps 2 and 3 are no different from each other; they can be replaced by a function that receives a list of templates as input and then takes an unused variable, "expands" the templates, and calls itself again, and so on until as long as there is an unused variable.

The call tree will look like Figure 7-2.

CHAPTER 7   IMPLEMENTATION OF OPTIMIZATION ALGORITHMS

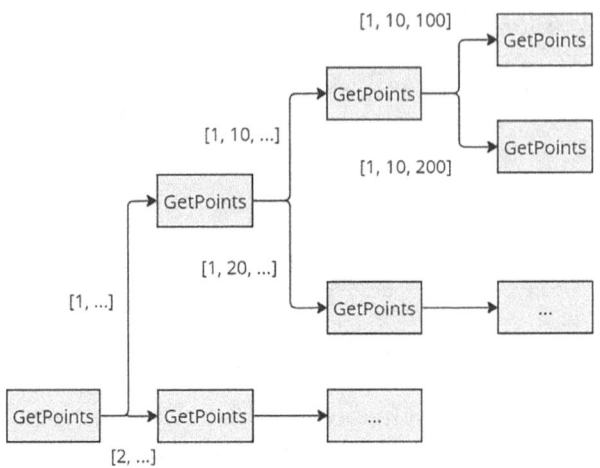

Figure 7-2. *GetPoints recursion*

Listing 7-11 demonstrates my simplest implementation of the GetPoints function.

Listing 7-11. GetPoints Function

```
private List<AlgorithmPoint> GetPoints(AlgorithmPoint?
pointTemplate = null)
{
    pointTemplate ??= new AlgorithmPoint();

    FunctionVariable? remainderVariable =
    GetRemainderVariable();
    if (remainderVariable == null)
        return new List<AlgorithmPoint>(){ pointTemplate };

    var newTemplates = GetTemplates();

    var result = new List<AlgorithmPoint>();
    foreach (AlgorithmPoint template in newTemplates)
    {
```

```
        List<AlgorithmPoint> points = GetPoints(template);
        result.AddRange(points);
    }

    return result;

    FunctionVariable? GetRemainderVariable()
    {
        foreach (FunctionVariable functionVariable in _
        functionVariables)
        {
            if (!pointTemplate!.Values
                    .Exists(v => v.Id.Equals
                    (functionVariable.Id)))
                return functionVariable;
        }

        return null;
    }

    IEnumerable<AlgorithmPoint> GetTemplates()
    {
        List<decimal> values = remainderVariable.GetValues();
        var templates = new List<AlgorithmPoint>();
        foreach (decimal value in values)
        {
            AlgorithmPoint newTemplate = new AlgorithmPoint();
            newTemplate.Values
                .Add(new FunctionVariableValue(remainder
                Variable.Id, value));

            foreach (FunctionVariableValue item in
            pointTemplate.Values)
```

```
            {
                newTemplate.Values
                    .Add(new FunctionVariableValue(item.Id,
                    item.Value));
            }
            templates.Add(newTemplate);
        }
        return templates;
    }
}
```

The condition for exiting recursion is the fact that the algorithm no longer finds unused variables, that is, when the `remainderVariable` variable is equal to null. Of course, this algorithm is far from optimal, but it is easy to understand. You can store hashes of used variables in some variable and not loop through all sets of variables each time. But I tried to implement an algorithm that is understandable to everyone. If your skills and knowledge allow you to optimize it, then that's great!

How to Use

So, BruteForceAlgorithm has been implemented. Let's try to connect our library and see if it is convenient to use. Listing 7-12 presents the simplest implementation of the algorithm.

Listing 7-12. Example of Using the Algorithm

```
var services = new ServiceCollection();
services.AddOptimizationAlgorithms();
ServiceProvider provider = services.BuildServiceProvider();

AlgorithmFactory algorithmFactory = provider.GetRequiredService
<AlgorithmFactory>();
```

```
AlgorithmInfo info = new(AlgorithmTypes.BruteForce);
info.Params.Add(new AlgorithmInfo_Param(ParamTypes.
PointsCount, 2));

List<FunctionVariable> functionVariables = new();
functionVariables.Add(new FunctionVariable(new
VariableId("First"), 1, 2, 1));
functionVariables.Add(new FunctionVariable(new
VariableId("Second"), 10, 20, 10));
functionVariables.Add(new FunctionVariable(new
VariableId("Third"), 100, 200, 100));

IOptimizationAlgorithm? algorithm = algorithmFactory.
GetOptimizationAlgorihm(info, functionVariables);
List<ObjectiveFunctionResult>? previousResults = new();

List<AlgorithmPoint> points = algorithm!.
GetNextPoints(previousResults).ToList();
List<(int step, List<AlgorithmPoint>)> result = new();
int step = 0;
while (points.Any())
{
    result.Add((step, points));
    step++;

    points
        .ForEach(p => previousResults.Add(new
        ObjectiveFunctionResult(p, 1)));

    points = algorithm!.GetNextPoints(previousResults).
    ToList();
}
```

CHAPTER 7   IMPLEMENTATION OF OPTIMIZATION ALGORITHMS

In this code, I created an algorithm that returns sets of values of 2. Also, the target function contains variables as in the example we discussed earlier. As a result, this piece of code will return the following result:

Step	First	Second	Third
0	1	10	100
0	1	10	200
1	1	20	100
1	1	20	200
2	2	10	100
2	2	10	200
3	2	20	100
3	2	20	200

Of course, work on the implementation of this algorithm is far from finished, because the library does not have a single test. But I will leave testing this code outside the scope of the book to focus your attention on the main thing.

CHAPTER 7 IMPLEMENTATION OF OPTIMIZATION ALGORITHMS

Genetic Algorithm

It's time to implement the genetic algorithm. We already have the foundation of the library. Let's build a new algorithm into this. I will recall its main aspects. This is one of the population algorithms, the idea of which is based on the creation of several independent agents (population), which, according to some logic, migrate across the range of acceptable values in search of the optimal value of the objective function.

The general scheme of any population algorithm is as follows:

1. According to some logic, an initial population or first set of agents is generated.

2. The agent migration process is in progress. If we take the genetic algorithm into consideration, then for it the migration process is presented as a set of operators. During the migration process, a new population or the next set of agents is generated.

3. The search completion conditions are checked. If this is done, then the calculations stop. Otherwise, go to step 2.

The most interesting and difficult part of creating this algorithm is the migration process. As mentioned earlier, for genetic algorithms, it looks like a set of operators.

These are the types of operators:

- **Mutation.** The idea of this operator is to use some algorithm to change the values of the agent's genes and thereby create a new population. That is, the result of this operator is the creation of a new population.

- **Crossover.** In this operator, two agents (individuals) are crossed using some algorithm, resulting in the creation of one or more agents. This operator also entails the emergence of a new population.

- **Selection.** This operator does not entail the creation of new agents, but it is necessary for selecting pairs for the crossover operator. It turns out that you cannot apply the crossover operator until you use the selection operator.

- **Filtering.** This operator is necessary for selecting the fittest individuals. It does not entail the creation of a new population but filters the old one so that poorly adapted individuals do not participate in other operators in the future.

Steps

In a general sense, a genetic algorithm is not some kind of strict set of rules but rather a set of instructions with which you can construct as many of your own variations of optimization algorithms as you want. It was this knowledge that prompted me to create the concept of the *step*. Each step will have its own type, order, and set of parameters, as well as a list of child steps. I have identified four types of steps for myself.

1. **Initialization.** At this stage, the first population is created.

2. **Mutation.** In this step, a mutation operator is applied to the current population.

3. **Filtering.** At this step, a filtering operator is applied to the current population.

CHAPTER 7   IMPLEMENTATION OF OPTIMIZATION ALGORITHMS

4. **Breeding.** This step contains two steps: Selection Step and Crossing Step. I found it inappropriate to separate these two steps into two different units because you can't cross without first selecting.

The idea is that you can construct your own algorithms using and combining steps 2, 3, and 4 in any number and in any order. For example, thanks to this architecture, you can create an algorithm like this:

1. **Initialization.** An initial population is created using the flat operator. That is, agents are created uniformly over the entire range of acceptable values.

2. **Mutation.** The mutation is performed using the random operator.

3. **Breeding.** Using the panmixia method for selection, we produce the crossovering fuzzy operator.

4. **Filtering.** We filter the current population using the elitism-based method.

5. **Mutation.** This happens using the gauss operator.

6. And so on. This list can go on forever.

In this book I will show the simplest implementation of this algorithm, so I will implement the simplest condition for ending the search: by the number of iterations. It turns out that the algorithm itself will have only one parameter equal to the number of generations.

Getting Info

Let's start the implementation with the `GetTypeInfo` method. Obviously, the genetic algorithm class itself should not know anything about what parameters are needed for each of the steps.

CHAPTER 7   IMPLEMENTATION OF OPTIMIZATION ALGORITHMS

This means that these are the steps:

1. The GetTypeInfo method of the GeneticAlgorithm class will call the GetTypeInfo method of all available step types.

2. You need to create an IAlgorithmStep interface with the GetTypeInfo function. It turns out that each step will be a class that implements this interface.

3. Since each step will have its own parameters, it is necessary to implement a factory that will help create a step of each type.

Since the concept of steps and their sequences appeared, it is necessary to change the AlgorithmInfo and AlgorithmTypeInfo types.

Listing 7-13 presents a new implementation of the `AlgorithmTypeInfo` type. In this case, I added the `AllowedSteps` field, because now each algorithm can contain steps.

Listing 7-13. AlgorithmTypeInfo Record

```
public record AlgorithmTypeInfo(AlgorithmTypes Type)
{
    public List<AlgorithmTypeInfo_AllowedStep> AllowedSteps {
    get; } = new();
    public List<AlgorithmTypeInfo_Param> Params { get; }
    = new();
}
```

Listing 7-14 shows an implementation of the `AlgorithmTypeInfo_AllowedStep` type. Note that the constructor has an `Index` parameter. The point is that we need to somehow indicate that a certain step is mandatory and also indicate its sequence number in advance. This concerns the initialization phase. This is mandatory and should always come first. I didn't create a separate type for the step parameters because I think the AlgorithmTypeInfo_Param type I created earlier is perfect for this task.

Listing 7-14. AlgorithmTypeInfo_AllowedStep Record

```
public record AlgorithmTypeInfo_AllowedStep(StepTypes Type,
int? Index)
{
    public List<AlgorithmTypeInfo_Operator> AllowedOperators {
    get; } = new();
    public List<AlgorithmTypeInfo_AllowedStep> Steps { get; }
    = new();
    public List<AlgorithmTypeInfo_Param> Params { get; } = new();
}
```

The AlgorithmTypeInfo_Operator class, shown in Listing 7-15, includes only a set of parameters and a type.

Listing 7-15. AlgorithmTypeInfo_Operator Record

```
public record AlgorithmTypeInfo_Operator(OperatorTypes Type)
{
    public List<AlgorithmTypeInfo_Param> Params = new();
}
```

Listing 7-16 demonstrates the IAlgorithmStep interface. For now there is only one function in this, but as the functionality expands, this will also grow.

Listing 7-16. IAlgorithmStep Interface

```
public interface IAlgorithmStep
{
    public AlgorithmTypeInfo_AllowedStep GetInfo();
}
```

CHAPTER 7   IMPLEMENTATION OF OPTIMIZATION ALGORITHMS

Since we have a new set of classes, we somehow need to add them to the collection and create a factory for them. I don't want the central part of the library to know anything about the steps and their presence in the algorithm, so I created my own implementation of the extension for IServiceCollection for each algorithm. Listing 7-17 presents a new implementation of the AddOptimizationAlgorithms function. As you can see, now work with IServiceCollection is hidden in each of the algorithms, which is very convenient.

Listing 7-17. Adding Dependencies

```
public static IServiceCollection AddOptimizationAlgorithms(this IServiceCollection services)
{
    services.AddSingleton<AlgorithmFactory>();

    services.AddBruteForceAlgorithm();
    services.AddGeneticAlgorithm();

    return services;
}
```

Listing 7-18 shows an implementation of the AddGeneticAlgorithm method. In it I add the GeneticAlgorithm class, a factory for creating steps and all the step classes.

Listing 7-18. AddGeneticAlgorithm Dependencies

```
public static IServiceCollection AddGeneticAlgorithm(this IServiceCollection services)
{
    services
        .AddKeyedTransient<IOptimizationAlgorithm,
        GeneticAlgorithm>(
```

```
        AlgorithmTypes.Genetic);

services.AddSingleton<StepFactory>();

services
    .AddKeyedTransient<IAlgorithmStep,BreedingStep>(
        StepTypes.Breeding);
services
    .AddKeyedTransient<IAlgorithmStep,FilteringStep>(
        StepTypes.Filtering);
services
    .AddKeyedTransient<IAlgorithmStep,InitializationStep>(
        StepTypes.Initialization);
services
    .AddKeyedTransient<IAlgorithmStep,MutationStep>(
        StepTypes.Mutation);

return services;
}
```

Now that we have the steps already added to the `IServiceCollection`, it's time to implement the `GetTypeInfo` method in the `GeneticAlgorithm`. Listing 7-19 shows my implementation. I added one parameter that controls the number of generations. Please note that this is the number of generations, not populations. I did this on purpose because many steps, such as mutation, will generate a population. I call a generation the complete passage of the algorithm through all steps. The interesting thing about this code is how I implemented obtaining information for all steps. I took all the classes that implement the `IAlgorithmStep` interface and one by one called their methods for obtaining information.

Listing 7-19. GetTypeInfo Method

```
public AlgorithmTypeInfo GetTypeInfo()
{
    var info = new AlgorithmTypeInfo(AlgorithmTypes.Genetic);
    info.Params.Add(
        new AlgorithmTypeInfo_Param(ParamTypes.
        GenerationsCount, 10));

    IEnumerable<IAlgorithmStep> steps =
        _stepFactory.GetAll();
    foreach (IAlgorithmStep step in steps)
        info.AllowedSteps.Add(step.GetInfo());

    return info;
}
```

Let's dive into the implementation of the GetInfo functions of each of the steps. Obviously, to obtain complete information about the step, it is necessary to obtain information for each of the implemented operators. This means that another IOperator interface is needed. Moreover, each step will have its own, because the purpose and functionality of each of them differs.

Let's start with InitializationStep. For this step I implemented two statements: FlatOperator and FlatManagedOperator.

The idea of FlatOperator is to uniformly distribute a predetermined number of initial individuals over the range of acceptable values.

FlatManagedOperator is very similar to FlatOperator, but it does not specify the size of the initial population but rather a percentage of the maximum possible number of individuals.

I won't bore you with showing the implementation of the InitializationStepCollectionExtensions and OperatorFactory classes, because their code is very similar to the code implemented earlier.

CHAPTER 7 IMPLEMENTATION OF OPTIMIZATION ALGORITHMS

Listing 7-20 shows my implementation of the GetInfo method of the InitializationStep class. The only interesting thing about this code is that I immediately define the order for this step. This means this step should always come first and cannot be skipped.

Listing 7-20. Get Step Function

```
public AlgorithmTypeInfo_AllowedStep GetInfo()
{
    AlgorithmTypeInfo_AllowedStep info = new(StepTypes.
    Initialization, 0);

    IEnumerable<IOperator> operators = _operatorFactory.
    GetAll();
    foreach (IOperator @operator in operators)
        info.AllowedOperators.Add(@operator.GetInfo());

    return info;
}
```

Next, in each of the statements, I implemented the GetInfo method approximately, as shown in Listing 7-21.

Listing 7-21. Get Operator Info Function

```
public AlgorithmTypeInfo_Operator GetInfo()
{
    var @operator = new AlgorithmTypeInfo_
    Operator(OperatorTypes.Flat);
    @operator.Params.Add(
        new AlgorithmTypeInfo_Param(ParamTypes.
        PopulationSize, 10));

    return @operator;
}
```

CHAPTER 7   IMPLEMENTATION OF OPTIMIZATION ALGORITHMS

I think we can stop here. I hope the information I gave you will be enough to implement the GetInfo method for the remaining steps and their operators.

Getting a Set of Values

Let's move on to the central function of this algorithm, namely, the GetNextPoints function. First, let's decide on the sequence of actions.

Let's imagine that a user has designed the following genetic algorithm:

- Initialization
- Mutation
- Filtering
- Breeding
- Filtering

The stopping condition will be the creation of GenerationsCount generations.

So, the application calls the GetNextPoints method of our algorithm in a loop, gets a new list of sets of values to calculate, calculates the objective function values for each of them, and calls the GetNextPoints method again. This continues until GetNextPoints returns an empty list of value sets.

Obviously, to count the number of generations, the optimization algorithm needs to know what generation and step it is at the next time GetNextPoints is called. It would be logical to store this counter in the very instance of the class that implements the optimization algorithm. But you can't do this, because in reality several instances of the application will be raised, one for each pod. And if so, then there will be several instances of classes.

We cannot guarantee that GetNextPoints will be called by only one specific instance of the class. Also, do not forget that the pod can cease to exist at any time and then the application will lose information about the current generation and step, which is unacceptable. There are two options left: store information about the current generation somewhere in external storage, such as Redis or PostgreSQL, or entrust this task to the calling application.

I really don't like both options; in the first one our library forces the application to use a certain kind of storage, and in the second one we expose some implementation details of the library.

I chose the second option. That is, I entrusted the storage of information to the calling application. But at the same time, I tried to make this information as impersonal as possible in order not to disclose implementation details and to allow other algorithms to use this field.

Listing 7-22 demonstrates how I changed the GetNextPoints function of the IOptimizationAlgorithm interface.

Listing 7-22. GetNextPoints Function

```
(List<AlgorithmPoint> points, string? magicString)?
    GetNextPoints(
        List<ObjectiveFunctionResult>? previousResults = null,
        string? magicString = null);
```

As you can see, I added the magicString parameter. Great name, isn't it? This is returned every time the GetNextPoints method is called. The calling application must save it and then pass it back as a parameter the next time the function is called.

Listing 7-23 demonstrates my implementation of the MagicData class for a genetic algorithm. It shows that magicString is a JSON string into which the class instance is parsed.

Listing 7-23. MagicData Class

```
public class MagicData
{
    public int GenerationNumber { get; set; }
    public int StepIndex { get; set; }

    public MagicData(string? jsonString = null)
    {
        if (jsonString != null)
        {
            MagicData? obj = JsonSerializer
                .Deserialize<MagicData>(jsonString);
            if (obj == null)
                throw new ArgumentException(nameof(jsonString));

            GenerationNumber = obj.GenerationNumber;
            StepIndex = obj.StepIndex;
        }
    }

    public MagicData(){}

    public override string ToString()
    {
        return JsonSerializer.Serialize(this);
    }
}
```

Let's go through all the steps:

1. The first call to GetNextPoints occurs. previousResults = null, magicString = null. We deserialize magicString and get GenerationNumber=0, StepIndex=0.

CHAPTER 7   IMPLEMENTATION OF OPTIMIZATION ALGORITHMS

2. We get an instance of the Initialization class of the step, because StepIndex = 0.

3. We turn to the method for obtaining a list of sets of values of this step and obtain the following points or the current population.

4. We get the identifier of the next step, write GenerationNumber=0, StepIndex=1 in magicData and return all the information to the calling method.

5. GetNextPoints is called. We were returned a certain set of previousResults and GenerationNumber=0, StepIndex=1.

6. We get an instance of the step Mutation class, because StepIndex = 1. To get the next population, you need to pass the current population to the mutation step method so that it can mutate all agents using the selected operator.

When this is the first generation, it is easy to get the current population, but imagine that this is not the first generation. How do you select only the necessary instances from previousResults?

It is for this purpose that I added the Id field to the ObjectiveFunctionResult class. And in the `MagicData` class is the PopulationIds field, which contains a list of solution identifiers. An application that will use a library of optimization algorithms will be able to provide this identifier, because in essence `ObjectiveFunctionResult` is a mapping of the Task entity, which of course has an identifier.

Let's continue:

1. The Mutation step returned a list of new sets of values to calculate, which we passed to the calling function.

297

But what's important is that this set of values is not a new generation. The new generation consists of the population obtained in the previous step plus the list of sets obtained in the Mutation step. It is also necessary to take into account that the mutation step can create a new generation by joining mutated individuals to the previous generation, or it can do this by replacing parents. It turns out that each step must implement two functions: one to get a list of parameter sets and the second to get a new population. The first entails transferring control to the calling function so that it can calculate the objective function for new agents, and the second generates a new population.

There is another fact that speaks in favor of creating two functions. This is the presence of such a step as Filtering. At this step, new agents are not formed, but a part of the current population is eliminated, and this is how this step forms a new population.

Let's say the Mutation step now has two functions. One of them generates a new list of parameter sets, and the second generates a new population. It seems reasonable to first call the function to get new individuals and then get a new population. But this order is not convenient, because after receiving a list of new individuals, it is necessary to transfer control to the calling function, which means there can be no talk of a subsequent call to the function for obtaining a new population.

Before we continue, I would like to draw your attention to one more point. I mentioned that the Mutation step can have the option of replacing parents with children, which means that each set of values must have its own MagicData. Therefore, I added a field of type string `MagicData` to the `AlgorithmPoint` class. And I created the `PointMagicData` class for this.

Since the logic of the algorithm has changed, it's probably worth starting to describe the steps again.

1. The first call to GetNextPoints occurs. previousResults = null, magicString = null. We deserialize magicString and get GenerationNumber=0, StepIndex=0. Based

CHAPTER 7 IMPLEMENTATION OF OPTIMIZATION ALGORITHMS

on this data, we obtain the current population currentPopulation and the results of calculations obtained from the previous list of new individuals currentPreviousResults. Of course, both of these lists are empty because we called the function for the first time.

2. We start the loop with the condition that the list of new individuals that need to be returned to the calling function—nextPoints—is empty. On each pass of this loop, the algorithm will call the functions of the next step. Not all steps generate new individuals.

3. In this loop, we get an instance of the current, zero step and call this GetNextPopulation method. This method does not spawn new individuals, so for the Initialization step, it will always return the list passed to it.

4. Next we get the next step. In this logic, we will have to make an exception for the Initialization step, because we cannot get the next step but need to stop at the current one.

5. We call the GetNextPoints method of the current Initialization step, which, of course, will return new individuals that the function will pass to the calling function.

6. And so on.

Listing 7-24 shows my implementation of the first step of the GetNextPoints method. This code fragment initializes three important variables: currentMagicData, currentPopulation, and currentPreviousResults, which will be needed in the loop from step 2.

Listing 7-24. Start of GetNextPoints Function

```
public (List<AlgorithmPoint> points, string magicString)?
GetNextPoints(
    List<ObjectiveFunctionResult>? previousResults = null,
    string? magicString = null)
{
    previousResults ??= new();
    MagicData currentMagicData = new MagicData(magicString);
    List<ObjectiveFunctionResult> currentPopulation =
        GetCurrentPopulation(currentMagicData,
        previousResults);
    List<ObjectiveFunctionResult> currentPreviousResults =
        GetCurrentPreviousResults(currentMagicData,
        previousResults);
...
```

Listing 7-25 shows a code snippet that implements the loop from step 2.

Listing 7-25. Second Part of GetNextPoints Function

```
List<AlgorithmPoint>? nextPoints = null;
var nextMagicData = new MagicData();
while (nextPoints == null || !nextPoints.Any())
{
    AlgorithmInfo_Step currentStepInfo = _info.Steps
        .First(s => s.Index == currentMagicData.StepIndex);
    IAlgorithmStep currentStep = _stepFactory
        .GetStep(currentStepInfo, _functionVariables);
    currentPopulation = currentStep
        .GetNextPopulation(currentPopulation,
        currentPreviousResults);
```

```
nextMagicData.PopulationIds = currentPopulation
    .ConvertAll(i => i.Id);
AlgorithmInfo_Step? nextStepInfo =
GetNextStep(currentMagicData, currentPopulation);
bool stoppingConditionFulfilled =
    CheckStoppingCondition(nextStepInfo, currentMagicData,
    currentStepInfo);
if (stoppingConditionFulfilled)
    return null;
nextMagicData.GenerationNumber = currentMagicData.
GenerationNumber;
nextMagicData.StepIndex = nextStepInfo.Index;
if (nextStepInfo!.Index <= currentStepInfo.Index
&& currentPopulation.Any())
    nextMagicData.GenerationNumber++;

IAlgorithmStep nextStep = _stepFactory.
GetStep(nextStepInfo, _functionVariables);
nextPoints = nextStep
    .GetNextPoints(
        currentPopulation,
        new PointMagicData(
            nextMagicData.GenerationNumber,
            nextMagicData.StepIndex));
currentMagicData = nextMagicData;
}
```

In this piece of code, I do the following:

1. I get information about the current step, currentStepInfo. It is necessary to obtain an instance of the class that implements the step.

CHAPTER 7   IMPLEMENTATION OF OPTIMIZATION ALGORITHMS

2. Using the factory, I get an instance of the currentStep step class.

3. I call the GetNextPopulation method of the current step and save the result to the currentPopulation variable.

4. Since we now know the identifiers of individuals in the current population, we need to write them into our magicData.

5. I receive information about the next step. In Listing 7-26, I provided my implementation of the GetNextStep method.

6. Based on the new step index, we can conclude whether this is the next generation or not. This means we can check the condition for completing the calculations. If the condition has not yet occurred, then we continue the calculations.

7. If the index of the new step is less than the index of the current one, this means that the algorithm has gone through all the steps and will now begin to generate a new generation. This means you can increase the generation number in the nextMagicData variable.

8. The GetNextPoints method of the new step is called. If it returns new individuals, then control is transferred to the calling function.

Listing 7-26. Implementation of a Method to Get the Next Step

```
private AlgorithmInfo_Step GetNextStep(
    MagicData currentMagicData,
    List<ObjectiveFunctionResult> previousResults)
{
    if (!previousResults.Any())
        return _info.Steps.Single(s => s.Index == 0);

    AlgorithmInfo_Step? nextStep =
        _info.Steps
            .Where(s => s.Index > currentMagicData.StepIndex)
            .MinBy(s => s.Index);
    if (nextStep == null)
        nextStep = _info.Steps
            .Where(s => s.Index > 0)
            .MinBy(s => s.Index);

    return nextStep!;
}
```

Initialization Step

Let's implement our first step, namely, the Initialization Step. Let me remind you that I plan to implement two operators in this, FlatOperator and FlatManagedOperator.

Listing 7-27 demonstrates the implementation of the Init function. There is nothing special about this, except that an instance of the operator class is immediately obtained.

Listing 7-27. Init Function

```
public void Init(
    AlgorithmInfo_Step step,
    List<FunctionVariable> functionVariables)
```

```
{
    _step = step;
    _functionVariables = functionVariables;
    _operator = _operatorFactory.GetOperator(_step.Operator);
}
```

The GetNextPopulation function, as I said earlier, returns the previousResults sent. Listing 7-28 shows a simple implementation of the GetNextPoints method. This is where the Generate operator function is called.

Listing 7-28. GetNextPoints Function

```
public List<AlgorithmPoint> GetNextPoints(
    List<ObjectiveFunctionResult>? population = null,
    PointMagicData? magicData = null)
{
    return _operator.Generate(_functionVariables, magicData);
}
```

Let's start implementing the operators. Let me remind you what their logic is.

The idea of FlatOperator is to uniformly distribute a predetermined number of initial individuals over the range of acceptable values.

FlatManagedOperator is very similar to FlatOperator, but it does not specify the size of the initial population but rather a percentage of the maximum possible number of individuals. It turns out that in both operators the same function is called to generate individuals; the difference is only in the desired number of new individuals.

Listing 7-29 shows the implementation of the Generate method for FlatOperator. As you can see, there is practically no logic in this.

CHAPTER 7 IMPLEMENTATION OF OPTIMIZATION ALGORITHMS

Listing 7-29. Generate Points Function

```
public List<AlgorithmPoint> Generate(
    List<FunctionVariable> functionVariables,
    PointMagicData? magicData)
{
    return PointsFactory.Flat(functionVariables, magicData,
    _populationSize);
}
```

It gets more interesting when we turn to the implementation of the same method, but for the FlatManagedOperator in Listing 7-30. In fact, I call the same PointsFactory.Flat function, but with a pre-calculated number of required individuals.

Listing 7-30. Generate Points for FlatManagedOperator

```
public List<AlgorithmPoint> Generate(
    List<FunctionVariable> functionVariables,
    PointMagicData? magicData)
{
    int populationSize = GetPopulationSize(functionVariables);
    return PointsFactory.Flat(functionVariables, magicData,
    populationSize);
}

private int GetPopulationSize(List<FunctionVariable>
functionVariables)
{
    long variablesCount = 1;
    foreach (var variable in functionVariables)
    {
        List<decimal> values = variable.GetValues();
        variablesCount *= values.Count;
    }
```

```
    long populationSizeLong = (long)(_coveredPercent / 100 *
    variablesCount);

    int populationSize = (int)Math.Min(populationSizeLong, _
    maxPopulationSize);
    populationSize = Math.Max(populationSize, _
    minPopulationSize);

    return populationSize;
}
```

I showed you the basic idea of implementing this step. I also laid down a fairly simple architecture for the solution, in which to add a new operator. It is enough to add only one class that implements the IOperator interface.

Mutation Step

I will show the implementation of this step using the random operator as an example. The essence of this method is to replace a certain number of parent genes with random values located in the range of acceptable values.

Listing 7-31 shows an implementation of the method for obtaining a population. It contains a simple logic of combining the previous population with all the mutated individuals. This means that at this step the number of individuals always doubles.

Listing 7-31. GetNextPopulation for Mutation Step

```
public List<ObjectiveFunctionResult>
    GetNextPopulation(List<ObjectiveFunctionResult>
    previousPopulation,
        List<ObjectiveFunctionResult> previousResults)
{
```

CHAPTER 7 IMPLEMENTATION OF OPTIMIZATION ALGORITHMS

```
    List<ObjectiveFunctionResult> nextPopulation = new();
    nextPopulation.AddRange(previousPopulation);
    nextPopulation.AddRange(previousResults);
    return nextPopulation;
}
```

The GetNextPoints method presented in Listing 7-32 is also quite simple. In this cycle, all parents undergo a mutation procedure.

Listing 7-32. GetNextPoints Function

```
public List<AlgorithmPoint> GetNextPoints(
    List<ObjectiveFunctionResult>? population = null,
    PointMagicData? magicData = null)
{
    var points = new List<AlgorithmPoint>();
    if (population == null)
        return points;

    foreach (ObjectiveFunctionResult parent in population)
    {
        AlgorithmPoint mutant = Mutate(parent);
        if (magicData != null)
            mutant.MagicData = magicData.ToString();
        points.Add(mutant);
    }

    return points;
}
```

Listing 7-33 shows an implementation of this procedure.

CHAPTER 7 IMPLEMENTATION OF OPTIMIZATION ALGORITHMS

It implements the following algorithm:

1. We take all the variables that can contain more than one value and put them in the changeableVariables variable.

2. After this, we randomly select the required number of genes for the mutation procedure.

3. Call the Mutation function of the selected operator and replace the parent gene with the resulting value.

Listing 7-33. Mutate Function

```
private AlgorithmPoint Mutate(ObjectiveFunctionResult parent)
{
    var mutant = new AlgorithmPoint();

    List<IVariableId> changeableVariables = new();
    foreach (FunctionVariable functionVariable in _
    functionVariables)
    {
        List<decimal> variations = functionVariable.
        GetValues();
        if (variations.Count>1)
            changeableVariables.Add(functionVariable.Id);
    }

    var random = new Random();
    List<IVariableId> variablesForMutation =
        random.GetList(changeableVariables, _mutationCount);
    foreach (var parentVariableValue in parent.Point.Values)
    {
        if (variablesForMutation.
        Contains(parentVariableValue.Id))
```

```
    {
        FunctionVariable functionVariable =
            _functionVariables.First(v => v.Id.
            Equals(parentVariableValue.Id));
        decimal parentValue = parentVariableValue.Value;
        decimal mutationValue = _operator.
        Mutation(functionVariable, parentValue);
        mutant.Values.Add(new FunctionVariableValue(parentV
        ariableValue.Id, mutationValue));
    }
    else
        mutant.Values.Add(parentVariableValue);
}

return mutant;
}
```

Filtering Step

Let's start implementing the filtering step. As a result of this step, new individuals are not created, but a new population is created by selecting more fit individuals. It follows that the `GetNextPoints` function of the class that implements this step will return null.

The `GetNextPopulation` function is very simple. Its implementation is presented in Listing 7-34. This calls the selected operator and returns the population that it generated.

Listing 7-34. GetNextPopulation for Filtering Step

```
public List<ObjectiveFunctionResult> GetNextPopulation(
    List<ObjectiveFunctionResult> previousPopulation,
    List<ObjectiveFunctionResult> previousResults)
```

```
{
    return _operator.GetNextPopulation(previousPopulation);
}
```

I have implemented two operators for this step.

Roulette Operator

We discussed this method in detail in the previous chapter. I will just remind you of the basic principle. The essence of the method is to present individuals in the form of a roulette wheel, which is divided into sectors. Each sector is assigned to a specific individual. The size of the sector depends on the fitness level of the individual.

The selection algorithm looks like this:

1. For each individual, the probability of its selection is calculated. To do this, take the value of its objective function and divide it by the sum of the values of all individuals in the population.

2. We divide the interval from 0 to 1 into subintervals proportional to the values from step 1.

3. We generate a random number from 0 to 1. Depending on which interval it falls in, that individual will be selected.

4. Repeat step 3 as many times as required.

It follows from the algorithm that this operator has only one free parameter: the required population size.

Listing 7-35 shows an implementation of the RouletteOperator's GetNextPopulation method. It does not yet have the basic logic of the roulette method. I moved this to another class because the roulette method will be used in other operators. Please note that a list of individuals with the weight of each of them is passed to the Roulette.Selection method.

CHAPTER 7 IMPLEMENTATION OF OPTIMIZATION ALGORITHMS

Listing 7-35. GetNextPopulation Function

```
public List<ObjectiveFunctionResult> GetNextPopulation(
    List<ObjectiveFunctionResult> previousPopulation)
{
    List<(ObjectiveFunctionResult Entity, double
    ProbabilityWeight)> listForRoulette =
        previousPopulation.ConvertAll(i => (i, (double)
        i.Value));
    List<ObjectiveFunctionResult> nextIndividuals =
        Roulette.Selection(listForRoulette, _populationSize);

    return nextIndividuals;
}
```

Listing 7-36 shows an implementation of the Roulette.Selection method. This involves initializing the list of roulette sectors by calling the GetProbabilityElements function. Next, the NextDouble function of the Random class is called, which returns a random number from 0 to 1. After this, the sector in which this number falls is selected and places the selected individual in the resulting list. Please note that this method does not check whether the individual has already entered the new population. As mentioned earlier, it is normal when, as a result of the roulette method, some individuals enter a new population several times.

Listing 7-36. Selection Function

```
public static List<T> Selection<T>(
    List<(T Entity, double ProbabilityWeight)> list,
    int size,
    Random? rand = null)
{
    var result = new List<T>();
```

CHAPTER 7 IMPLEMENTATION OF OPTIMIZATION ALGORITHMS

```
    List<ProbabilityElement<T>> probabilityElements =
        GetProbabilityElements(list);
    var random = rand ?? new Random();
    for (int i = 0; i < size; i++)
    {
        double u = random.NextDouble();
        ProbabilityElement<T> nextPoint =
            probabilityElements
                .First(e => u > e.MinInterval && u <=
                e.MaxInterval);
        result.Add(nextPoint.ListElement.Entity);
    }
    return result;
}
```

Elitism Operator

This method was developed to ensure that the best individuals are guaranteed to be included in the new population. It consists of two steps. At the first stage, the best individuals are selected. They are placed on the list of individuals of the new population. The second completely copies the roulette method. That is, the missing number of individuals is added to the new population using the roulette method.

Based on this logic, this operator has two parameters: the percentage of individuals out of the total number that are considered elite and the required size of the new population.

Listing 7-37 shows an implementation of the GetNextPopulation method.

Listing 7-37. GetNextPopulation Function

```
public List<ObjectiveFunctionResult> GetNextPopulation(
    List<ObjectiveFunctionResult> previousPopulation)
{
    var individuals = new List<ObjectiveFunctionResult>();
    int eliteCount = (int)(_elitePercent / 100 *
    previousPopulation.Count);
    individuals.AddRange(
        previousPopulation
            .OrderByDescending(i => i.Value).ToList()
            .GetRange(0, elitCount-1));
    int remainder = _populationSize - individuals.Count;

    List<(ObjectiveFunctionResult Entity, double
    ProbabilityWeight)> listForRoulette =
        previousPopulation.ConvertAll(i => (i, (double)
        i.Value));
    List<ObjectiveFunctionResult> rouletteIndividuals =
    Roulette.Selection(listForRoulette, remainder);
    individuals.AddRange(rouletteIndividuals);

    return rouletteIndividuals;
}
```

In Listing 7-37 I first calculate the size of the elite and put that value into the eliteCount variable. After that, I sort the previous population in descending order of the value of the objective function and take the top elements in the resulting eliteCount list. After this, I call the roulette method Roulette.Selection that we previously implemented.

CHAPTER 7 IMPLEMENTATION OF OPTIMIZATION ALGORITHMS

Breeding Step

The purpose of the breeding step is to create new individuals by crossing individuals of the parents. The algorithm for this step is quite simple. First, we select pairs for crossing using some algorithm. Second, we cross them using one of the previously described operators.

Listing 7-38 shows an implementation of the GetNextPoints method. In this function, I first check that the current population consists of at least two individuals; otherwise, further steps are meaningless. Then, I call the GetParentsList function configured by the selection step and save the resulting pairs of parents into the parentsList variable. After this, I perform the crossing by calling the Crossing function for each group of parents.

Listing 7-38. GetNextPoints Function for Breeding Step

```
public List<AlgorithmPoint> GetNextPoints(
    List<ObjectiveFunctionResult>? population = null,
    PointMagicData? magicData = null)
{
    var nextGeneration = new List<AlgorithmPoint>();
    if (population != null && population.Count < 2)
        return nextGeneration;

    List<List<ObjectiveFunctionResult>> parentsList =
        _selectionStep.GetParentsList(population, _
        groupsCount);
    foreach (List<ObjectiveFunctionResult> parents in
    parentsList)
    {
        List<AlgorithmPoint> children = _crossingStep
            .Crossing(parents, _functionVariables);
```

```
        if (magicData != null)
        {
            string magicDataString = magicData.ToString();
            children.ForEach(c => c.MagicData =
            magicDataString);
        }
        nextGeneration.AddRange(children);
    }

    return nextGeneration;
}
```

The GetNextPopulation function, shown in Listing 7-39, creates a new population based on a previous, or parent, population and a set of descendant individuals. In this step I added the ReplaceWorst parameter. If this flag has a positive value, then the descendant individuals will completely replace the worst parent individuals. Otherwise, the new population will consist of both offspring and parent individuals. If we look in the long term, then thanks to this logic, offspring individuals will compete not only with individuals of their generation but also with all parent individuals. Of course, this is impossible to find in the real world, because there are no immortal living beings.

Listing 7-39. GetNextPopulation Function

```
public List<ObjectiveFunctionResult> GetNextPopulation(
    List<ObjectiveFunctionResult> previousPopulation,
    List<ObjectiveFunctionResult> previousResults)
{
    if (previousPopulation.Count == 1)
        return previousPopulation;

    var individuals = new List<ObjectiveFunctionResult>();
```

```
if (_replaceWorst)
{
    int needParentsCount =
        previousPopulation.Count>previousResults.Count
            ? previousPopulation.Count -
            previousResults.Count
            : 0;
    var needParents = previousPopulation
        .OrderByDescending(p => p.Value).
        Take(needParentsCount);
    individuals.AddRange(needParents);
    individuals.AddRange(previousResults);
}
else
{
    individuals.AddRange(previousPopulation);
    individuals.AddRange(previousResults);
}
individuals = individuals.GroupBy(i => i.Id)
    .Select(g => g.First()).ToList();

return individuals;
}
```

Selection Step

The purpose of this step is to create a set of parent groups for crossing. The GetParentsList function of the class that implements this step has no logic. It calls the function of the same name of the selected operator.

Selection Operator

The idea of this operator is that only those individuals whose fitness is higher than or equal to the average fitness of the current population are included in the list of parents. Next, pairs are selected using the roulette method, where all elite individuals have an equal probability of being selected into a pair.

Listing 7-40 shows an implementation of this operator.

Listing 7-40. GetParentsList Function

```
public List<List<ObjectiveFunctionResult>> GetParentsList(List<
ObjectiveFunctionResult> individuals, int groupsCount)
{
    var parentsList = new List<List<ObjectiveFunction
    Result>>();

    var elite = new List<ObjectiveFunctionResult>();
    int eliteCount = _elitPercent / 100 * individuals.Count;
    elite.AddRange(individuals.OrderByDescending(i => i.Value).
    ToList()
        .GetRange(0, eliteCount-1));

    List<(ObjectiveFunctionResult Entity, double
    ProbabilityWeight)> listForRoulette =
        elite.ConvertAll(i => (i, (double)i.Value));
    for (int i = 0; i < groupsCount; i++)
    {
        List<ObjectiveFunctionResult> parentsGroup =
            Roulette.SelectionDistinct(listForRoulette, 2);
        parentsList.Add(parentsGroup);
    }

    return parentsList;
}
```

CHAPTER 7   IMPLEMENTATION OF OPTIMIZATION ALGORITHMS

Panmixia Operator

This is perhaps the simplest selection operator. The idea of this operator is to randomly select parental individuals with equal probability. Listing 7-41 shows its implementation.

Listing 7-41. GetParentsList Function

```
public List<List<ObjectiveFunctionResult>> GetParentsList(List<
ObjectiveFunctionResult> individuals, int groupsCount)
{
    var parentsList = new List<List<ObjectiveFunction
    Result>>();

    for (int i = 0; i < groupsCount; i++)
    {
        List<ObjectiveFunctionResult> parentsGroup = Roulette.
        SelectionDistinct(individuals, 2);
        parentsList.Add(parentsGroup);
    }

    return parentsList;
}
```

Crossing Step

The purpose of this step is to create offspring individuals based on the groups of parent individuals formed in the previous step. As in the case of the selection step, the Crossing function of the class that implements this step does not have logic. It calls the function of the same name of the selected operator.

Let's look at the flat operator implementation of this step. The idea is that the gene of a descendant is a random number located between the minimum and maximum values of the parents' genes.

Listing 7-42 shows an implementation of the Crossing function. Please note that to determine the interval within which the gene value of the descendant will be located, I select the best and worst individual from the group of parent individuals. This operation is actually meaningless for this operator, but it makes a lot of sense for other operators I have implemented, such as the heuristic operator, where the value of the child gene should be located closer to the best value of the parent gene.

Listing 7-42. Crossing Function

```
public List<AlgorithmPoint> Crossing(List<ObjectiveFunction
Result> parents, List<FunctionVariable> functionVariables)
{
    var nextGeneration = new List<AlgorithmPoint>();

    ObjectiveFunctionResult parent1 = parents[0];
    ObjectiveFunctionResult parent2 = parents[1];
    var point = new AlgorithmPoint();
    nextGeneration.Add(point);
    foreach (FunctionVariableValue value1 in parent1.
    Point.Values)
    {
        FunctionVariableValue value2 = parent2.Point.Values.
        First(v => v.Id.Equals(value1.Id));
        FunctionVariable functionVariable = functionVariables.
        First(v => v.Id.Equals(value1.Id));
        decimal best = parent1.Value > parent2.Value ? value1.
        Value : value2.Value;
        decimal worst = parent1.Value < parent2.Value ? value1.
        Value : value2.Value;
        decimal crossValue = Crossing(best, worst,
        functionVariable);
```

CHAPTER 7 IMPLEMENTATION OF OPTIMIZATION ALGORITHMS

```
            point.Values.Add(new FunctionVariableValue(value1.Id,
            crossValue));
        }

        return nextGeneration;
}
```

Listing 7-43 demonstrates the implementation of the Crossing function, but for a gene. And again in this code the already implemented Roulette class comes to our aid.

Listing 7-43. Crossing Variable

```
private decimal Crossing(decimal best, decimal worst,
FunctionVariable functionVariable)
{
    decimal crossValue = best;

    if (best != worst)
    {
        decimal minValue = Math.Min(best, worst);
        decimal maxValue = Math.Max(best, worst);

        List<decimal> accessValues =
            functionVariable.GetValues()
                .Where(v => v >= minValue && v <= maxValue).
                ToList();
        crossValue = Roulette.Selection(accessValues);
    }

    return crossValue;
}
```

CHAPTER 7　IMPLEMENTATION OF OPTIMIZATION ALGORITHMS

Test Functions

One of the requirements for the module was the requirement for the implementation of mathematical functions, thanks to which you can check the performance of the created algorithm. One of the requirements for such a function is the need for a large number of local extrema. One of the most common functions that satisfies this condition is the Rastrigin function. This is exactly what I was one of the first to implement.

The formula for this is as follows:

$$f(X) = \sum_{i=1}^{|X|}(x_i^2 - 10\cos(2\pi x_i) + 10)$$

Obviously, the minimum and, accordingly, optimal solution to this function will be 0, with the value of all variables equal to 0.

I want to draw your attention to the fact that although the optimization problem often sounds like minimizing the value of the objective function, our task in finding the most profitable strategy is a maximization problem. This shouldn't bother you. If you multiply the value of the objective function by -1, then the maximization problem becomes a minimization problem.

Listing 7-44 shows an implementation of the Rastrigin function.

Listing 7-44. Test Calculate Function

```
public static decimal Calculate(
    List<FunctionVariable> functionVariables,
    AlgorithmPoint point)
{
    double result = 0;
    foreach (FunctionVariable variable in functionVariables)
    {
        double x = (double)point.Values.First(v => v.Id ==
        variable.Id).Value;
```

CHAPTER 7 IMPLEMENTATION OF OPTIMIZATION ALGORITHMS

```
        result += x * x - 10 * Math.Cos(2 * Math.PI * x) + 10;
    }
    return (decimal)result;
}
```

SubTheory Example

The optimization algorithms module has been implemented. Let's look at the use case for this in more detail. Let's imagine that we have a SubTheory with the following parameters:

Signal to open a position:

    Group AND:

        Volume < Const

        Bbw < Const

        Lp < BbwL

Signal to close a position:

    Group AND:

        Hp > BbwU

Risk control will be presented in the form of a stop-loss order.

Volume is the trading volume of the candle. The candle itself can be obtained thanks to three parameters.

- **CandleIntervalId:** Candle interval identifier (1min, 2min, and so on)

- **CandleFrom:** Parameter that determines how many candles back you need to move away from the current one

CHAPTER 7　IMPLEMENTATION OF OPTIMIZATION ALGORITHMS

- **CandleTo:** Parameter that determines how many candles back you need to move away from CandleFrom

Thanks to these parameters, you can get a set of candles for which the Volume indicator is calculated. The search for candles for all other indicators that require this occurs in a similar way. If the condition involves two indicators that require information about the candle, then for condition = true, the condition must be met for all candles in the left and right parts.

Const is a constant or a specific number that does not depend on trading data. For this there is only one parameter, which is volume, that is, the value of the constant itself.

Bbw (bollinger bands width) is the indicator with two parameters: lookbackPeriods and standardDeviations. This indicator also contains three parameters to determine the candle on which this will be calculated.

Lp is the low price of the selected candle. It has no specific parameters other than the three (CandleIntervalId, CandleFrom, and CandleTo) described earlier.

BbwL (bollinger bands lower band) is an indicator with two parameters: lookbackPeriods and standardDeviations. This indicator also contains three parameters to determine the candle on which this will be calculated.

HP is high price. It has no specific parameters other than the parameters necessary to define a candle.

BbwU (bollinger bands upper band) is an indicator with two parameters: lookbackPeriods and standardDeviations. This indicator also contains three parameters to determine the candle on which this will be calculated.

Stop-loss order has only one parameter: protected coefficient. Using this, you can calculate the limit price. If the current price of a financial asset is above this level, the position is closed.

CHAPTER 7 IMPLEMENTATION OF OPTIMIZATION ALGORITHMS

I would like to draw your attention to the way I decided to set the parameters for the CandleFrom and CandleTo variables. If you use standard from, to, and step, then there is a high probability of intersection of values, as well as invalid data, such as when CandleFrom = 5 and CandleTo = 1. To avoid this, I decided to vary the CandleFrom and CandleInterval parameters. Then CandleTo is easy to define: CandleTo = CandleFrom + CandleInterval.

If we take all the signal parameters, we get a list of variables for the optimization algorithm, as shown in Table 7-2. As you can see, the transition from SubTheory parameters to optimization algorithm variables is quite easy to implement.

Table 7-2. *Open Position Signal Params*

Object	Name	Param	From	To	Step
Open signal					
	Volume	CandleIntervalId	1min, 5min, 10min, 1h, 4h		
		CandleFrom	0	2	1
		CandleInterval	0	5	1
	Const	Volume	10	2000	10
	Bbw	LookbackPeriods	7	500	1
		StandardDeviations	2	5	1
		CandleIntervalId	1min, 5min, 10min, 1h, 4h		
		CandleFrom	0	2	1
		CandleInterval	0	5	1
	Const	Volume	10	2000	10
	Lp	CandleIntervalId	1min, 5min, 10min, 1h, 4h		
		CandleFrom	0	2	1

(continued)

Table 7-2. (*continued*)

Object	Name	Param	From	To	Step
		CandleInterval	0	5	1
	BbwL	LookbackPeriods	7	500	1
		StandardDeviations	2	5	1
		CandleIntervalId	1min, 5min, 10min, 1h, 4h		
		CandleFrom	0	2	1
		CandleInterval	0	5	1
Close signal					
	Hp	CandleIntervalId	1min, 5min, 10min, 1h, 4h		
		CandleFrom	0	2	1
		CandleInterval	0	5	1
	BbwU	LookbackPeriods	7	500	1
		StandardDeviations	2	5	1
		CandleIntervalId	1min, 5min, 10min, 1h, 4h		
		CandleFrom	0	2	1
		CandleInterval	0	5	1
Stop-loss	Protected Coefficient	Coeff	0.1%	10%	0.1%

Summary

In this chapter, I showed one of the options for implementing the optimization algorithms module. Two algorithms were implemented: brute-force and genetic. But the module is implemented in such a way that adding a new algorithm will not pose a big problem.

CHAPTER 7   IMPLEMENTATION OF OPTIMIZATION ALGORITHMS

In the generic algorithm, several operators were implemented for each of the steps. This will allow you to design a large number of your own variations of the optimization algorithms. I also showed how to implement one of the mathematical functions that can be used to check and test your optimization algorithms.

Now the module of optimization algorithms is ready.

CHAPTER 8

Implementation of the Core Module

In this chapter, I will show my implementation of the main component, namely, the kernel of the entire system. This will be used both in the subsystem for searching for a profitable strategy and in the subsystem for real trading. The main purpose of this module is to give signals to the broker to place or close orders on the exchange, based on trading information (see Figure 8-1).

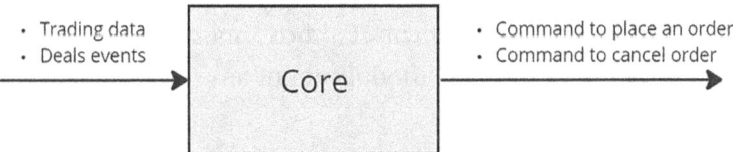

Figure 8-1. *Core module input and output data*

Use Cases

Before we begin, I would like to remind you of the operating logic of the parts of the subsystem for searching for a profitable strategy and the real trading subsystem, which directly interact with the Core module.

CHAPTER 8   IMPLEMENTATION OF THE CORE MODULE

The logic of searching for a profitable strategy is based on the generation of theories, which in turn generate subtheories. Subtheories, using optimization algorithms, generate strategies. To calculate a strategy on a certain interval of historical data, a task is created, which contains the strategy identifier and the TestCandleInterval identifier. For a task to be calculated, it must be placed in the queue for calculation. A queue is a separate table in the database. Queue processing will be handled by a special application, for which several pods will be created in Kubernetes.

The scenario for using the Core module in the subsystem for searching for a profitable strategy is as follows:

1. One of the task queue handler pods picks up the next task.

2. This loads information about historical data in the form of an array of candles and starts a loop to process them.

3. At each iteration, this notifies Sandbox Exchange when new candles appear. Sandbox Exchange, in turn, notifies the Core module about any changes in the order statuses.

4. After notifying Sandbox Exchange, the application notifies the Core module about the appearance of a new candle.

5. The Core module performs calculations and gives a command to place or close an order on the exchange.

We have decided on the logic of using the Core module in the strategy search subsystem; let me remind you how this module will be used in the real trading subsystem:

CHAPTER 8   IMPLEMENTATION OF THE CORE MODULE

1. The Tasks App of the Strategy Manager Service, based on information about the types of instruments and the list of profitable strategies, "decides" that it is necessary to activate the strategy-instrument pair.

2. The Tasks App of the Strategy Manager Service calls the API App method of the Strategy Service indicating that this pair needs to be activated.

3. The Strategy Service API App makes a note in its database that the strategy-instrument pair is now active.

4. One of the free Worker App pods of the Strategy Service starts working with a new pair.

5. This subscribes to events about the appearance of new candles of the selected instrument.

6. When an event occurs about the appearance of a new candle, the Worker App notifies the Core module.

7. The Core module performs calculations and gives a command to place or close an order on the exchange.

8. The Worker App sends an Exchange Gateway API command to place or close an order.

9. When information about a change in order status comes from the exchange, the Worker App again notifies the Core module about this.

Both of these scenarios are designed for the Core module to work with only one strategy-instrument pair at a time. I specifically focused on this in the chapter where we discussed the architectural solution. There were two reasons for this.

First, the instrument can be very volatile, and therefore, with a large number of strategies running on one pod, a situation may arise in which the pod will not have time to process all messages about candle changes. Second, this approach allows you to further isolate running strategies from each other, because they will cache frequently used information.

As a result, I identified the following list of external commands and events to which the Core module will respond:

- **InitContextCommand.** This command is used to initialize frequently used information.

- **UpdateCandleEvent.** This message is generated when candles are updated.

- **CancelExchangeOrderEvent.** This message notifies the module about the fact that the order has been cancelled by the broker.

- **CloseExchangeOrderEvent.** This message notifies the module about the fact of complete execution of the order on the exchange.

- **CreateDealEvent.** This message comes when a deal is executed on the exchange.

In turn, the Core service calls only one command, a handler, which must be implemented in an external application—PlaceOrderCommand—a command to place an order on the exchange. I did not add a command to cancel the order. We discussed this point in Chapter 4. Since the system will implement system orders, which

CHAPTER 8   IMPLEMENTATION OF THE CORE MODULE

are responsible for the logic of order execution, it was decided in this implementation to place only market orders on the exchange, which are usually executed instantly.

I would also like to draw your attention to the fact that events about changes in candles will only come on candles at intervals of a minute, because other candles can be easily calculated based on minute candles. This is also because many exchanges and brokers require a subscription to a separate web socket connection channel for each candle interval and, of course, limit the number of such subscriptions and connections.

Context

At this stage, I will not fill the context with all the necessary information, because I still don't know what might be needed. But I will lay the foundation for this mechanism. The context will be a singleton, which is filled with information in the InitContextCommand command handler.

I leave the job of ensuring that there is a single instance of the StrategyContext context class entirely to IServiceCollection. To do this, I created a static CoreServiceCollectionExtensions class and added a line to it that declared the StrategyContext context, as shown in Listing 8-1.

Listing 8-1. Core Module Connection Function

```
public static IServiceCollection AddCore(
this IServiceCollection services)
{
    services.AddSingleton<StrategyContext>();

    return services;
}
```

In the context initialization command class, `InitContextCommand` has so far added only the minimal required information, as shown in Listing 8-2.

Listing 8-2. InitContextCommand Class

```
public class InitContextCommand: IRequest<bool>
{
    public required int ExchangeId;
    public required int InstrumentId;
    public required int StrategyId;
}
```

Update Candle Event

This event is emitted by an application that uses the Core library. Core contains a handler for this. I implemented the event class very simply, as shown in Listing 8-3. For this we only need a candle. You may need more information later, but for now this is enough.

When implementing `Event`, I use a new feature of .NET 8 called *primary constructors*, which allow you to increase code readability. You can get more information about this at https://learn.microsoft.com.

Listing 8-3. UpdateCandleEvent Class

```
public class UpdateCandleEvent(Candle candle) : INotification
{
    public readonly Candle Candle = candle;
}
```

Perhaps it's worth revealing the implementation of `Candle`. At the same time, I will remind you of what fields this concept consists of. Listing 8-4 shows the implementation of this, as well as all the values of the

CHAPTER 8   IMPLEMENTATION OF THE CORE MODULE

CandleInterval enum. I implemented all the fields as required to make sure they were filled out in addition to the necessary fields that identify the candle, such as ExchangeId, InstrumentId, and Interval. This, of course, contains the Open, Close, High, and Low prices: the open, close, highest, and lowest price for the period of the candle, respectively. In addition to prices, candles also contain the volume of all past transactions (Volume) and the opening date of the candle (OpenDate).

Listing 8-4. Candle Record

```
public record Candle
{
    public required int ExchangeId;
    public required int InstrumentId;
    public required CandleInterval Interval;

    public required decimal Open;
    public required decimal Close;
    public required decimal High;
    public required decimal Low;
    public required decimal Volume;
    public required DateTime OpenDate;
}

public enum CandleInterval
{
    _1min = 1,
    _2min = 2,
    _3min = 3,
    _5min = 5,
    _10min = 10,
    _15min = 15,
    _30min = 30,
```

```
    hour = 60,
    _4hour = 240,
    day = 1440,
    week = 10080,
    month = 43200
}
```

When the event about the appearance of a new minute candle arrives, you need to do these three things:

- Check that the candle belongs to the current context.
- Check system orders, as they require certain actions when trading information arrives.
- Calculate signals and, if necessary, emit commands to place orders.

Listing 8-5 shows my implementation of a handler for this minute candle event. In this, I performed basic checks to ensure that the candle matches the context. Next, I called the UpdateCandle function on the context. Very soon I will show the implementation of this function, but now I will say that all candles of the required intervals are updated. This will be needed when calculating signal values. After all, they can use not only minute candles but also candles of other intervals. After updating the candles in the context, I sequentially processed the commands for checking orders and signal values.

Listing 8-5. Handle Function of UpdateCandleEvent Handler

```
public async Task Handle(UpdateCandleEvent notification,
CancellationToken cancellationToken)
{
    Candle newCandle = notification.Candle;
```

CHAPTER 8   IMPLEMENTATION OF THE CORE MODULE

```
if (newCandle.ExchangeId != _strategyContext.ExchangeId)
    return;

if (newCandle.InstrumentId !=           _strategyContext.
                                        InstrumentId)
    return;

_strategyContext.UpdateCandle(newCandle);

await _mediator.Send(new CheckSystemOrdersCommand(),
cancellationToken);
await _mediator.Send(new CheckSignalsCommand(),
cancellationToken);
}
```

Check Signals

Signal values are checked in the `CheckSignalsCommand` command handler. Listing 8-6 shows the implementation of the signal check command handler.

Here's what happens:

1. `SignalData` is being calculated, and then I will analyze this class in detail. The most important thing is that it contains a field `SignalValue` of type `bool?`, containing the value of the signal true, false, or null. If this is null, then this means that signal calculation is currently impossible. The fact is that many indicators require the availability of historical candle data, which means that if the data has not been accumulated, then the calculation is impossible.

CHAPTER 8   IMPLEMENTATION OF THE CORE MODULE

2. If at least one of the signals cannot be calculated, then the processing of the command stops, because it is impossible to say whether it is possible to open or close a position.

3. Further, if the signal to open a position and close a position is positive, then this situation is considered contradictory, and a position is not opened or closed.

4. If the opening signal is triggered, the position opening command is called.

5. If the close signal is triggered, all open positions are closed. As my experience has shown, the ability to open multiple positions has a positive effect on the quality of strategies.

Listing 8-6. CheckSignalsCommand Handler

```
public async Task<bool> Handle(
    CheckSignalsCommand request,
    CancellationToken cancellationToken)
{
    int openSignalId = _strategyContext.Strategy.OpenSignalId;
    int closeSignalId = _strategyContext.Strategy.
    CloseSignalId;

    SignalData openSignalData =
        await _mediator.Send(new CalculateSignalCommand(openS
        ignalId));
    SignalData closeSignalData =
        await _mediator.Send(new CalculateSignalCommand(closeS
        ignalId));
```

```csharp
    bool? openPosition = openSignalData.SignalValue;
    bool? closePosition = closeSignalData.SignalValue;
    if (!openPosition.HasValue
        || !closePosition.HasValue
        || openPosition.Value && closePosition.Value)
        return true;

    if (openPosition.Value)
        await _mediator.Send(new OpenPositionCommand());
    else if (closePosition.Value)
        await _mediator.Send(new ClosePositionsCommand());

    return true;
}
```

Strategy Model

Before we move on to implementing the signal calculation command, it is necessary to implement a model of this. Let me remind you the main aspects of this entity.

- The purpose of the signal is to calculate a yes/no response.
- The yes/no answer is obtained by calculating the value of the root group conditions.
- There are two types of groups: with an AND condition and with an OR condition. .
- Each conditions group can contain both child groups and conditions.
- Conditions represent a condition for comparing the values of two indicators.

CHAPTER 8   IMPLEMENTATION OF THE CORE MODULE

Listing 8-7 shows an implementation of the Signal class. Since this is an entity, it contains an Id field. The Name field contains a description for the UI. In addition, it contains a Condition field. As was said earlier, Condition has a hierarchical structure, so Condition is not a list.

Listing 8-7. Signal Class

```
public class Signal
{
    public required int Id;
    public required string Name;
    public required Condition Condition;
}
```

The Condition class presented in Listing 8-8 looks more interesting.

Listing 8-8. Condition Class

```
public class Condition
{
    public required Guid Code;
    public required int Index;
    public required bool IsGroup;
    public required List<Condition> Conditions = new ();
    public required ConditionGroupType? GroupType;
    public required int? Indicator1Id;
    public required ConditionType? ConditionType;
    public required int? Indicator2Id;
}
```

I added the following fields to this class:

- **Code.** This will be needed in many places in our program, for example, when setting the value of a parameter of one of the condition indicators.

CHAPTER 8　IMPLEMENTATION OF THE CORE MODULE

- **Index.** This field is required to determine the order in which the UI will be displayed to the user. It is very unpleasant when the sequence of conditions changes after saving and updating the page with the signal.

- **IsGroup.** This field is necessary to understand whether the condition is a group or a full-fledged condition with indicators.

- **Conditions.** If the condition is a group, then of course it contains children. They are stored in this parameter.

- **GroupType.** This is a field of type enum with only two values AND and OR.

- **Indicator1Id.** This is the ID of the first indicator.

- **ConditionType.** This is the type of condition for comparing identifier values. It is represented as an enum with six possible values: Equality, Inequality, Less, LessOrEqual, Greater, and GreaterOrEqual.

- **Indicator2Id.** This is the second indicator ID.

Knowing the structure of the class that represents a signal, we can describe the `SignalData` class. Listing 8-9 shows an implementation of this. I added Id to this field so that `SignalData` and the list of indicator values can be linked. Please note that in the `SignalDataIndicatorValues` class I did not use the IndicatorId field but instead introduced an `IsIndicator1` field of type *bool*. That is, if it is true, then this is the value of `Indicator1Id` in the condition; otherwise, it's `Indicator2Id`. I did this on purpose, because there are strategies where the values of the same indicator are compared, but at different candle intervals.

CHAPTER 8 IMPLEMENTATION OF THE CORE MODULE

Listing 8-9. SignalData Class

```
public class SignalData
{
    public long Id;
    public required int ExchangeId;
    public required int InstrumentId;
    public required int StrategyId;
    public required DateTime CandleTime;
    public required int SignalId;
    public bool? SignalValue;

    public List<SignalDataIndicatorValues> IndicatorValues
    = new();
}
public class SignalDataIndicatorValues
{
    public required string ConditionCode;
    public required bool IsIndicator1;
    public required decimal? IndicatorValue;
    public required int CandleBackNumber;
}
```

At this stage, we have everything we need to implement the strategy model. Let me remind you that the main goal of the strategy is to contain the identifiers of signals for opening and closing a position, as well as the values of all parameters necessary to calculate all identifiers of the selected signals. Listing 8-10 shows an implementation of the Strategy class. This is an entity, which means it has its own identifier. I also added the Name field to contain a description for U. OpenSignalId and CloseSignalId are identifiers of the selected signals.

CHAPTER 8 IMPLEMENTATION OF THE CORE MODULE

Pay attention to the three fields SignalId, ConditionCode, and IsIndicator1 in the classes StrategySignalParam and StrategySignalCandle, which are used to accurately determine the parameters of which indicator were set. StrategySignalParam contains information about the values of all indicator parameters; this is a list of values for the IndicatorParamTypeId field, which will be provided by a separate library for calculating indicators. The StrategySignalCandle class contains the CandleIntervalId field, which is the identifier of the candle interval at which the indicator value is calculated, as well as CandleFrom and CandleTo, which determine at what depth this calculation should be performed.

Listing 8-10. Strategy Class

```
public class Strategy
{
    public required int Id;
    public required string Name;
    public required int OpenSignalId;
    public required int CloseSignalId;

    public required List<StrategySignalParam>
    StrategySignalParams;
    public required List<StrategySignalCandle>
    StrategySignalCandles;
}

public class StrategySignalParam
{
    public required int SignalId;
    public required string ConditionCode;
    public required bool IsIndicator1;
```

CHAPTER 8   IMPLEMENTATION OF THE CORE MODULE

```
    public required int IndicatorParamTypeId;
    public required decimal ParamValue;
}
public class StrategySignalCandle
{
    public required int SignalId;
    public required string ConditionCode;
    public required bool IsIndicator1;
    public required int CandleIntervalId;
    public required int CandleFrom;
    public required int CandleTo;
}
```

Since strategy and signals have become complex entities whose parameters will most likely be needed in command handlers, it is necessary to add repository interfaces for retrieving entities, as well as enrich the StrategyContext class with new parameters.

Listings 8-11 shows a new implementation of the InitContextCommand command handler. I get the object of the strategy and the necessary signals. Since these entities are received only once when the strategy is launched, it is necessary to keep in mind that when the strategy or signals change, it is necessary to restart the strategy.

Listing 8-11. InitContextCommand Handler

```
public async Task<bool> Handle(
    InitContextCommand request,
    CancellationToken cancellationToken)
{
    _strategyContext.ExchangeId = request.ExchangeId;
    _strategyContext.InstrumentId = request.InstrumentId;
```

CHAPTER 8 IMPLEMENTATION OF THE CORE MODULE

```
    _strategyContext.Strategy =
        await _strategyRepository.GetAsync(request.StrategyId);

    _strategyContext.Signals =
        await _signalRepository.GetAsync([
            _strategyContext.Strategy.OpenSignalId,
            _strategyContext.Strategy.CloseSignalId,
        ]);

    return true;
}
```

Calculate Signal

Let's start implementing the `CalculateSignalCommand` command handler. The task is to return the result of calculating signal data in the form of an instance of the `SignalData` class and also save this data to the database. The user will need this data to check the correctness of the calculations and the operation of the entire algorithm.

Listing 8-12 shows the implementation of the central command handler function. I fill in some fields of the command handler class that I will need in other functions. Then I create an instance of the `SignalData` class. I call the calculation function condition `CalculateCondition`. Please note that I have placed the `SignalData` instance into the class fields. I did this so that the calculation functions could add the calculated indicator values to this.

Listing 8-12. CalculateSignalCommand Handler

```
public async Task<SignalData> Handle(
    CalculateSignalCommand request,
    CancellationToken cancellationToken)
{
```

```
    _signal = _strategyContext.Signals
        .First(s => s.Id == request.SignalId);

    _signalData = new()
    {
        ExchangeId = _strategyContext.ExchangeId,
        InstrumentId = _strategyContext.InstrumentId,
        StrategyId = _strategyContext.Strategy.Id,
        CandleTime = _strategyContext.LastCandle!.OpenDate,
        SignalId = _signal.Id,
    };

    _signalData.SignalValue = CalculateCondition(_signal.
    Condition);

    _signalData = await _signalDataRepository.SaveAsync
    (_signalData);
    return _signalData;
}
```

The implementation of the CalculateCondition function is quite simple. This is where the calculation function is selected. If this is a condition group, then the CalculateGroupCondition function is called; otherwise, CalculateNotGroupCondition is called. Listing 8-13 shows my implementation of the CalculateCondition function.

Listing 8-13. CalculateCondition Function

```
private bool? CalculateCondition(Condition condition)
{
    bool? conditionValue = false;
    if (condition.ItsGroup)
        conditionValue = CalculateGroupCondition(condition);
    else
```

CHAPTER 8   IMPLEMENTATION OF THE CORE MODULE

```
        conditionValue = CalculateNotGroupCondition(condition);

    return conditionValue;
}
```

The condition group calculation function is a loop in which each child condition is calculated and a decision is made about the value of the entire group depending on its type. If it is of type AND, then all the conditions of the groups and conditions contained in it must be satisfied. If it is of type OR, then only one condition is sufficient. To calculate the value of child conditions, I use the previously written `CalculateCondition` function. The interesting thing about this function is the fact that I calculate all child conditions, although I could stop at the first false condition for a group with type AND, for example. This is because to check the correctness of the calculations, I want to see all the indicator values, and for this they need to be calculated. Listing 8-14 shows the implementation of this function.

Listing 8-14. CalculateGroupCondition Function

```
private bool? CalculateGroupCondition(Condition condition)
{
    bool? conditionValue = condition.GroupType ==
    ConditionGroupType.And;
    bool oneOfChildIsNull = false;
    foreach (Condition childCondition in condition.Conditions)
    {
        bool? childConditionValue = CalculateCondition(childC
        ondition);
        if (!childConditionValue.HasValue)
        {
            oneOfChildIsNull = true;
            break;
        }
```

```
        conditionValue = (condition.GroupType ==
        ConditionGroupType.And)
            ? conditionValue.Value &&
            childConditionValue!.Value
            : conditionValue.Value ||
            childConditionValue!.Value;

    }

    conditionValue = oneOfChildIsNull ? null : conditionValue;

    return conditionValue;
}
```

Please note how I solved the problem that some of the conditions could not be calculated. I created a variable oneOfChildIsNull, and if it is true, then only the child conditions are calculated, and the result of executing the entire function will be null.

A more interesting function is the function for calculating nongroup conditions. To do this, you need to obtain the depths of the candles from the signal settings and then check the conditions on each of the candles. For example, if the condition is configured like this:

indicator_1 candle from = 0 - candle to = 2

<

Indicator_2 candle from = 3 - candle to = 4

then the calculation is made on five-minute candles and the new candle has an opening date equal to 2024-02-10T10:45:00; then for the condition value to be positive, all conditions must be met.

- indicator_1 on 2024-02-10T10:**45**:00 < Indicator_2 on 2024-02-10T10:**30**:00 (minus 3 times for 5 minutes)
- indicator_1 on 2024-02-10T10:**45**:00 < Indicator_2 на 2024-02-10T10:**25**:00 (minus 4 times for 5 minutes)

CHAPTER 8 IMPLEMENTATION OF THE CORE MODULE

- indicator_1 on 2024-02-10T10:**40**:00 < Indicator_2 на 2024-02-10T10:**30**:00 (minus 3 times for 5 minutes)
- indicator_1 on 2024-02-10T10:**40**:00 < Indicator_2 на 2024-02-10T10:**25**:00 (minus 4 times for 5 minutes)
- indicator_1 on 2024-02-10T10:**35**:00 < Indicator_2 на 2024-02-10T10:**30**:00 (minus 3 times for 5 minutes)
- indicator_1 on 2024-02-10T10:**35**:00 < Indicator_2 на 2024-02-10T10:**25**:00 (minus 4 times for 5 minutes)

Listing 8-15 shows an implementation of the CalculateNotGroupCondition function. I get from the settings from and to candle. Next I work with two cycles. In each iteration, I calculate the values of each indicator, and if both values are not null, then I check the condition.

Listing 8-15. CalculateNotGroupCondition Function

```
private bool? CalculateNotGroupCondition(Condition condition)
{
    bool? conditionValue = false;
    var (candleFrom1, candleTo1) =
        GetFromToCandles(condition.Code, true);
    var (candleFrom2, candleTo2) =
        GetFromToCandles(condition.Code, false);
    for (int i1 = candleFrom1; i1 <= candleTo1; i1++)
    {
        for (int i2 = candleFrom2; i2 <= candleTo2; i2++)
        {
            decimal? indicator1Value =
                CalculateIndicatorValue(condition.Code,
                    true, i1);
```

CHAPTER 8 IMPLEMENTATION OF THE CORE MODULE

```
                decimal? indicator2Value =
                    CalculateIndicatorValue(condition.Code,
                    false, i2);

                bool? currentConditionValue = false;
                if (!indicator1Value.HasValue || !indicator2Value.
                HasValue)
                    currentConditionValue = null;
                else
                    currentConditionValue =
                        CalculateConditionValue(
                            condition.ConditionType!.Value,
                            indicator1Value.Value,
                            indicator2Value.Value);

                conditionValue = currentConditionValue;
                if (conditionValue != true)
                    return conditionValue;
            }
        }

        return conditionValue;
    }
```

Listing 8-16 shows implementations of the GetFromToCandles and CalculateConditionValue helper functions. Of course, the from and to candles settings are stored in the strategy itself, so the GetFromToCandles function accesses an instance of the Strategy class.

The CalculateConditionValue function is a simple switch. Starting with version c# 8, working with this has become truly convenient.

CHAPTER 8 IMPLEMENTATION OF THE CORE MODULE

Listing 8-16. GetFromToCandles Function

```
private (int from, int to) GetFromToCandles(
    string conditionCode,
    bool isIndicator1)
{
    int candleFrom =
        _strategyContext.Strategy.StrategySignalCandles
            .FirstOrDefault(d =>
                d.SignalId == _signal.Id
                && d.ConditionCode == conditionCode
                && d.IsIndicator1 == isIndicator1)?.CandleFrom
        ?? 0;
    int candleTo =
        _strategyContext.Strategy.StrategySignalCandles
            .FirstOrDefault(d =>
                d.SignalId == _signal.Id
                && d.ConditionCode == conditionCode
                && d.IsIndicator1 == isIndicator1)?.CandleTo
        ?? 0;
    return (candleFrom, candleTo);
}

private bool CalculateConditionValue(
    ConditionType conditionType,
    decimal indicator1Value,
    decimal indicator2Value
) => conditionType switch
{
    ConditionType.Equality => indicator1Value ==
    indicator2Value,
    ConditionType.Inequality => indicator1Value !=
    indicator2Value,
```

CHAPTER 8 IMPLEMENTATION OF THE CORE MODULE

```
    ConditionType.Greater => indicator1Value > indicator2Value,
    ConditionType.GreaterOrEqual => indicator1Value >=
    indicator2Value,
    ConditionType.Less => indicator1Value < indicator2Value,
    ConditionType.LessOrEqual => indicator1Value <=
    indicator2Value,
    _ => throw new ArgumentOutOfRangeException(nameof(condition
    Type), conditionType, null)
};
```

The `CalculateIndicatorValue` function performs two actions. First, the indicator value is calculated, and second, the calculated value is added to `SignalData`. Of course, the indicator value is calculated in the `Calculate` function of the special class `IndicatorCalculatorManager`. Next, I will analyze in detail the logic for calculating indicators. Listing 8-17 shows the implementation of the `CalculateIndicatorValue` function.

Listing 8-17. CalculateIndicatorValue Function

```
private decimal? CalculateIndicatorValue(
    string conditionCode,
    bool isIndicator1,
    int candleBackNumber)
{
    decimal? indicatorValue = _indicatorCalculatorManager.
    Calculate(
        _signal.Id,
        conditionCode,
        isIndicator1,
        candleBackNumber,
        _strategyContext.Candles);
```

```
    _signalData.IndicatorValues.Add(new
    SignalDataIndicatorValues
    {
        ConditionCode = conditionCode,
        IsIndicator1 = true,
        IndicatorValue = indicatorValue,
        CandleBackNumber = candleBackNumber,
    });

    return indicatorValue;
}
```

Calculation of Indicators

Why IndicatorCalculatorManager? After all, calculators, by their nature and by name, should not contain a state. But as practice has shown, this is not entirely true. First, we need an entity that will store the already calculated indicator values for the required number of candles back to calculate conditions of type indicator_1 < indicator_2 on the last three candles. Second, many indicators contain variables in their formulas, the values of which depend on historical data. For example, Adx (Average Directional Index), Atr (Average True Range), Bbw (Bollinger Bands Width) and others depend on the previous value, which means that this value must be stored somewhere.

As a result, I built the following class architecture to solve the problem of calculating indicators:

- **IndicatorCalculatorManager.** This is a Singleton that creates a list of calculators and stores it. This is exactly what you turn to when calculating the indicator. The purpose of this class is to generate and store a list of calculators.

- **HistoryCalculator.** This is a wrapper over classes that implement the indicator calculation interface. This is where the calculated data for the required number of candles back will be stored. The purpose of this class is to provide the ability to calculate indicators with the ability to pass the candleBackNumber parameter, which helps to find the candle on which the indicator is calculated.

- The classes implement the IIndicatorCalculator interface. There are specific classes containing all the necessary logic required for calculating indicators.

Listing 8-18 shows an implementation of the Init function of the IndicatorCalculatorManager class. This generates calculators for each of the indicators. The Init method is called in the InitContextCommand command handler. Please note that the GenerateCalculators function is recursive; in fact, it initializes generator classes for each condition. This means it is called for each child condition in a condition with the type group.

Listing 8-18. Init Function

```
public void Init(
    Strategy strategy,
    List<Signal> signals)
{
    _calculators.Clear();

    foreach (Signal signal in signals)
        GenerateCalculators(strategy, signal.Id, signal.
        Condition);
}
```

CHAPTER 8 IMPLEMENTATION OF THE CORE MODULE

```
private void GenerateCalculators(Strategy strategy, int
signalId, Condition condition)
{
    if (condition.IsGroup)
    {
        foreach (Condition childCondition in condition.
        Conditions)
            GenerateCalculators(strategy, signalId,
            childCondition);
    }
    else
    {
        var calculator1 = GetCalculator(strategy, signalId,
        condition, true);
        _calculators.Add(calculator1);

        var calculator2 = GetCalculator(strategy, signalId,
        condition, false);
        _calculators.Add(calculator2);
    }
}
```

The GetCalculator method is quite simple. This involves obtaining a class that implements IIndicatorCalculator from the collection and subsequent initialization of the HistoryCalculator class. To obtain a calculator linked to an indicator, it is necessary to store the signal identifier, the condition code, and the flag indicating that this is a left or right indicator. I decided to store these parameters in the HistoryCalculator class. See Listing 8-19.

CHAPTER 8　IMPLEMENTATION OF THE CORE MODULE

Listing 8-19. GetCalculator Function

```
private HistoryCalculator GetCalculator(
    Strategy strategy,
    int signalId,
    Condition condition,
    bool isIndicator1)
{
    int indicatorId =
        isIndicator1
            ? condition.Indicator1Id!.Value
            : condition.Indicator2Id!.Value;
    IIndicatorCalculator indicatorCalculator =
        _serviceProvider
            .GetRequiredKeyedService<IIndicatorCalculator>
            ((IndicatorIds) indicatorId);

    StrategySignalCandle candleParam = strategy.
    StrategySignalCandles
        .First(c =>
            c.SignalId == signalId
            && c.ConditionCode == condition.Code
            && c.IsIndicator1 == isIndicator1
        );
    var calculator = new HistoryCalculator
    {
        SignalId = signalId,
        ConditionCode = condition.Code,
        IsIndicator1 = isIndicator1,
        MaxCandlesCount = candleParam.CandleTo + 1,
        CandleInterval = (CandleInterval)candleParam.
        CandleIntervalId,
```

```
        Calculator = indicatorCalculator
    };

    return calculator;
}
```

In the GetCalculator function, I get instances of calculator classes from IServiceCollection by indicator ID. To have this opportunity, you must first place the class in this collection. Listing 8-20 shows the implementation of the IServiceCollection extension and the IIndicatorCalculator interface.

To implement the ability to automatically add new classes that implement the IIndicatorCalculator interface, I added a static field called static IndicatorIds Id { get; } in IIndicatorCalculator. In the AddIndicators function, I select all the classes that implement the IIndicatorCalculator interface in the current assembly and then add each of the classes using the AddKeyedTransient function.

Listing 8-20. IIndicatorCalculator Interface

```
public interface IIndicatorCalculator
{
    static IndicatorIds Id { get; }

    public void Init(
        Dictionary<IndicatorParamTypes, decimal>
        indicatorParams);
    public decimal? Calculate(Candle newCandle);
}
public static IServiceCollection AddIndicators(this
IServiceCollection services)
{
    services.AddSingleton<IndicatorCalculatorManager>();
```

```
    var calculators = AppDomain.CurrentDomain
        .GetAssemblies()
        .SelectMany(assembly => assembly.GetTypes())
        .Where(type =>
            typeof(IIndicatorCalculator).IsAssignableFrom(type)
            && !type.IsInterface
            && !type.IsAbstract);

    foreach (var calculator in calculators)
    {
        IndicatorIds indicatorId =
            (IndicatorIds) calculator!
                .GetProperty("Id")!
                .GetValue(null, null)!;
        services.AddKeyedTransient(
            typeof(IndicatorIds),
            indicatorId,
            calculator);
    }

    return services;
}
```

Let's move on to the implementation of the HistoryCalculator class. It has only one public function, Calculate, the implementation of which is shown in Listing 8-21. First it finds a candle with the required interval. Let me remind you that candle update events will come only at minute intervals, but based on this, you can calculate candles for all other intervals. The Calculate function will receive candles for all time intervals as a parameter, which means you need to find the right one among them. Next, the NeedCalculation check is performed. This checks for changes in the parameters of the required candle. If the candle has changed, then the calculator is contacted for the calculation, and the new result is stored in a field of the HistoryCalculator class. After this, the requested value is received.

Listing 8-21. Calculate Function

```
public decimal? Calculate(int candleBackNumber, List<Candle> candles)
{
    Candle newCandle = candles.First(c => c.Interval == CandleInterval);

    if (NeedCalculation(newCandle))
    {
        decimal? newValue = Calculator.Calculate(newCandle);
        PutNewValue(newCandle, newValue);
    }

    return GetValue(candleBackNumber);
}
```

Average True Range (Atr)

I would like to demonstrate the implementation of the indicator calculator using the example of calculating the Atr (Average True Range) indicator. Atr is one of the market volatility indicators widely used in technical analysis. Since atr is the average value of the true range, then, of course, its parameter is the number of candles on the basis of which the average value of the indicator will be determined.

CHAPTER 8　IMPLEMENTATION OF THE CORE MODULE

The formula for calculating Atr is as follows:

$$\frac{\sum_i^n Tr_i}{n}$$

That is, in essence, this is the sum of the True Range at the required number of candle intervals divided by their number.

True Range is calculated using the following formula:

$$Tr = \max\left(H-L, |H-C_p|, |L-C_p|\right)$$

H is the High price of the current candle.

L is the Low price of the current candle.

C_p is the Close price of the previous candle.

To implement this, I created a separate abstract class for calculating Average indicators. I put this logic in a separate class because so many indicators use the average value, so it makes sense to make the calculation of the average value common to all indicators of this type.

Listing 8-22 demonstrates an implementation of the `AverageCalculator` class. In addition to the `Calculate` method, it also implements the `Init` method. Why `Init` and not a `constructor`? Because indicator parameters can be initialized only through the Init method, since classes are created using `IServiceProvider`. And the required number of candles can be found only from the indicator parameters.

The logic of the `Calculate` method comes down to monitoring the required list of candles and calling the `calculateValue` function passed as a parameter from the child class.

Listing 8-22. AverageCalculator Abstract Class

```
public abstract class AverageCalculator
{
    private int _maxCandlesCount;
    private SortedList<DateTime, Candle> _lastCandles;

    protected void Init(int maxCandlesCount)
    {
        _lastCandles = new();
        _maxCandlesCount = maxCandlesCount;
    }

    protected decimal? Calculate(
        Candle newCandle,
        Func<List<Candle>, decimal?> calculateValue)
    {
        _lastCandles.TryAdd(newCandle.OpenDate, newCandle);
        _lastCandles[newCandle.OpenDate] = newCandle;

        decimal? value = null;
        if (_lastCandles.Count >= _maxCandlesCount)
        {
            if (_lastCandles.Count > _maxCandlesCount)
                _lastCandles.Remove(_lastCandles.
                    GetKeyAtIndex(0));

            value = calculateValue(_lastCandles.Values.
            ToList());
        }

        return value;
    }
}
```

CHAPTER 8 IMPLEMENTATION OF THE CORE MODULE

As a result, the implementation of the AtrIndicatorCalculator class is quite simple. This is demonstrated in Listing 8-23. This calculates Tr for each candle. These values are summed and divided by the total number of candles.

Listing 8-23. AtrIndicatorCalculator Class

```
public class AtrIndicatorCalculator : AverageCalculator,
IIndicatorCalculator
{
    public static IndicatorIds Id => IndicatorIds.Atr;

    private int _lookbackPeriods;

    public void Init(Dictionary<IndicatorParamTypes, decimal>
    indicatorParams)
    {
        _lookbackPeriods = (int) indicatorParams[IndicatorParam
        Types.LookbackPeriods];
        base.Init(_lookbackPeriods);
    }

    public decimal? Calculate(Candle newCandle)
    {
        decimal? value = base.Calculate(newCandle,
        CalculateValue);
        return value;
    }

    private decimal? CalculateValue(List<Candle> lastCandles)
    {
        decimal sumTr = 0;
        for (int i = 1; i < lastCandles.Count; i++)
        {
```

CHAPTER 8　IMPLEMENTATION OF THE CORE MODULE

```
        Candle candle = lastCandles[i];
        Candle prevCandle = lastCandles[i - 1];
        decimal tr = Math.Max(candle.High - candle.Low,
            Math.Max(Math.Abs(candle.High -
            prevCandle.Close),
                Math.Abs(candle.Low - prevCandle.Close)));
        sumTr += tr;
    }

    decimal value = sumTr / lastCandles.Count;

    return value;
    }
}
```

I'd also like to show you the implementation of the HighPriceCalculator class in Listing 8-24, which returns the high price of the current candle and is another indicator. This will show you how easy it is to expand the library's capabilities without changing the essence of it.

Listing 8-24. HighPriceCalculator Class

```
public class HighPriceCalculator : IIndicatorCalculator
{
    public static IndicatorIds Id => IndicatorIds.HighPrice;

    public void Init(Dictionary<IndicatorParamTypes, decimal>
    indicatorParams)
    {
    }

    public decimal? Calculate(Candle newCandle)
```

361

```
    {
        return newCandle.High;
    }
}
```

Process of Positions

At this stage, a signal calculation command handler is implemented. Based on this, the library makes a decision to open or close a position. Moreover, only one position is opened, but all are closed. This is why the commands are named `OpenPositionCommand` and `ClosePositionsCommand`. Initially, I created a system that allowed me to open only one position. And, as practice has shown, this approach is less profitable than the possibility of opening several positions. The main thing is to set a rule by which you will limit the number and frequency of positions opened.

The position processing process is also important. For example, the system opened a position and then placed a buy order on the exchange, but you did not have enough funds on the exchange account, and this returned a callback with error information. In this case, the process is quite simple, but what if the financial asset was purchased. Next, based on the rules described in risk control, several specific system orders were opened and the signal to close positions came. You must remember to close all auxiliary orders.

Or what if the system sent a command to place a buy order but somewhere something went wrong and the message about the status of this order was never received. What do you do in this case?

I tried implemented position processing based on statuses and transitions between them. But as the system became more complex, the process of position processing became more complicated, and in the end I got confused in the statuses, and the logic of transitions between them became difficult. After another unsuccessful attempt to introduce

CHAPTER 8   IMPLEMENTATION OF THE CORE MODULE

another branch of the process, I gave up. I realized it was time to change something. Then I remembered that I already have a state machine implemented in my system, in which I am satisfied with everything except the asynchrony.

An already implemented state machine uses a database to store the current state of the entity. Jobs run periodically, read this table, and process the entity state. But in Core, there is no question of any background job; I simply do not have the opportunity to wait even one millisecond (and most likely more) for this job to be processed. It is necessary to respond to the event immediately! And I thought: What if we create a "lite" version of the state machine, where all steps are fast and the entity will move along the process map only at the moment the event arrives?

There were two problems with this solution. The first is the uncontrollable number of entities being processed in parallel; in other words, we won't be able to control the load. If in the implemented version of the state machine the number of processed entities is specified in the settings, then what about the lite version? Imagine that events will come for hundreds of entities at once! Will the system be able to cope with this? But will there really be hundreds of positions open on one pod? It is unlikely, so I decided to ignore this danger, because the architecture of the entire system will not allow this to happen. In the real trading subsystem, I have a rule: one pod = one strategy-instrument pair. And in the strategy search subsystem, one pod processes only one task at a time. That is, the rule is also followed: a one-for-one strategy-instrument pair.

The second problem is the probability of two events arriving simultaneously for one entity. If the process handles them simultaneously, then disaster will occur. The main idea of a state machine, based on the fact that at one point in time an entity can be in only one state, will be violated. The fact that only one strategy-instrument pair is processed on one pod will not help in solving this problem, because several orders can be placed with the broker for one position, which means there is a possibility that they will receive status change events simultaneously. Also, do not forget about the position closing event.

How do you get out of this situation? What helped me in solving the problem was the understanding that event processing is a very fast process, and I also knew that there would not be many events (let me remind you that the system is not designed for scalping trading, when orders are created quite often). These two points gave me an idea: what if, when an event arrives, the entire bot process is blocked for all threads? That is, the lite version will be able to process only one event of one entity at a time. There is one drawback to this approach; there is a possibility that the pod will not have time to process the entire queue of events. But I decided to try anyway, because I was going to implement the handlers as quickly as possible, and the number of open positions was controlled to be small.

Process Bot (Lite Version)

Before we move on to the actual implementation, let's define the operating logic of this version of the state machine.

Here are some points:

- Any actions with the entity are performed only when an event is received.
- In this version, the waiting node type does not wait for a certain amount of time, after which it steps further, but always stays at this step until the event arrives.
- When processing an event, the robot steps either to the end of the map or to the first node with the waiting type.
- At one time, the state machine can work with only one entity.

- I intended to store the current state of the entity in a database. But the integration itself with this should not be implemented in this library, but rather an event about a state change should be published.

As a result, the input to this library is as follows:

- We input a list of process map nodes. I assumed that it would be stored not in the database but directly in the code, which would ensure that it would be the same in both subsystems (the search subsystem and the real trading subsystem).

- We implement the `IProcessActFactory` interface with a single method for getting `IProcessAct` by its type identifier. Also, obtaining a class that implements `IProcessAct` could be implemented in another way, by creating a command in the state machine library and a handler for this in the application that uses it. However, I don't like this approach for one reason. In the case of a factory implementation, I can "force" the application to pass me the class by implementing it in the `IServiceCollection AddProcessBotLite` extension method. In the case of a team, I will not be able to do this.

- We also need the calling library to implement the `IProcessEntityQueries` interface with a single `GetCurrentNodeIdAsync` method, which returns the current state of the entity.

CHAPTER 8   IMPLEMENTATION OF THE CORE MODULE

As a result, this library provides an implementation of the `MoveEntityCommand` command. This is what drives the entity along the process map. See Figure 8-2.

Figure 8-2. *Input and output functionality of the library*

The implementation of the `MoveEntityCommandHandler` class is simple. I just get an instance of the `ProcessMap` class from serviceCollection and call its `MoveAsync` method.

The algorithm for the `MoveAsync` function is as follows:

1. This handles the event. That is, it moves the entity to the nearest trigger of this one.

2. After this, the nodes are moved and processed in a loop until the entity stands on a node with the waiting type or the map runs out.

Listing 8-25 shows the implementation of part of the `MoveAsync` function, before the loop from step 2. First, notice that this function returns a bool type. If it is false, then this means that the workflow for this entity is over; that is, the robot has reached the end of the process map.

I isolated the state machine blocking logic for other threads in the `LockAsync` function. Also note that `eventId` can come with the value null; this is done specifically for the first entry into this function with a new entity, that is, to start the process.

First, the `GetCurrentNodeIdAsync` function is called to understand which node the entity is currently on. After this, the entity is moved to the nearest trigger in the `HandleEvent` function.

Listing 8-25. MoveAsync Function, Part 1

```
public Task<bool> MoveAsync(Guid entityId, int? eventId)
{
    return LockAsync(async () =>
    {
        Guid? currentNodeId =
            await _processEntityQueries.GetCurrentNodeIdAsync(
            entityId);
        if (!currentNodeId.HasValue && eventId.HasValue)
            return false;
        Guid? triggerNodeId =
            await HandleEvent(entityId, currentNodeId,
            eventId);
        if (!triggerNodeId.HasValue)
            return true;
```

Listing 8-26 shows the second part of the implementation of the MoveAsync function. The loop determines the identifier of the next node by calling the GetNextNodeId function. If there is no next node, this means that the process map is completed and the workflow is closed. After receiving the nextNodeId, the application is notified about the change in the state of the entity MoveEntityEvent and of course processing the node by calling the HandleNode function.

Pay attention to the nodeHandleResult variable. There are two fields in this. Move is precisely what makes it possible to understand whether it is necessary to stop the cycle and NodeId. NodeId is necessary for nodes that make transitions; for example, if the condition is met, then go to NodeId_1, and if not, then move on.

CHAPTER 8 IMPLEMENTATION OF THE CORE MODULE

Listing 8-26. MoveAsync Function, Part 2

```
        currentNodeId = triggerNodeId;
        (bool move, Guid? nodeId) nodeHandleResult = (true,
        currentNodeId);

        while (nodeHandleResult.move)
        {
            Guid? nextNodeId =
                GetNextNodeId(nodeHandleResult,
                currentNodeId!.Value);
            if (!nextNodeId.HasValue)
                return false;

            currentNodeId = nextNodeId.Value;

            await _mediator.Publish(
                        new MoveEntityEvent(entityId,
                        currentNodeId.Value));
            nodeHandleResult =
                await HandleNode(entityId,
                currentNodeId.Value);
        }

        return true;
    });
}
```

Listing 8-27 shows the implementation of the LockAsync method. I am using the SemaphoreSlim class provided by Microsoft. If you look at the documentation, it says that "The SemaphoreSlim class represents a lightweight, fast semaphore that can be used for waiting within a single process when wait times are expected to be very short." That is, this class provides functionality that allows you to block code execution by other processes.

368

Listing 8-27. LockAsync Function

```
private readonly SemaphoreSlim _semaphore =
    new(initialCount: 1, maxCount: 1);

private async Task<T> LockAsync<T>(Func<Task<T>> act)
{
    await _semaphore.WaitAsync();
    try
    {
        return await act();
    }
    finally
    {
        _semaphore.Release();
    }
}
```

Listing 8-28 shows an implementation of the HandleEvent function. In this, if the currentNodeId does not yet have a value, that is, the state machine processes the entity for the first time, the first node of the map is searched. If the entity is not processed for the first time, then the first node is searched for by code, which is a trigger for the transmitted event and whose code is greater than the code of the current node.

If a trigger is found, the entity moves to it, and the application is notified about the entity's movement.

Listing 8-28. HandleEvent Function

```
private async Task<Guid?> HandleEvent(
    Guid entityId,
    Guid? currentNodeId,
    int? eventId)
{
    Guid? triggerNodeId;
```

```csharp
    if (currentNodeId.HasValue)
    {
        Node currentNode = _nodes.First(n => n.Id ==
        currentNodeId);
        triggerNodeId = _nodes
            .Where(n =>
                n.Code > currentNode.Code
                && n.EventId == eventId)
            .MinBy(n => n.Code)
            ?.Id;
    }
    else
    {
        triggerNodeId = _nodes
            .Where(n => n.EventId == eventId)
            .MinBy(n => n.Code)
            ?.Id;
    }

    if (triggerNodeId.HasValue)
        await _mediator
            .Publish(
                new MoveEntityEvent(entityId, triggerNodeId.
                Value));

    return triggerNodeId;
}
```

Listing 8-29 shows the implementation of the GetNextNodeId function for finding the next node identifier. In this, if the result of processing the previous node contains the ID of the next node, then a transition is made to this one; otherwise, the first node with a code greater than the current one is selected.

Listing 8-29. GetNextNodeId Function

```
private Guid? GetNextNodeId(
    (bool move, Guid? nodeId) prevHandleResult,
    Guid currentNodeId)
{
    Guid? nextNodeId;
    if (prevHandleResult.nodeId.HasValue)
        nextNodeId = prevHandleResult.nodeId.Value;
    else
    {
        Node currentNode = _nodes.First(n => n.Id ==
        currentNodeId);
        nextNodeId =
            _nodes
                .Where(n => n.Code > currentNode.Code)
                .MinBy(n => n.Code)
                ?.Id;
    }
    return nextNodeId;
}
```

Listing 8-30 shows an implementation of the node handler function. In this, the action is performed depending on the type of node. Of interest is the processing of a node with type Act. This involves getting an instance of a class that implements the IProcessAct interface. After this, the Make method is called. This result of executing this is true, which means you need to move to the node from the parameter of the current node; otherwise, you can move on.

Listing 8-30. HandleNode Function

```
private async Task<(bool move, Guid? nodeId)> HandleNode(
    Guid entityId,
    Guid nodeId)
{
    Node currentNode = _nodes.First(n => n.Id == nodeId);

    (bool move, Guid? nodeId) nodeHandleResult = currentNode.
    Type switch
    {
        NodeTypes.Act => await MakeAction(),
        NodeTypes.Waiting => (false, null),
        NodeTypes.Trigger => (true, null),
        NodeTypes.Description => (true, null),
        _ => throw new Exception($"unknown node type
        {currentNode.Type}")
    };

    return nodeHandleResult;

    async Task<(bool move, Guid? nodeId)> MakeAction()
    {
        IProcessAct? act =
            _processActFactory.GetAct(currentNode.
            ActId!.Value);
        if (act == null)
            throw new Exception($"act is unknown {currentNode.
            ActId!.Value}");
        bool moveTo = await act.Make(entityId, currentNode.
        MagicString);
```

```
        Guid? moveToNodeId = null;
        if (moveTo)
            moveToNodeId = currentNode.MoveToNodeId!.Value;

        return (true, moveToNodeId);
    }
}
```

Process Steps

The ProcessBot Lite library has been implemented. It is necessary to think over a Process map for the position processing process. First, you need to define a list of events to which the process map will react.

In the end, I came up with the following list:

- **Start.** This event begins the processing of the position process.

- **Open order executed.** Immediately after creating a position, you need to buy a certain number of lots of a financial instrument. To do this, a system order will be created, which in turn gives a command to the broker to place an order on the exchange. When the exchange order is executed, the system order will also be executed. This event is generated by the fact that a system order is executed.

- **Open order error.** Sometimes a broker fails to place an order on the exchange. There can be many reasons for this, from insufficient funds in your account to a temporary stoppage of the broker's work. Our system must competently handle such situations.

- **Close position.** This event can occur in several cases: first, when a signal to close a position is triggered, and second, when a signal comes from the risk control module; in our implementation, this is equivalent to closing one of the auxiliary system orders, for example, a take profit order. Third, an event about closing a position can occur at the user's request, when he explicitly instructs the system in the UI to close the position.

- **Close order executed.** As a result of closing a position, it is necessary to reduce the amount of the financial asset in the portfolio to zero for this position. This means that if there is a certain amount of a financial asset left in the portfolio, it must be sold. That is, place a sell order. As a result of this action, two events can occur: the closing order is executed, and the closing order is an error.

- **Close order error.** This is the second type of event for the action of placing an order to sell a financial asset.

As a result, I got a list of position states presented in Table 8-1. Perhaps the controversial point in this is the "Stop and alert" state. This occurs in the event of an unsuccessful order to sell assets when closing positions. It might make sense to try placing the order again. But this approach can be unprofitable, since it is unclear at what price the asset will be sold. I decided to take a conservative route and send myself an alert in case of unforeseen circumstances.

It is also worth paying attention to the actions "Add to queue of active positions" and "Remove from queue of active positions." When opening a new position, it is necessary to understand the number of open positions in order to control them. The number of positions will grow steadily, and therefore the request for a selection of active positions will also grow. To prevent this, I added another table to store a list of open positions.

Table 8-1. List of Actions

Name	Type
Trigger: 'Start'	Trigger
Set the status 'Created'	Act
Add to queue of active positions	Act
Create an opening order	Act
Wait	Wait
Trigger: 'Open order executed'	Trigger
Set the status to 'Open'	Act
Create auxiliary orders	Act
Wait	Wait
Trigger: 'Close position'	Trigger
Cancel all auxiliary orders	Act
Go to 'Sell All' if the opening order is filled	Act
Wait	Wait
Trigger: 'Open order error'	Trigger
Go to 'Ending the process'	Act
Trigger: 'Open order executed'	Trigger
Sell All	Description
Place a closing order	Act
Wait	Wait
Trigger: 'Close order executed'	Trigger
Go to 'Ending the process'	Act
Trigger: 'Close order error'	Trigger

(*continued*)

Table 8-1. (*continued*)

Name	Type
Stop and alert	Act
Ending the process	Description
Set the status to 'Closed'	Act
Remove from queue of active positions	Act
End of process	Description

This scheme is highly expandable. For example, when you develop a capital management block, steps will be added to this scheme for placing orders for additional purchase of a financial asset or its partial sale to fix part of the profit.

Events

Now is the time to describe the functionality that sets positions on the process map in motion. More precisely, let's write command handlers that lead to the emission of process events.

First, this is, of course, `Start`. This event occurs immediately after a position is created and recorded in the database. Listing 8-31 shows the implementation of the position creation command handler `OpenPositionCommandHandler`. Let me remind you that the `OpenPositionCommand` command is called from the `CheckSignalsCommand` command if the result of calculating a signal to open a position is positive.

In this handler, the command for generating a new position is called with a further call to the ProcessBot.Lite handler. Note that the position generator may return `null` instead of a reference to an instance of the position class. This is because you can limit the number of positions open at the same time.

Listing 8-31. OpenPositionCommandHandler

```
public async Task<bool> Handle(
    OpenPositionCommand request,
    CancellationToken cancellationToken)
{
    var position =
        await _mediator.Send(new GeneratePositionCommand());
    if (position == null)
        return false;

    position = await _positionRepository.SaveAsync(position);
    await _mediator.Send(
        new MoveEntityCommand(position.Id, (int)EventIds.
        Start));

    return true;
}
```

Listing 8-32 presents one of the simplest implementations of the GeneratePositionCommand command handler. First, this involves searching for active positions. If at least one is found, then a new position will not be created. You can change this condition according to your capital management. In general, I separated position generation into a separate command with the aim of using the capital management block in this. Because this is where the calculation of the required amount of a financial instrument for purchase occurs.

Since capital management is quite simple, I did not separate it into a separate entity but added settings to the strategy. I only need PositionBalanceCoeff, which determines the share of the current balance for which a position should be opened.

CHAPTER 8 IMPLEMENTATION OF THE CORE MODULE

Please note the positionCount calculation and rounding. This can be improved by adding a decimals field to the goods entity. Goods is one of the halves of a financial instrument. This contains two goods: base goods and quantity goods. For example, let's look at the financial instrument POWI_USD. Base goods are shares of Power Integrations Inc. Quantity goods are United States dollar. That is, when we place a buy order, we are going to buy base goods and spend quantity goods. For POWI, decimals will be equal to 0, but what if the base goods are not a company share but a cryptocurrency such as Ethereum? Ethereum has 18 decimal places, which means decimals are very important.

This code can also be improved by adding lots. The fact is that not all exchanges are ready to trade in small volumes and use lots. For example, often to purchase a currency it is necessary to indicate not the quantity of the desired currency but the number of lots. For example, you cannot buy 15,000 Costa Rican Colon (CRC), but you can place an order to buy 10 lots, each of which is equal to 10,000 CRC.

Also in this code it is worth taking into account the broker's restrictions on the purchase or sale of a financial asset. All brokers limit order sizes. You can't buy a CRC for one cent, any more than you can place an order to sell a CRC worth $1 billion.

Listing 8-32. GeneratePositionCommand Handler

```
public async Task<Position> Handle(
    GeneratePositionCommand request,
    CancellationToken cancellationToken)
{
    List<Position> activePositions =
        await _positionRepository.GetActivePositions(
            _strategyContext.ExchangeId,
            _strategyContext.Instrument.Id,
            _strategyContext.Strategy.Id);
```

```
    if (activePositions.Count > 0)
        return null;

    decimal currentQuoteBalance = await _balanceQueries.
    GetBalanceAsync(
        _strategyContext.ExchangeId,
        _strategyContext.Instrument.Id,
        _strategyContext.Strategy.Id,
        _strategyContext.Instrument.QuoteGoodsId
        );
    decimal currentPrice = _strategyContext.Candles.
    First().Close;
    decimal positionTotal =
        _strategyContext.Strategy.PositionBalanceCoeff *
        currentQuoteBalance;
    decimal positionCount =
        Math.Round(positionTotal / currentPrice, 0,
        MidpointRounding.ToZero);

    Position position = new()
    {
        Id = Guid.NewGuid(),
        ExchangeId = _strategyContext.ExchangeId,
        InstrumentId = _strategyContext.Instrument.Id,
        StrategyId = _strategyContext.Strategy.Id,
        Count = positionCount,
    };

    return position;
}
```

The events "Open order executed," "Open order error," "Close order executed," and "Close order error" are emitted only in response to events of changes in the status of orders at the broker. To process them, I created

CHAPTER 8   IMPLEMENTATION OF THE CORE MODULE

one command, HandleFinalOrderStatusCommand, which parses the order status into a new system order status and events for position processing. Listing 8-33 shows the first part of the implementation of a handler for this command. This is where the new status of the system order is parsed and saved.

Listing 8-33. HandleFinalOrderStatusCommand Handler, Part 1

```
public async Task<bool> Handle(
    HandleFinalOrderStatusCommand request,
    CancellationToken cancellationToken)
{
    SystemOrder systemOrder =
        await _systemOrderRepository
            .GetAsync(request.Order.SystemOrderId);

    systemOrder.Status = request.Status switch
    {
        OrderStatus.Canceled => SystemOrderStatus.Canceled,
        OrderStatus.Error => SystemOrderStatus.Error,
        _ => SystemOrderStatus.Closed
    };

    await _systemOrderRepository.UpdateAsync(systemOrder);
```

Listing 8-34 shows the implementation of the second half of the function. Depending on the new status of the system order, the required EventId type is selected, with a further call to the position process handler command. Please note that the "Open order executed" event is generated not only in response to the Closed status of the system order but also to the Cancelled status. I also introduced another PositionOrderType field for the system order. This is necessary to understand the purpose of creating this order within the position. And it can take three values: Open, Auxiliary, and Close. As a consequence, the reaction of position movement

CHAPTER 8   IMPLEMENTATION OF THE CORE MODULE

through the process is carried out only if the status of Open or Close system orders changes. In this implementation, we agreed that Auxiliary system orders are created only according to the settings in Risk Control; that is, they affect only the position closing command.

Listing 8-34. HandleFinalOrderStatusCommand Handler, Part 2

```
EventIds eventId  = systemOrder.PositionType switch
    {
        (PositionOrderType.Open) => systemOrder.Status switch
        {
            SystemOrderStatus.Closed
                or SystemOrderStatus.Canceled => EventIds.
                OpenOrderDone,
            SystemOrderStatus.Error => EventIds.OpenOrderError,
            _ => throw new Exception("unknown order status")
        },
        PositionOrderType.Close => systemOrder.Status switch
        {
            SystemOrderStatus.Closed
                or SystemOrderStatus.Canceled => EventIds.
                CloseOrderDone,
            SystemOrderStatus.Error => EventIds.
            CloseOrderError,
            _ => throw new Exception("unknown order status")
        },
        _ => throw new Exception("unknown position type")
    };
```

```
    await _mediator.Send(
        new MoveEntityCommand(systemOrder.PositionId, (int)
        eventId));

    return true;
}
```

I won't bore you with the implementation of event handlers for changing order statuses at the broker. They perform only two important actions: saving the new status to the database and calling the `HandleFinalOrderStatusCommand` command. I will only note that these events can be implemented in different ways. You can create several events for each status, or you can create one `ChangeOrderStatusEvent` and pass the new order status as a parameter.

we still need to implement the initiation of the last event from the position processing process; this is "Close position." This event can be emitted from two command handlers. In the first case, it is emitted when checking the signal to close positions, `ClosePositionsCommand`, and all active positions are closed. And in the second case, it is emitted when processing the `CheckSystemOrdersCommand` command. `CheckSystemOrdersCommand` is called in the event handler for the arrival of new candles.

Listing 8-35 shows the implementation of the `ClosePositionsCommand` command handler. This checks for active positions. And if there are any, then the position process is processed with the `ClosePosition` event.

Listing 8-35. CloVsePositionsCommand Handler

```
public async Task<bool> Handle(
    ClosePositionsCommand request,
    CancellationToken cancellationToken)
{
```

```
    var openPositions =
        await _positionRepository
            .GetActivePositions(
                _strategyContext.ExchangeId,
                _strategyContext.Instrument.Id,
                _strategyContext.Strategy.Id);

    if (!openPositions.Any())
        return true;

    foreach (Position openPosition in openPositions)
        await _mediator
            .Send(
                new MoveEntityCommand(
                    openPosition.Id,
                    (int)EventIds.ClosePosition));

    return true;
}
```

The HandleFinalOrderStatusCommand command handler looks more interesting. But first, let's look at auxiliary system orders. I implemented three types of such orders, and to configure them, I allocated a separate RiskControl entity. The identifier of this was placed in the field of the Strategy class.

Stop loss order. This order sends a signal to close a position if the current price of an asset is lower than the price of the asset at the time of creating this order minus a certain percentage specified in the settings. In other words, this system order outlines the lower limit of the asset price. And if the price drops below this level, then the position is closed.

Take profit order. The logic of this order is similar to the logic of the Stop loss order. Only it outlines the upper limit. If the asset price rises above this level, the position is closed.

Trailing stop order. I covered this in detail in Chapter 3 when we discussed risk control.

The idea of this order is to set three boundaries.

- The Profit border behaves exactly the same as the Take Profit order, except that this level does not depend on the initial price of the asset, but on the price, which moves according to a certain logic.

- The Stop border is the opposite of Profit border. That is, if the asset price falls below this value, the position is closed.

- The Decision border is the line for making a decision to change the target price, relative to which the Profit and Stop borders are calculated. When the asset price reaches this, a special signal is checked, and if it is true, then the target price is changed. I also introduced the BorderChangeCoeff parameter into the settings, which is responsible for reducing the shift of the Profit and Stop borders. That is, these boundaries become closer to each other with each change in the target price. This means that with each positive decision, the probability of this system order being triggered increases.

Listing 8-36 shows the implementation of the main `CheckSystemOrdersCommand` command handler function. This is triggered when new candles arrive. I get all active positions and their system orders. Next, depending on their type, I check the conditions.

CHAPTER 8 IMPLEMENTATION OF THE CORE MODULE

Listing 8-36. CheckSystemOrdersCommand Handler

```
public async Task<bool> Handle(
    CheckSystemOrdersCommand request,
    CancellationToken cancellationToken)
{
    List<Position> activePositions =
        await _positionRepository.GetActivePositions(
            _strategyContext.ExchangeId,
            _strategyContext.Instrument.Id,
            _strategyContext.Strategy.Id);
    List<SystemOrder> systemOrders =
        await _systemOrderRepository.GetByPositionIdAsync(
            activePositions.ConvertAll(p => p.Id).Distinct());

    foreach (SystemOrder systemOrder in systemOrders)
    {
        var result = systemOrder.Type switch
        {
            OrderType.StopLoss =>
                await StopLoss_UpdatePrice(systemOrder),
            OrderType.TakeProfit =>
                await TakeProfit_UpdatePrice(systemOrder),
            OrderType.Trailing =>
                await Trailing_UpdatePrice(systemOrder),
            _ => true
        };
    }

    return true;
}
```

385

CHAPTER 8 IMPLEMENTATION OF THE CORE MODULE

Listing 8-37 shows the implementation of handlers for stop loss and take profit orders. In fact, both of these processors differ from each other only by the sign of comparison with the current price.

Listing 8-37. Stop Loss and Take Profit Orders Handlers Implementation

```
private async Task<bool> StopLoss_UpdatePrice(SystemOrder 
systemOrder)
{
    decimal currentPrice = _strategyContext.CurrentPrice();
    double protectOrderLessPriceCoeff =
        _strategyContext.RiskControl.ProtectOrderLess
        PriceCoeff!.Value;
    decimal protectPrice =
        systemOrder.Price!.Value * (1 - (decimal)
        protectOrderLessPriceCoeff);
    if (currentPrice <= protectPrice)
        await ClosePosition(systemOrder);

    return true;
}

private async Task<bool> TakeProfit_UpdatePrice(SystemOrder 
systemOrder)
{
    decimal currentPrice = _strategyContext.CurrentPrice();
    double protectOrderHighPriceCoeff =
        _strategyContext.RiskControl.
        ProtectOrderHighPriceCoeff!.Value;
    decimal protectPrice =
        systemOrder.Price!.Value * (1 + (decimal)
        protectOrderHighPriceCoeff);
```

CHAPTER 8　IMPLEMENTATION OF THE CORE MODULE

```
    if (currentPrice >= protectPrice)
        await ClosePosition(systemOrder);

    return true;
}
```

The code snippet for the trailing order check function, as presented in Listing 8-38, shows the basic logic for checking this type of system order. In this case, the intersection of price boundaries is checked, and if this happens, the position is closed, and the function is exited. If this does not happen, then the decision border is checked; if the price has reached the target value, then the target price is shifted. I also added the ChangedCount field to the system order entity. This is necessary to narrow the price limits.

Listing 8-38. Trailing Order Handler

```
private async Task<bool> Trailing_UpdatePrice(
    SystemOrder systemOrder)
{
    decimal currentPrice = _strategyContext.CurrentPrice();

    if (CheckProfitBorder() || CheckStopBorder())
    {
        await ClosePosition(systemOrder);
        return true;
    }

    if (await CheckBorder())
    {
        systemOrder.ChangedCount++;
        systemOrder.Price = _strategyContext.CurrentPrice();
        await _systemOrderRepository.UpdateAsync(systemOrder);
    }

    return true;
```

CHAPTER 8   IMPLEMENTATION OF THE CORE MODULE

The CheckProfitBorder and CheckStopBorder functions look almost identical to the StopLoss_UpdatePrice and TakeProfit_UpdatePrice functions. With one difference, the new border depends not only on the coefficient specified in the settings but also on the number of shifts of the border itself (the ChangedCount field in the system order). Listing 8-39 shows an implementation of one of these functions. Pay attention to the formula for calculating the boundary.

> **trailingProfitBorderCoeff:** The coefficient by which the border is higher than the target price. For example, if you set this to 0.1, it means that if the current price of the asset exceeds the target price by 10%, then you need to close the position.
>
> **trailingBorderChangeCoeff:** The coefficient by which the border narrows as the number of target price shifts increases. For example, if you set this value to 0.05, this means that with each border shift, trailingProfitBorderCoeff will decrease by 5%.

Let's look at an example.

If ChangedCount = 0, then trailingBorderChangeCoeff will be equal to 95% of the power of zero. And any number to the zero power is always equal to 1. That is, the upper limit will be equal to Price * (100% + 10%*1) = 110% Price.

When ChangedCount = 1, then trailingBorderChangeCoeff will be equal to 95% to the first power, that is, equal to 95%. This means the limit will be equal to Price * (100% + 10% * 95%) = 109.5% Price. That is, the upper limit shifted from the target price not by 10% but by 9.5%.

When ChangedCount = 2, then the upper limit will be equal to Price * (100% + 10% * 95% * 95%) = 109.025% Price. And so on. The more shifts, the narrower the border.

CHAPTER 8　IMPLEMENTATION OF THE CORE MODULE

Listing 8-39. CheckProfitBorder Function

```
bool CheckProfitBorder()
{
    double trailingProfitBorderCoeff =
        _strategyContext.RiskControl
            .TrailingProfitBorderCoeff!.Value;
    double trailingBorderChangeCoeff =
        _strategyContext.RiskControl
            .TrailingBorderChangeCoeff!.Value;
    trailingBorderChangeCoeff =
        Math.Pow((1-trailingBorderChangeCoeff), systemOrder.
        ChangedCount!.Value);
    trailingProfitBorderCoeff *= trailingBorderChangeCoeff;

    decimal protectPrice =
        systemOrder.Price!.Value * (1 + (decimal)
        trailingProfitBorderCoeff);
    return currentPrice >= protectPrice;
}
```

The CheckBorder function, the implementation of which is presented in Listing 8-40, is a check for crossing a price border. If this happens, the signal is checked. And it is the significance of this that determines the need to shift the target price.

Listing 8-40. CheckBorder Function

```
async Task<bool> CheckBorder()
{
    double trailingDecisionCoeff =
        _strategyContext.RiskControl.
        TrailingDecisionCoeff!.Value;
    decimal decisionPrice =
```

CHAPTER 8   IMPLEMENTATION OF THE CORE MODULE

```
        systemOrder.Price!.Value
        * (1 + (decimal)trailingDecisionCoeff);
    if (currentPrice <= decisionPrice)
        return false;

    SignalData signalData = await _mediator.Send(
        new CalculateSignalCommand(
            _strategyContext.RiskControl.
            TrailingDecisionSignalId!.Value));
    return signalData.SignalValue ?? false;
}
```

Process Acts

I showed the implementation of all the commands that create events that affect position processing. Now it's time to implement the step handlers. First you need to add them to the IServiceCollection. I'll remind you that every step in a process must implement the IProcessAct interface, but that won't be enough for us. Because in the future we will also need to implement a class that implements the IProcessActFactory interface, this has only one function for getting the IProcessAct implementation by the identifier specified in the process step. To create the steps, I will use IServiceProvider, and I will receive acts using the GetRequiredKeyedService function.

This means that each of the classes must contain a key. So I created another interface, shown in Listing 8-41, called ICoreAct, with a static ActId field. All acts will implement this interface.

CHAPTER 8   IMPLEMENTATION OF THE CORE MODULE

Listing 8-41. ICoreAct Interface

```
public interface ICoreAct : IProcessAct
{
    static ActIds ActId { get; }
}
```

Listing 8-42 shows part of the IServiceCollection implementation where I add all the acts. To do this, I find all classes of the current assembly that implement the ICoreAct interface, and then I find the actId for each of them with the name of the static field ActId. Then I add them to the IServiceCollection with a key equal to actId.

Listing 8-42. Add Acts to IServiceCollection

```
var acts = AppDomain.CurrentDomain.GetAssemblies()
    .SelectMany(assembly => assembly.GetTypes())
    .Where(type =>
        typeof(ICoreAct).IsAssignableFrom(type)
        && !type.IsInterface);

foreach (var act in acts)
{
    ActIds actId =
        (ActIds) act!
            .GetProperty(nameof(ICoreAct.ActId))!
            .GetValue(null, null)!;
    services.AddKeyedTransient(typeof(IProcessAct),
    actId, act);
}
```

Accordingly, the function for obtaining an instance of a class that implements IProcessAct will look like that shown in Listing 8-43.

391

Listing 8-43. GetAct Function

```
public IProcessAct? GetAct(int actId)
{
    return
        serviceProvider
            .GetKeyedService<IProcessAct>(actId);
}
```

The required list of steps that need to be implemented is as follows:

- **SetStatusAct.** This will be used in several steps such as "Set the status Created," "Set the status to Open," and so on. This step obtains the ID of the desired status in the parameter and then executes the Update procedure in the database to update the status of the item.

- **PutToQueueAct.** This performs the procedure of placing a position in the queue of active positions.

- **CreateAuxiliaryOrdersAct.** If necessary, this creates auxiliary orders. I implemented three options for such orders: stop loss, take profit, and trailing.

- **CancelAuxiliaryOrdersAct.** This performs the procedure for canceling all previously created auxiliary orders.

- **MoveToIfOpenOrderCompletedAct.** At this step, the status of the opening order is checked. And if it is in the final status, then the transition occurs to the step specified in the parameter.

- **MoveToAct.** This is the action of unconditionally moving to the step specified in the node parameter. The act data is needed for the step "Go to 'Ending the process.'"

CHAPTER 8   IMPLEMENTATION OF THE CORE MODULE

- **CreateCloseOrderAct.** This is the action to create a closing order.

- **AlertAct.** At this step, the position will stop and make a log entry marked error.

- **RemoveFromQueueAct.** This removes a position from the active list.

I won't go into simple steps like AlertAct or PutToQueueAct. The logic behind this is quite simple. Let's look at the CreateAuxiliaryOrdersAct step. Listing 8-44 shows a partial implementation of the Make function. The greatest interest in this fragment is the process of determining the target price for a new system order. Because an opening order can be executed involving two deals with different prices, I decided that the target price in this case would be the average of the prices of all deals of the opening order.

In this I get all system position orders. After that, I select an opening order. I assume in advance that it has already been created. If not, then it is logical that the step will end with an error. After that, I receive an order placed by the broker and call the AvgPrice function to obtain the average price value.

Listing 8-44. Make Function of CreateAuxiliaryOrdersAct

```
List<SystemOrder> systemOrders = await
    _systemOrderRepository.GetByPositionIdAsync(entityId);
SystemOrder openSystemOrder =
    systemOrders.First(o => o.PositionType ==
    PositionOrderType.Open);
List<Order> orders = await _orderRepository.GetBySystemOrder
Async(openSystemOrder.Id);
```

CHAPTER 8   IMPLEMENTATION OF THE CORE MODULE

```
Order openOrder = orders.First();

decimal avgPrice = openOrder.AvgPrice();

if (riskControl.CreateProtectOrderLess)
{
    await _mediator.Send(new CreateSystemOrderCommand
    {
        PositionId = entityId,
        Type = OrderType.StopLoss,
        PositionType = PositionOrderType.Auxiliary,
        Count = openOrder.Count,
        Price = avgPrice
    });
}
public class Order
{
    public decimal AvgPrice()
    {
        if (Deals == null || !Deals.Any())
            return 0;
        decimal price =
            Deals.Sum(d => d.Price * d.Count)
            / Deals.Sum(d => d.Count);
        return price;
    }
```

I would also like you to pay attention to CreateCloseOrderAct, where all the purchased assets are sold as a result of the position process. Since I intend to complicate the process of working on a position, the logic of selling all assets purchased as a result of executing an opening order would be incorrect. This is because as a result of position processing, steps may

CHAPTER 8 IMPLEMENTATION OF THE CORE MODULE

be added for an additional purchase or partial sale of a financial asset. Therefore, in this step, I select all orders placed on the exchange and calculate the volume of the asset based on the deals executed as a result of their execution. Listing 8-45 shows an implementation of this algorithm.

Please note that in this case it is necessary not to forget about side orders to correctly determine the sign of the amount of the asset in the transaction.

Listing 8-45. Make Function of CreateCloseOrderAct

```
public async Task<bool> Make(Guid entityId, string magicString)
{
    List<Order> orders = await _orderRepository.GetBySystemOrde
    rAsync(entityId);
    decimal balance = orders
        .Sum(o =>
            o.Deals.Sum(
                deal =>
                    o.Side ==
                    OrderSide.Buy
                        ? deal.Count
                        : -deal.Count));
    if (balance > 0)
    {
        await _mediator.Send(new CreateSystemOrderCommand
        {
            PositionId = entityId,
            Type = OrderType.MarketSell,
```

```
            PositionType = PositionOrderType.Auxiliary,
            Count = balance
        });
    }

    return false;
}
```

Summary

In this chapter, I tried to reveal the implementation of the main module of the system in as much detail as possible. I showed how to work with the context, which significantly speeds up the calculation of strategies. We also implemented a block for calculating signals and indicators. We created a process bot lite and used it to describe the life cycle of the position. This is what determines whether the system will bring you income or not.

Increasing the complexity and changing the calculation logic, adding indicators, and changing the process map will have the greatest impact on the efficiency of your system.

CHAPTER 9

Approaches to Final Implementation

In previous chapters, I described in detail how to create the main blocks of a trading system. I provided a large amount of information to improve and build a trading system, right down to the architectural solution. There is another important aspect that has never been sufficiently explored: the infrastructure issues. In this chapter, I will cover how to deploy your services. Of course, this book is not as comprehensive as the documentation of tools discussed, but it will give you resources for further research and show how you can build a fairly complex infrastructure on your home computer.

In this chapter, I would like to provide you with information on how to deploy and run a project using Docker and Kubernetes. I will also tell you how I deploy the infrastructure I need.

Binance Adapter

Before launching the application, you need to create it. In previous chapters, I paid a lot of attention to the internal services of the system, or rather even just the domain layer of it, without details of the interaction between the database and peripheral services.

CHAPTER 9   APPROACHES TO FINAL IMPLEMENTATION

In this chapter, I will show how to create a working application. Let's launch an adapter to one of the largest and most popular cryptocurrency exchanges: Binance.

I described in detail the part of the system related to interaction with exchanges in Chapter 4. Here I would like to remind you of the main goals and architectural features of this block.

The following is the main functionality that I included in the block of interaction with exchanges:

- Possibility of placing orders
- Possibility of order cancellation
- Providing information on updating order statuses and executing trade transactions
- Providing trade data

In this chapter, I show how to implement the last point because it clearly demonstrates how much data you have to deal with.

My goal is to implement an application that connects to Binance to receive small candlestick updates and put this data into a Kafka topic.

Implementation

To implement the application, I created an ASP.NET project. In the Main function, which was added by the only hosted service `CollectDataHostedService`, I implement the receiving data from Binance, as shown in Listing 9-1. This is also where I configured the logging and controller explorer.

Listing 9-1. Main Function

```
public static void Main(string[] args)
{
    var builder = WebApplication.CreateBuilder(args);
```

CHAPTER 9 APPROACHES TO FINAL IMPLEMENTATION

```
    builder.Services.AddControllers();
    builder.Services.AddEndpointsApiExplorer();

    builder.Services.AddHostedService<CollectDataHostedS
    ervice>();

    string logLevel = Environment
        .GetEnvironmentVariable("LOG_LEVEL") ?? "Trace";
    builder.Services.AddLogging(c =>
    {
        c.AddConsole()
            .SetMinimumLevel(Enum.
            Parse<LogLevel>(logLevel, true));
    });

    WebApplication app = builder.Build();

    app.MapControllers();

    app.Run();
}
```

To quickly check the functionality of the application, I added a single controller, HealthCheckController (see Listing 9-2). Here I have implemented two functions: liveness and readiness. I will tell you later why there are two of them and what purposes each of them serves. But for now they just return a response with a status of 200 Success. Please note that when you call the /status/liveness method, you will receive the response "It's alive!!!" I added this as a simple visual check of the app's functionality.

CHAPTER 9   APPROACHES TO FINAL IMPLEMENTATION

Listing 9-2. Status Controller

```
[ApiController]
[Route("status")]
public class HealthCheckController: Controller
{
    [HttpGet("liveness")]
    public ActionResult Liveness()
    {
        return Ok("It's alive!!!");
    }

    [HttpGet("readiness")]
    public ActionResult Rediness()
    {
        return Ok();
    }
}
```

Listing 9-3 shows the implementation of the constructor for the CollectDataHostedService class. For this I use two popular packages: one for integration with Binance (*https://www.nuget.org/packages/Binance.NET*) and the other for interaction with Kafka (*https://www.nuget.org/packages/Confluent.Kafka*). In the constructor, I instantiate the Binance and producer client class for Kafka. The Kafka producer is a Kafka client that writes messages to a topic.

Listing 9-3. Hosted Service, Part 1

```
public CollectDataHostedService(
    ILogger<CollectDataHostedService> logger)
{
    _logger = logger;
```

CHAPTER 9   APPROACHES TO FINAL IMPLEMENTATION

```
    _exchange = "binance";
    _symbol = Environment
        .GetEnvironmentVariable("SYMBOL")
        ?? "btcusdt";

    _bootstrapServers =
        Environment
            .GetEnvironmentVariable("KAFKA_BOOTSTRAP_
            SERVERS")!;
    _binanceSocketClient = new BinanceSocketClient();

    _producer =
        new ProducerBuilder<Null, string>
            (new ProducerConfig()
            {
                BootstrapServers = _bootstrapServers
            })
            .Build();
}
```

The StartAsync function subscribes to the Binance exchange candle update event. When subscribing, you must pass the message arrival event handler. Listing 9-4 shows an implementation of this; here I log the message with a LogLevel trace and produce to a Kafka topic.

Listing 9-4. Hosted Service, Part 2

```
public Task StartAsync(CancellationToken cancellationToken)
{
    var klineSubscriptionResult =
        _binanceSocketClient.SpotApi.ExchangeData
            .SubscribeToKlineUpdatesAsync(
                symbol: _symbol,
                interval: KlineInterval.OneMinute,
```

CHAPTER 9   APPROACHES TO FINAL IMPLEMENTATION

```
                onMessage: HandleDataEvent,
                cancellationToken);

    return klineSubscriptionResult;
}
public Task StopAsync(CancellationToken cancellationToken)
{
    return _binanceSocketClient.UnsubscribeAllAsync();
}
private void HandleDataEvent(DataEvent<IBinanceStreamKlineData> message)
{
    string KafkaMessage = JsonConvert.SerializeObject(message);
    _logger.LogTrace(KafkaMessage);

    string topic = $"{_exchange}_{_symbol}";
    _producer
        .ProduceAsync(
            topic,
            new Message<Null, string>()
                {Value = KafkaMessage});
}
```

If you set the KAFKA_BOOTSTRAP_SERVERS environment variable with the current URL to your Kafka server instance and run the application, then in the logs you will see a stream of messages with current information about the minute candles of the BTC_USDT pair.

Docker

In this section, I will expand on Docker. I'll explain how to create a Docker container based on your application and run it on your computer.

History

Before we begin, I will explain how containerization technology came to be.

Once upon a time, when computers started to connect to networks, companies called *providers* were involved in developing the infrastructure. For example, if in those days you wanted your project or website to be present on the Internet, then you had to buy or rent an entire server from a provider, which, of course, was not cheap.

There was a big problem with this approach: idle resources. Imagine that you had a news site whose peak load occurred only in the morning hours. Of course, you would have to rent a server designed for peak load. But what would happen the rest of the time? Your server would simply be idle. That is, it would cost money as if your site were constantly experiencing peak load.

The solution to this problem was the development of virtual machine technology, which led to cloud providers. Cloud providers purchased and set up physical servers, and they rent these virtual machines to their clients. Virtualization technology has made it possible to run many independent operating systems on one physical server and allocate the required amount of resources to each of them. Previously, you were forced to rent an entire physical server. Now you can rent the resources of the physical server or servers you need and, if necessary, easily increase these resources.

It was at this time that companies such as Amazon Web Services, DigitalOcean, Google Cloud, Microsoft Azure, and others were created. These companies took care of all the low-level work, such as optimizing physical servers and improving network performance. Thanks to this approach, a separation of application programmers and system administrators occurred. Now you, as a developer, no longer need to understand the intricacies of setting up a network or operating a physical server. Now the programmer can fully concentrate on writing code.

This approach ensured a boom in Internet projects and startups. And as applications grew, so did the complexity. This complexity was expressed not only in the algorithmic or logical complexity of the project but also in infrastructural complexity. Projects began to consist not of one large monolithic service but of many different components, each of which requires its own set of dependencies. For example, two different applications might use two versions of TypeScript. See Figure 9-1.

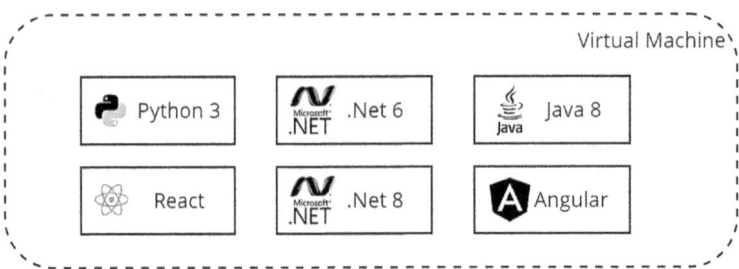

Figure 9-1. *Virtual machine*

Because of increasing complexity, keeping all applications within a single operating system has become difficult. An obvious idea arose about distributing applications across different virtual machines. This approach works and is used in many companies. But there are two problems with this approach.

The first is the growing complexity. The more virtual machines you have, the more different types of applications you have, and the more difficult it is to support it all. Not to mention, there's updating or changing the configuration. Added to all this complexity is the difficulty of monitoring all these virtual machines and of deploying different

CHAPTER 9 APPROACHES TO FINAL IMPLEMENTATION

environments. Developers need a development environment, and testers need a test environment. A good practice before releasing a build is to do a final check of a new version in a stage environment, which is as similar as possible to the production environment.

The second problem is that the virtual machine takes up a lot of server resources. Each virtual machine requires its own operating system. When you have dozens of them, this is not so noticeable, but when you have a lot of them, they begin to consume a significant amount of server resources and therefore money.

To solve this problem, containerization technology was invented. Currently, the most popular platform for this is Docker. The point of Docker is that instead of running the application directly on the operating system, it launches a Docker process within which the target application runs. From the operating system's point of view, such a process looks like just another process; that is, it looks like just another application that does something. And inside each Docker process, each running application thinks that it is unique in the entire operating system with all its dependencies, users, and environment variables.

Docker, unlike a virtual machine, is very lightweight; it only provides security. That is, it ensures that one application cannot access other applications and processes on this system and ensures that the network operates to ensure communication between containers.

Why Is This Needed?

How will this technology be useful for our system? Our trading system is built on the microservices architecture. I described in detail the advantages of this approach in Chapter 4. Here I will highlight the main advantages of this approach, which are scalability and independence.

Scalability is necessary to quickly and easily increase the resources needed for a portion of the system. For example, with an increase in the number of active strategies, we need to increase the resources of the application responsible for processing trading information. At the same time, there is no need to increase the resources for the UI part of the application.

Independence is one of the main reasons to choose a microservices architecture. If problems are identified in one part of the system, the remaining parts will not be affected. Imagine an example when you discovered an error in the integration block with one of the exchanges and you need to update the application to fix this error. In the case of a monolithic architecture, the entire application will restart, which means that all strategies that do not even trade on this exchange will stop working. For me this option is unacceptable.

The presence of a large number of microservices presupposes the presence of a convenient infrastructure. Containerization technology is perfect for this.

The trading system also uses third-party applications for its work, such as Postgres and Kafka. Both of these applications are easier and more convenient to run as containers rather than as processes on your operating system.

In summary, knowledge and understanding of Docker is key to developing the trading system described in this book.

Docker Components

Understanding Docker is built on understanding the basic concepts of it. The entire Docker technology is built on several key concepts.

- **Docker engine.** This is the main Docker application. This is also called a *platform*. This is what ensures the operation of Docker processes and network interactions between them. One easy way to install the Docker engine is to use Docker Desktop. Docker

Desktop contains the Docker engine and many other components. Installation distributions can be downloaded from the official Docker website.

- **Docker container.** This is a running Docker process on the operating system. This is a running container that runs your application with all its dependencies.

- **Docker image.** This is a prototype of a container or an image of it. Based on the Docker image, you can run as many Docker containers as you like. Thanks to Docker image, it is guaranteed that each of the Docker container instances will have the same version of the target application, as well as all dependencies.

- **Dockerfile.** This is a file describing how to create a Docker image. That is, this is a manifest thanks to which Docker understands what the future Docker image consists of.

A short algorithm for working with Docker is as follows:

1. You need to install the Docker engine. I use Docker Desktop on my work computer, which contains the Docker engine as one of the components.

2. Create a Docker file describing how the target application will be built as a Docker image.

3. Using the `docker build` command, create a Docker image.

4. Run the Docker container using the `docker run` command.

In this chapter we will go through all the steps except the first. Because it is specific to each operating system and is well described in the documentation on the Docker website.

CHAPTER 9   APPROACHES TO FINAL IMPLEMENTATION

Launching the Application

Before starting a Docker container, you need to create an image of the application. To do this, I created a Docker file in the project directory. This file can be called anything, but it is usually called Dockerfile, with a capital letter and without specifying the file type. Listing 9-5 shows the contents of my Docker file.

To create an image, you first need to do the following:

1. Download all the project dependencies. Our project links to external libraries from NuGet packages. The Docker file runs the dotnet restore command. When this command is executed, .NET searches for dependencies and downloads them.

2. Publish the application. To publish an application, use the dotnet publish command. This compiles the application and publishes the resulting files to the specified directory.

3. Give Docker a command to run the application.

Listing 9-5. Dockerfile

```
FROM mcr.microsoft.com/dotnet/sdk:8.0 AS builder     (1)
WORKDIR /app                                         (2)

COPY . ./                                            (3)
RUN dotnet restore                                   (4)
RUN dotnet publish --no-restore -c Release -o out    (5)

FROM mcr.microsoft.com/dotnet/aspnet:8.0             (6)
WORKDIR /app                                         (7)
COPY --from=builder /app/out .                       (8)
ENTRYPOINT ["dotnet", "GatewaysApi.Binance.dll"]     (9)
```

CHAPTER 9   APPROACHES TO FINAL IMPLEMENTATION

Let's figure out what happens on each line of this file.

1. The `FROM` statement is executed. This specifies the image with which the application's build commands will be executed. For my application I am using `image dotnet/sdk` version 8.0 located on the Microsoft Artifact Registry server.

2. In this step, I execute the `WORKDIR` instruction. This changes the current directory in the container to the one specified in the instructions.

3. The `COPY` statement tells Docker to copy files and folders into the container. In our example, it instructs Docker to copy everything from the directory from which the build command is launched to the app directory of the container.

4. Run the `dotnet restore` command.

5. Execute the `dotnet publish` command. The `-o` option instructs Docker to put the final compiled files in the `out` directory. It turns out that the resulting files will be stored at `app/out` in the container. The `--no-restore` option indicates that there is no need to check the dependency packages since we ran the `restore` command first. `-c` specifies the name of the build configuration; in our case it is `Release`. After running this command, the assembly files (all kinds of `.dll`) will appear in the `app/out` folder.

6. This is where the second stage of image assembly begins. At this step, the `FROM` statement already points to the base or parent image of the

CHAPTER 9   APPROACHES TO FINAL IMPLEMENTATION

application. I created an ASP.NET application so I am using the parent image dotnet/aspnet version 8.0.

7. Since a new build step has begun due to the FROM statement, you must again specify the current container directory using the WORKDIR statement.

8. At this stage, all files from the /app/out directory from the previous build stage are copied to the current directory. As a result, the resulting .dll files will be located in the current app directory.

9. The ENTRYPOINT instruction tells Docker which command and with which arguments should be called during container execution. In our case, the dotnet GatewaysApi.Binance.dll command will be called.

The Docker file and applications are ready. Let's collect the image and launch the container. Before we begin, we need to make sure the Docker engine is working. To do this, you can run the docker -v command; this will give you information about the current Docker version.

Also on the Docker hub registry, this is the place where people or companies publish Docker images. The image hello-world (https://hub.docker.com/_/hello-world) contains a single static file. Thanks to this image, you can check the performance of the Docker engine on your computer.

If you run the docker run hello-world command, you will see information similar to Listing 9-6. In this fragment, Docker could not find the image hello-world, so it downloaded this. After that, Docker launched the application, and we see the message "Hello from Docker!" This means that Docker is working correctly.

Listing 9-6. docker run hello-world

```
$ docker run hello-world
Unable to find image 'hello-world:latest' locally
latest: Pulling from library/hello-world
c1ec31eb5944: Pull complete
Digest: sha256:d000bc569937abbe195e20322a0bde6b2922d805332fd6d
        8a68b19f524b7d21d
Status: Downloaded newer image for hello-world:latest

Hello from Docker!
This message shows that your installation appears to be working
correctly.
```

If you now run the command to view the list of Docker images, you will see an entry similar to Listing 9-7. You can see the image `hello-world` and the tag `latest`. Any tag for the image can be assigned, but usually the version is used. This information also contains the image identifier, its creation date, and its size.

Listing 9-7. Docker Images

```
$ docker images
REPOSITORY     TAG      IMAGE ID        CREATED         SIZE
hello-world    latest   d2c94e258dcb    10 months ago   13.3kB
```

Since there is obviously no need for the `hello-world` container anymore, let's delete this image. If you run the `docker rmi hello-world` command, Docker will unsuccessfully try to remove the image `hello-world`. Listing 9-8 demonstrates the error you will encounter.

Listing 9-8. docker rmi

```
$ docker rmi hello-world
Error response from daemon: conflict: unable to remove
repository reference "hello-world" (must force) - container
375244b990d2 is using its referenced image d2c94e258dcb
```

This happens because there is a running container that uses this image. To remove image and dependent containers, you need to run the same command but with the -force parameter. Then Docker will delete the image and all dependent containers. Listing 9-9 shows the output of the command. Now if you run a Docker image, you will get an empty list.

Listing 9-9. docker rmi force

```
$ docker rmi hello-world --force
Untagged: hello-world:latest
Untagged: hello-world@sha256:d000bc569937abbe195e20322a0bde
          6b2922d805332fd6d8a68b19f524b7d21d
Deleted:  sha256:d2c94e258dcb3c5ac2798d32e1249e42ef01cba484
          1c2234249495f87264ac5a
```

After you are convinced that the Docker engine is working, let's create an image of our application using a ready-made Docker file. To do this, you need to run the command docker build -t gateways-binance -f Dockerfile . (note the dot at the end!). I call the docker build command with the -t option, which points to the tag gateways-binance. The -f parameter specifies the name of the Docker file according to which the image will be built. Listing 9-10 shows the result of the command.

First of all, auxiliary images are loaded. After this, the commands specified in the Docker file are executed.

CHAPTER 9 APPROACHES TO FINAL IMPLEMENTATION

Listing 9-10. Docker Build

```
$ docker build -t gateways-binance -f Dockerfile .
[+] Building 0.1s (14/14) FINISHED
docker:default => [internal] load .dockerignore
 => => transferring context: 2B
 => [internal] load build definition from Dockerfile
 => => transferring dockerfile: 328B
 => [internal] load metadata for mcr.microsoft.com/dotnet/
    aspnet:8.0
 => [internal] load metadata for mcr.microsoft.com/
    dotnet/sdk:8.0
 => [builder 1/5] FROM mcr.microsoft.com/dotnet/sdk:8.0
 => [stage-1 1/3] FROM mcr.microsoft.com/dotnet/aspnet:8.0
 => [internal] load build context
 => => transferring context: 6.03kB
 => CACHED [stage-1 2/3] WORKDIR /app
 => CACHED [builder 2/5] WORKDIR /app
 => CACHED [builder 3/5] COPY . ./
 => CACHED [builder 4/5] RUN dotnet restore
 => CACHED [builder 5/5] RUN dotnet publish --no-restore -c
    Release -o out                                     0.0s
 => CACHED [stage-1 3/3] COPY --from=builder /app/out .
 => exporting to image
 => => exporting layers
 => => writing image sha256:d7b014f94643b51fc7465ea104a47075e
       330681922101d9a1ad7b3840883ed18
 => => naming to docker.io/library/gateways-binance
```

As a result, if you run the docker images command, you will see the result, as in Listing 9-11.

413

Listing 9-11. docker images

```
$ docker images
REPOSITORY         TAG     IMAGE ID        CREATED         SIZE
gateways-binance   latest  d7b014f94643    15 minutes ago  293MB
```

It's time to launch the first container. To do this, you need to run the command `docker run -d -p 1234:8080 gateways-binance`. In this I am executing the `docker run` command. The `-d` (detach) parameter specifies that the container should be launched in the background, and only the identifier of this container should be displayed on the command line.

The `-p 1234:8080` option specifies port mapping. You will remember that the application "thinks" it is running on a separate virtual machine, and in that "virtual machine" it runs on port 8080, because ASP.NET applications run on port 8080 unless otherwise specified. If you want to access your application, you will have to do it as if you were accessing another computer. This is why it is necessary to determine port compliance. In this I specify that when a request occurs on port 1234, the Docker engine forwards it to port 8080 in the container's "virtual machine."

If you perform a GET request to `http://localhost:1234/status/liveness`, you will see the line "It's alive!!!" as shown in Listing 9-12.

Listing 9-12. get status

```
$ curl http://localhost:1234/status/liveness
It's alive!!!
```

Using the command `docker logs bbbe5ed2c573947bfa7b4c68d41d`, you can see the logs of your container. This should contain many messages with logs of trading information received from Binance. To find out the container ID, you can run the command `docker ps -f ancestor=gateways-binance`. This outputs all containers formed from image `gateways-binance`.

Let's launch another instance of our application, but on port 1235. To do this, just run the command `docker run -d -p 1235:8080 gateways-binance`. Now if you run the command `docker ps -f ancestor=gateways-binance`, you will see two containers and, accordingly, two instances of the application.

How easy is it to launch application instances using Docker? Now imagine that you can simply upload this application to the Docker hub and anyone running the Docker engine can run your application, completely unaware that it is written in .NET or that it has any dependencies. It is easy.

Kubernetes

So, we've launched two instances of the `gateways-binance` app, but what happens when you decide to release a new version of it?

You will need to do the following:

1. Release the image with a new version of your application.

2. Stop and remove all containers that were using the image with the old version.

3. Launch the required number of containers with the new version of the image.

There is one big drawback to this procedure. Your application will not work between steps 2 and 3. Steps 2 and 3 are done sequentially with each container and in reverse order. That is, they first launch the container with the new version of the application and then stop the container with the old version. Then the same actions are performed with the second container, and so on until the target number of containers is reached. This deployment strategy is called *zero downtime deployment*.

Of course, all these steps can be done manually. But the trading system will have not one, but at least 10, applications with different numbers of containers. Manually updating each application requires attention and is subject to a high probability of error.

In addition to the complexity of updating, there is another disadvantage of an infrastructure built on pure Docker: the lack of control and monitoring. Imagine if one of your containers stopped existing or the application in one of the containers stopped working? How can this be in this case? Manually check the number of containers and, in the case of problems, launch a new container manually. Such a system can hardly be called efficient.

To automate the task of updating, scaling, and managing containers, special applications—orchestrators—were created. The most popular of them is Kubernetes (`https://kubernetes.io/`).

In this section, I will show how to deploy our application in Kubernetes. As with Docker, I won't go into detail about installing this application on your computer because it is unique to each operating system. I will only say that for personal needs it is very convenient to use Docker Desktop. This includes the ability to run Kubernetes.

Components

The core component of Kubernetes (k8s) is Cluster. A cluster consists of several servers called *nodes*. There are two types of nodes. The worker node is the server on which the containers run, and the master node is the server that manages the work of the worker nodes. When you run commands on k8s, they are always sent to the master node.

For the normal functioning of a Kubernetes Cluster, one master node and one worker node are sufficient, but usually there are several worker nodes. By increasing the number of nodes in a cluster, your cluster can be scaled horizontally. That is, if you have a large number of running containers, you can always add another worker node to the cluster. See Figure 9-2.

CHAPTER 9   APPROACHES TO FINAL IMPLEMENTATION

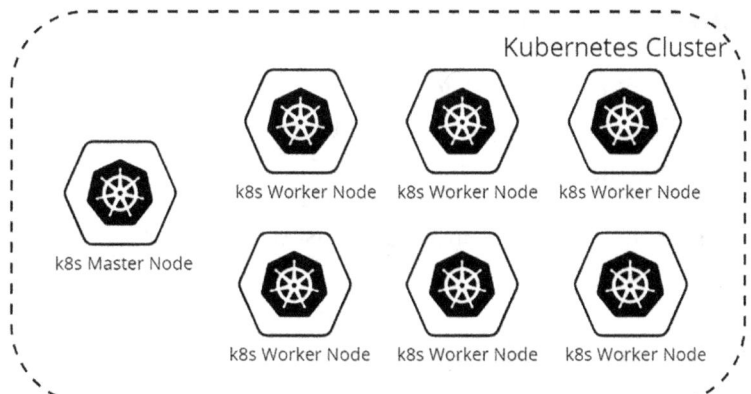

Figure 9-2. *Kubernetes Cluster*

Pods

Each worker node can run several minimal k8s units called *pods*. A pod is the smallest k8s object; it ensures the operation of containers. Let's create pods with our application.

First, you need to make sure Kubernetes is working. To do this, you can run a simple command to get a list of nodes, as shown in Listing 9-13. As you can see, I have one k8s node v1.27.2 running.

Listing 9-13. List of Nodes

```
$ kubectl get nodes
NAME             STATUS    ROLES           AGE     VERSION
docker-desktop   Ready     control-plane   215d    v1.27.2
```

To create a pod, simply run the kubectl run command, as shown in Listing 9-14. I pass the image from which the container inside the pod will be launched and the name of the container as parameters.

Listing 9-14. kubectl run

```
$ kubectl run gateways-binance-1
         --image=gateways-binance:latest
pod/gateways-binance created
```

Now, if we run the command to get a list of pods, our pod will be returned. See Listing 9-15.

Listing 9-15. List of Pods

```
$ kubectl get pods
NAME                   READY   STATUS    RESTARTS   AGE
gateways-binance-1     1/1     Running   0          2m31s
```

To view pod logs, you can use the kubectl logs gateways-binance-1 command.

How do you check the functionality of the application? I want to call the GET method /status/liveness. To do this, I need to forward port pod 8080 (this is the port on which ASP.NET runs the application by default) to a port on my computer. To do this, just run the port-forward command, as shown in Listing 9-16.

Listing 9-16. kubectl port forward

```
$ kubectl port-forward gateways-binance-1 1234:8080
Forwarding from 127.0.0.1:1234 -> 8080
Forwarding from [::1]:1234 -> 8080
```

Now, if you call the GET method at http://localhost:1234/status/liveness, you will see the response "It's alive!!!"

To delete a pod, just run the kubectl delete pods gateways-binance-1 command.

CHAPTER 9   APPROACHES TO FINAL IMPLEMENTATION

Knowing all these commands is great, but there is also an alternative way to manage Kubernetes: by using an IDE. For me, the most convenient are Kubernetes Dashboard (https://github.com/kubernetes/dashboard) or Lens (https://k8slens.dev/). I will continue to demonstrate working with k8s through the command line, because these are the basics that I would like you to know.

Deployments

So, at this stage we have a pod called `gateways-binance-1` with a running container built on the image of our application. But creating and deleting pods is essentially no different from running containers. To automate the deployment and scaling of pods in Kubernetes, there is a `deployments` entity.

We will create this not using the create command but using the so-called manifest file. Manifest files are required to save and control the configuration of Kubernetes settings. You can put these files in source control and always see changes that are made to it.

Let's create a manifest file for our deployment. Manifest files are of type `.yaml`. Create a `deployment.yaml` file in any directory on your computer. Typically, deployment-related files are stored in the `.ops` directory, which is located in the root directory of your application.

Be especially careful when working with `.yaml` files. It is very important to indicate this correctly. Listing 9-17 provides a minimal manifest file for deployment.

- `apiVersion`: `apps/v1` indicates the Kubernetes API version.

- `kind`: Deployment is a type of file manifest. For example, if you specify `kind: Pod`, this will mean that this file describes the creation of a pod.

CHAPTER 9   APPROACHES TO FINAL IMPLEMENTATION

- metadata: name is the name of the deployment.
- metadata: labels is necessary for many things. They can be used to manage Kubernetes objects. For example, delete all objects that have a certain set of labels, or they can be used to collect application logs to add additional information to your logs.
- spec: replicas is the target number of pods.
- spec: selector: matchLabels indicates by which labels the deployment and pods are matched.
- The spec: template section contains a description of future pods.
- template: metadata: labels specifies with which labels future pods will be created.
- template: metadata: containers: name is the prefix for the names of future containers.
- template: metadata: containers: image specifies which image will be used to launch the container on each pod.

Listing 9-17. deployment.yaml File

```
apiVersion: apps/v1
kind: Deployment
metadata:
  name: gateways-binance-deployment
  labels:
    app: gateways-binance
spec:
  replicas: 2
  selector:
```

```
    matchLabels:
      app: gateways-binance
  template:
    metadata:
      labels:
        app: gateways-binance
    spec:
      containers:
        - name: gateways-binance-pod
          image: gateways-binance
```

To use the manifest file, simply run the kubectl apply -f deployment.yaml command. That's all. If you look at the list of deployments, you will see a message like Listing 9-18.

Listing 9-18. List of Deployments

```
$ kubectl get deployments
NAME                              READY  UP-TO-DATE  AVAILABLE  AGE
gateways-binance-deployment       2/2    2           2          12m
```

If we request a list of pods, then we will have two of them, because the manifest file specifies spec: replicas = 2. See Listing 9-19.

Listing 9-19. List of Pods

```
$ kubectl get pods
NAME                                              READY  STATUS   RESTARTS  AGE
gateways-binance-deployment-656b7fd7d4-f76rh      1/1    Running  0         13m
gateways-binance-deployment-656b7fd7d4-rpn95      1/1    Running  0         13m
```

Let's check one of the Kubernetes functions for which we started using it: monitoring and controlling running pods. I suggest deleting one of the pods and, immediately after doing so, running the command to get a list of pods, as shown in Listing 9-20.

Listing 9-20. Deleting the Pod

```
$ kubectl delete pod gateways-binance-deployment-656b7fd7d4-f76rh
pod "gateways-binance-deployment-656b7fd7d4-f76rh" deleted
```

As you can see on Listing 9-21, Kubernetes immediately launched a new pod to replace the deleted one, because the actual number of running pods was not equal to the target, that is, two.

Listing 9-21. Listing of Pods

```
$ kubectl get pods
NAME                                              READY   STATUS    RESTARTS   AGE
gateways-binance-deployment-656b7fd7d4-rpn95      1/1     Running   0          16m
gateways-binance-deployment-656b7fd7d4-tnq5b      1/1     Running   0          3s
```

If you change the manifest file and set `replicas = 3` and then call the `apply` command again, you will see a message similar to Listing 9-22. Kubernetes automatically added another pod to the two existing ones.

Listing 9-22. Scale

```
$ kubectl apply -f deployment.yaml
deployment.apps/gateways-binance-deployment configured

$ kubectl get pods
NAME                                              READY   STATUS    RESTARTS   AGE
gateways-binance-deployment-656b7fd7d4-c9jvq      1/1     Running   0          3s
gateways-binance-deployment-656b7fd7d4-rpn95      1/1     Running   0          20m
gateways-binance-deployment-656b7fd7d4-tnq5b      1/1     Running   0          4m
```

CHAPTER 9   APPROACHES TO FINAL IMPLEMENTATION

In addition to the fact that the pod itself may cease to exist, there is also the possibility that the application running inside the container will suddenly cease to perform its functions. To check the functionality of the application, k8s periodically makes requests (takes probes). The URL and the frequency of this is set in the manifest file.

- The readiness probe is necessary for k8s to understand whether it is possible to switch traffic to this pod. If the readiness probe is negative, then requests will not be sent to this port.

- The liveness probe is taken at the moment that the pod is launched. From this, k8s understands that the application has been successfully launched and is operational.

Another important Kubernetes feature for us is HorizontalPodAutoscaler. Listing 9-23 shows the second part of the deployment.yaml file. I have added a manifest to this with a description of the HorizontalPodAutoscaler object.

- minReplicas specifies the minimum number of pods.

- maxReplicas indicates the maximum number of pods.

- spec: scaleTargetRef points to our deployment.

- The metrics section indicates the rules for regulating the number of pods. My rule specifies that if the average number of CPU utilization of all pods exceeds 50, then another pod will be launched and so on until maxReplicas is reached.

In metrics you can use not only system metrics but also your own metrics. For example, for the real trading subsystem, the metric of the number of active strategies will be relevant.

Listing 9-23. HorizontalPodAutoscaler in deployment.yaml

```yaml
---
apiVersion: autoscaling/v2
kind: HorizontalPodAutoscaler
metadata:
  name: gateways-binance-hpa
spec:
  scaleTargetRef:
    apiVersion: apps/v1
    kind: Deployment
    name: gateways-binance-deployment
  minReplicas: 2
  maxReplicas: 5
  metrics:
    - type: Resource
      resource:
        name: cpu
        target:
          type: Utilization
          averageUtilization: 50
```

Services

Currently, to access our application, we have to run the port-forward command, which is not only inconvenient but also ineffective. I want to access my service at a certain address and not think about which pods provided the service to me. Moreover, it is necessary that the traffic is distributed evenly between all my pods. To solve these problems, k8s has a special component: `service`. It is thanks to this that k8s provides the functionality described.

CHAPTER 9   APPROACHES TO FINAL IMPLEMENTATION

Services come in several types. In this chapter, I will show you how to work with a service of the NodePort type. The manifest file provided in Listing 9-24 is the minimum required to create a service.

An important section is the `spec: selector` section. This defines a set of labels, which is used to search for pods to bind to the service. The `spec: ports` section specifies the port of the service itself within the Kubernetes cluster, as well as the port through which the request to the pods occurs.

Listing 9-24. service.yaml

```
apiVersion: v1
kind: Service
metadata:
    name: gateways-binance-service
spec:
    selector:
        app: gateways-binance
    ports:
        - protocol: TCP
          port: 1234
          targetPort: 8080
    type: NodePort
```

After creating the `service.yaml` file, you need to run the `kubectl apply -f service.yaml` command to create a new service. Once the service is created, you can see it in the list of services, as shown in Listing 9-25.

Listing 9-25. List of Services

```
$ kubectl get svc
NAME                      TYPE       CLUSTER-IP      EXTERNAL-IP   PORT(S)
gateways-binance-service  NodePort   10.106.71.65    <none>        1234:30550/TCP
```

Pay attention to the PORT (S) section; this indicates the port inside the cluster, which is 1234, as well as external port 30550, through which you can access the service. Now if you make a request to http://localhost:30550/status/liveness, you will see the message "It's alive!!!" If you look at the pod logs, you can see that the request went to one of them.

Helm

We have created several manifest files with which you can quickly launch our application on the Kubernetes cluster. In the future, you will integrate not only with Binance but also with other trading exchanges and brokers, which means you will have many gateways-xxx applications. The main difference between them will be only the name and set of environment variables. Of course, you can store the manifest files along with the application source code, but what if you need to change something in them? For example, add one more container to each pod that collects logs. It turns out that you will have to change the manifest files in all repositories with a high probability of errors. Also, as the infrastructure becomes more complex, the list of your manifest files may contain not two files as in my example, but a dozen files, and in each of them you must remember to write the label app: gateways-binance.

To solve these problems, a solution called helm was created. You can find installation and configuration instructions on the official website at https://helm.sh. The idea behind this is quite simple. The application manifest files become templates, where individual values, for example gateways-binance, are replaced with variable names, and special files with the values of these variables are added to this. Now manifest files can be stored in one place, and files with individual variable values can be stored along with the source code. See Listing 9-26.

Listing 9-26. Helm Chart

```
    - HelmChart
    - templates
  - deployment.yaml
  - service.yaml
    - values.yaml
    - Chart.yaml
```

The new `Chart.yaml` file contains the technical information needed by `helm` to run your application. Listing 9-27 presents one version of such a file.

Listing 9-27. Chart.yaml

```
apiVersion: v2
name: basechart
type: application
version: 0.1.0
```

The new `values.yaml` file contains the default variable values. I have identified four variables. These are the number of replicas, images, ports, and targetPorts. In the end, my `values.yaml` file looks like the one shown in Listing 9-28.

Listing 9-28. values.yaml

```
replicaCount: 2
image: gateways-binance
port: 1234
targetPort: 3000
```

Now you need to register these variables in the manifest files. Listing 9-29 shows the modified `service.yaml` file. As you can see, this manifest file can be used for all `gateways-xxx` applications.

Here I have used the technical variable `.Release.Name`. I will indicate this when executing the `helm install` command.

Listing 9-29. service.yaml with helm Variables

```
apiVersion: v1
kind: Service
metadata:
    name: {{ .Release.Name }}-service
spec:
    selector:
        app: {{ .Release.Name }}
    ports:
        - protocol: TCP
          port: {{ .Values.port }}
          targetPort: {{ .Values.targetPort }}
    type: NodePort
```

To run the application using `helm`, you need to run the `helm install` command, as shown in Listing 9-30. I specified `gateways-binance` in the `Release.Name` parameter.

Listing 9-30. helm install Command

```
$ helm install gateways-binance HelmChart/
NAME: gateways-binance
LAST DEPLOYED: Wed Mar  6 19:35:40 2024
NAMESPACE: default
STATUS: deployed
REVISION: 1
TEST SUITE: None
```

CHAPTER 9   APPROACHES TO FINAL IMPLEMENTATION

Once the command has completed successfully, you can verify that all the required components have been created by running the `kubectl get pod` command. To update `helm-chart`, you need to call the `helm upgrade` command.

hHelm is a powerful mechanism that allows you to easily install complex applications that consist of several components.

For example, to install Kafka, you can use `helm-chart`. Perhaps the most popular set of charts at the moment is the set from Bitnami (https://bitnami.com). This provides everything you need to deploy various applications on your Kubernetes cluster. With these kits, you can run complex applications on your server using literally one command.

Summary

So, we have finished our journey. You have come a long way and learned how to build complex trading systems. I showed how to create the architecture of such systems and approach the implementation of this.

In this chapter, I covered one of the main topics of building a trading system, namely, the topic of infrastructure. I showed how to create your own Docker image using the example of a small application for integration with a cryptocurrency exchange. Together we launched a Docker container.

But we didn't stop there. I also showed how to work with the most popular orchestration: Kubernetes. I talked about the main components of this. I showed an example of creating pods, deployments, and services, as well as how these manifest files can be packaged in `helm-chart`.

After reading this chapter, you have enough knowledge to install all the necessary infrastructure on your server or personal computer. Now you have enough knowledge to create your own easily scalable trading system.

CHAPTER 9   APPROACHES TO FINAL IMPLEMENTATION

I want to remind you that the system described in this book is not the final solution. There is endless room for improvement here. For example, instead of using indicators in condition, you can start using entire formulas. Or you can create your own type of signal that does not use conditions but is built, for example, on the number of mentions of certain phrases in news reports.

Building a trading system is an endless process in which there is always room for improvement. And working on this is very pleasant, because you immediately see and feel feedback from your work in monetary terms, and this is one of the best motivators. I wish you success and big earnings.

Index

A

Adaptive maxing random search (AMRS), 252
Adaptive step size random search (ASSRS), 251
Anemic model, 177
Architectural solution
    requirements elicitation
        central entities, 75
        concepts, 71
        first view process, 78–82
        indicator entity, 73
        signal entity, 74–76
        strategy entity, 77
    services, 117
    steps, 69, 70
    theory generation, 78
Average directional index (ADX), 220
Average True Range (Atr) indicator, 357
    AtrIndicatorCalculator class, 360
    AverageCalculator class, 359
    formula, 358
    HighPriceCalculator class, 361

B

Binance adapter
    exchanges, 398
    goals/architectural features, 398
    implementation, 398
        hosted service, 400–402
        main function, 398, 399
        status controller, 400
Brute-force algorithm
    algorithm, 282–284
    AlgorithmTypeInfo class, 272
    dependencies, 271
    FunctionVariable record, 275, 276
    GetOptimizationAlgorithm function, 272, 274
    GetTypeInfo class, 273
    Init function, 274
    IOptimizationAlgorithm interface, 272
    IVariableId interface, 276
    library classes, 270
    set values, 277
        AlgorithmPoint class, 277
        GetNextPoints function, 277
        GetPoints recursion, 280, 282
        variables, 278

INDEX

C

Capital management
　anti-Martingale, 45
　fixed position sizing, 41
　fixed proportional
　　method, 46–49
　generating theories, 106
　Kelly criterion, 41–43
　Martingale, 44, 45
　methods, 40
　optimal f-ratio, 43, 44
Check signals, 335
Core module
　external commands/events, 330
　InitContextCommand, 332
　input/output data, 327
　context, 331, 332
　position, 362
　primary constructors, 332
　profitable strategies, 328
　signal check, 335
　UpdateCandleEvent
　　class, 332–335
　use cases, 327–331

D, E

Deoxyribonucleic acid (DNA), 220
Dependency injection (DI), 270
Docker
　algorithm, 407
　approach, 403
　containerization
　　technology, 405
　disadvantages, 416
　Dockerfile, 408
　file type, 408–415
　get status, 414
　hello-world, 411
　history, 403–405
　image creation, 408
　independence, 406
　key concepts, 406, 407
　platform, 406
　providers, 403
　rmi force command, 412
　scalability, 405
　virtualization, 403
　virtual machine, 404
Domain-driven design (DDD),
　177, 178

F

Fixed step size random search
　(FSSRS), 251

G, H, I, J

Generating theories
　capital management entity, 106
　condition/condition
　　group, 80–82
　financial instruments, 98
　indicator charts, 114, 115
　life cycle/position, 104
　modes, 78
　profitable strategies, 82

calculated strategies, 96
finding strategies, 100
local extremes, 87
quality condition, 91
real trading, 101–103
search settings, 100, 101
SubTheory entity, 92
theory generation
  process, 100
two-step system, 89–97
profitable strategiesone-step
  process, 89–96
regression line (LRC), 79
requirements, 79
risk control, 107
  financial instrument, 110
  position processing, 107, 108
  stop loss system, 108
  strategy parameter
    values, 111
  trailing system order, 108–114
  trolling order works, 109
scalability, 114, 115
selection/forward testing, 97, 98
signals, 79
system order process, 104
Genetic algorithm
  AddGeneticAlgorithm
    method, 290
  algorithm, 298
  AlgorithmTypeInfo_Operator
    class, 289
  AlgorithmTypeInfo record, 288
  AllowedStep record, 289

breeding step, 314–316
  GetNextPoints method, 314
  GetNextPopulation
    function, 315
  panmixia operator, 318
  crossing function, 318–320
  selection operator, 317, 318
chromosome, 220
crossover operators, 224
  arithmetical operator, 225
  blend, 225
  flat operation, 224, 225
  fuzzy, 226
  heuristic number, 225
  linear, 226
  simulated binary crossover,
    227, 228
dependencies, 290
filtering operators, 228
  clipping method, 232
  crowding method, 233
  elitism method, 232
  proportional sampling
    method, 229
  rank method, 231, 232
  roulette method, 228, 229
  stochastic universal
    method, 230
  tournament method,
    230, 231
filtering process
  elitism operator, 312–314
  GetNextPopulation
    function, 309

INDEX

Genetic algorithm (*cont.*)
    roulette operator, 310–312
    selection function, 311
  FlatManagedOperator, 305
  GetInfo method, 293, 294
  GetNextPoints function, 294, 295, 300, 301, 304
  GetNextPoints method, 294
  GetTypeInfo method, 287, 291
  IAlgorithmStep interface, 289
  initialization step, 303–306
  local unconstrained optimization, 249
    ASSRS algorithms, 251–254
    extremum search trajectory, 253
    multipoint algorithms, 255–260
    multistep algorithm, 254, 255
    random search, 249, 260–264
    RLS algorithm, 250
  MagicData class, 296
  method implementation, 302, 303
  multipoint algorithms
    complex algorithm, 255–259
    hypersphere, 259, 260
    reflected vertex, 257
  mutation operator
    arithmetic number, 223
    definition, 221
    Gaussian function, 223, 224
    random operator, 222, 223
    stages, 222

  mutation step, 298, 306–309
  objective, 285
  ObjectiveFunctionResult class, 297
  operators, 285
  random search
    algorithm diagram, 262
    iterated local search, 263
    Monte Carlo algorithm, 260
    perturbation, 263
    random restarts, 262
    requirements, 264
    simulated annealing, 261, 262
  restrictions
    behavioral memory method, 248
    components, 238
    conditional optimization, 239
    death penalty, 244
    dynamic penalty method, 245
    penalty function graphs, 241–243
    reduction method, 246–248
    segregated genetic algorithm, 246, 247
    sliding tolerance criterion, 240–242
    static penalties, 244
  selection operators
    inbreeding, 237

INDEX

outbreeding method, 238, 239
panmixia method, 235
principle, 234
selective selection, 236
source code, 301, 302
steps, 286, 287, 296

K, L

Kelly criterion, 41–43
Kubernetes (k8s)
    cluster, 416, 417
    components, 416, 417
    deployment/scaling
        deleting pods, 422
        deployment.yaml file, 420, 421
        helm chart, 426–429
        HorizontalPodAutoscaler, 423, 424
        manifest file, 419, 423
        pods, 421
        scale, 422
        services, 425–427
    nodes, 416
    pods, 417–419
    steps, 415
    zero downtime deployment, 415

M, N

Manual trading system, 2
Microservice architecture
    advantages, 119
    application update process, 123
    build systems, 118
    concepts, 121
    contextual constraint, 120
    disadvantages, 121
    distributed architecture, 120
    independence, 119
    Kubernetes, 122–124
    methods, 118, 119
    scaling, 119

O

Object relational mapper (ORM), 178
    DbConnector implementation, 181–183
    entity classes, 179, 180
    GetOrderAsync function, 183
    IExchangeOrderRepository interface, 182
    InsertOrderAsync function, 183
    migration, 184, 185
Optimization algorithm module
    advantages, 215, 216
    extrema/multiextremal, 217
    features, 215
    formulation, 216, 217
    genetic algorithms, 220
    multiparameter, 217
    multistart method, 219
    population agents, 218
    population algorithms, 217–219

INDEX

Optimization algorithms
    Brute-force, 270
    functional requirement, 267–269
    genetic algorithm, 285
    module/service, 265
    operation, 269
    Rastrigin function, 321
    scenarios, 266, 267
    SubTheory, 322–325
    test functions, 321, 322

P, Q

Position processing
    acts
        CreateAuxiliaryOrders Act, 393
        CreateCloseOrderAct, 395, 396
        GetAct function, 392
        ICoreAct interface, 391
        implemention, 392
        IProcessAct implementation, 390
        IServiceCollection, 391
    events
        boundaries, 384
        CheckBorder function, 389
        CheckProfitBorder function, 389
        CheckSystemOrders Command handler, 384
        ClosePositionsCommand handler, 382
        GeneratePositionCommand handler, 378, 379
        HandleFinalOrderStatus Command handler, 380, 381
        OpenPositionCommand Handler, 377
        stop loss and take profit orders, 386
        trailing order handler, 387
    meaning, 362
    probability, 363
    process bot (lite version)
        GetNextNodeId function, 370
        HandleEvent function, 369, 370
        HandleNode function, 371, 373
        implementation, 364
        input/output functionality, 366
        library, 365
        LockAsync function, 368, 369
        MoveAsync function, 366–368
    risk control, 362
    steps, 373–376
        process map, 373
    uncontrollable number, 363

R

Random line search (RLS) algorithm, 250
Real trading subsystem

INDEX

enabling/disabling
strategies, 158-160
financial instrument
databases and
applications, 162
general architectural
diagram, 163, 164
instruments App, 162
instrument service, 162, 166
options, 160, 161
profitability, 160
strategies, 161, 164
strategy manager
service, 163
Workers App, 165, 166
goals, 151
integration/exchanges
adapter service
architecture, 156
architectural solutions, 153
Kafka message, 155
message broker, 154
update information, 152
working process, 153
launch/operation, 156-158
master data, 167-169

S

Signal checking model
Atr indicator, 357-362
calculating signal data, 343-351
CalculateCondition
function, 344
CalculateGroup
Condition function, 345
CalculateIndicator
Value function, 350
CalculateNotGroup
Condition function, 347
command handler, 343
GetFromToCandles
function, 348
command handler, 335-337
indicator calculation
calculate function, 357
class architecture, 351
GetCalculator method, 353
IIndicatorCalculator
interface, 355, 356
Init function, 352
strategies, 337-343
concepts, 337
condition class, 338
InitContextCommand
handler, 342
signal class, 338
SignalData class, 340
strategy class, 341
Simulated Binary Crossover (SBX), 227, 228
Single-dimension perturbation
search (SDPS), 251
Subsystems/Services
architecture, 118
database table schema, 133
finite state machine, 134, 135
functionality/dependencies, 117

INDEX

Subsystems/Services (*cont.*)
   interaction diagram, 124
   processing generator, 126
      application structure, 129
      asynchronous
        option, 126
      automatic theory
        generation, 130
      back-end method, 129
      disadvantages, 128
      queue management, 128
      settings page, 127
   profitable strategies, 125
   queue requirements, 131–135
   real, 151
   subtheory calculation, 141
      application structure, 144
      generation process,
        142–145
      optimization algorithms,
        144, 145
      task queue, 146–149
      TestCandleInterval, 146
      working proccess, 147
   theory processing process
      Core module, 149, 150
      entities, 136
      processing process,
        137–141
      Sandbox Exchange
        module, 150, 151
      steps, 135
      subtheory
        calculation, 141–150

T, U, V

Technology stack/libraries
   application projects
      anemic model, 177
      architecture, 172
      clean architecture, 175–178
      command handler, 176
      data transfer objects
        (DTOs), 174
      domain-driven design
        (DDD), 177, 178
      SOLID principles, 175
      spaghetti code, 173
   background tasks
      AddBackworker
        function, 208
      BackworkerTask
        class, 210–213
      database table
        schema, 207
      RunAsync function, 209
   finite state machines
      hosted service, 189–207
      nodes, 186, 188
      principles, 186–189
      theory flow, 187
   hosted services
      ActiveQueue, 194
      database table schema, 193
      GetAndLockEntitiesAsync
        function, 195
      GetNextNodeId
        function, 206–208

INDEX

HandleEntitiesAsync function, 195
HandleEventsAsync function, 196
HandleProcessingQueueAsync function, 198
IProcessActFactory interface, 191
IServiceCollection, 190
IServiceCollection services, 190
MakeActAsync function, 203–205
MoveAsync function, 202
.NET application, 189
node class, 200, 201
ProcessingQueue, 194
RunAsync function, 194
StartAsync function, 192
language/framework, 172
ORM, 178
Theory trading strategies
  approaches, 27, 29, 35
  capital management, 40–50
  concepts, 18
  Depth of Market, 22
  dividends, 20
  drawdowns, 61
  effectiveness, 59
  financial instrument, 19, 20
  fundamental analysis, 34
  leverage, 24, 25
  margin, 24, 25
  modules, 25–27
  optimization process, 63–67
  order execution, 21–24
  performance indicators, 59–63
  profitability, 60
  profit factor, 60
  quote/spread, 24
  risk control
    actions/calculations, 49
    approaches, 49
    diversification methods, 56–58
    maximum loss amount, 50
    monitoring market volatility, 57
    stop loss levels, 51, 52
    take profit, 52, 53
    trailing stop, 53–55
  shareholders, 19
  signals, 37–39
  technical analysis, 18
    definition, 29
    Fibonacci retracements and extensions, 34
    functions, 29
    graphical analysis, 30
    indicators/oscillators, 30–32
    trend analysis, 33
  testing approaches, 58, 59
  tickers, 20
  underlying asset, 19
  volatility, 36, 37
Trading system development, 1
  advantages/disadvantage, 10, 13–15

439

INDEX

Trading system development (*cont.*)
- algorithmic systems, 5–9
- approaches, 10, 13, 14
- automatic robots, 8
- brute-force method, 11
- general theory, 17
- hire third-party developers, 13, 14
- independent testing, 12
- manual trading, 2
- Martingale, 8
- short-term signals, 7
- signals, 3, 4
- single strategy, 10, 11
- specialized services, 9
- theory, 26

W, X, Y, Z

Weighted moving average (WMA), 79

GPSR Compliance

The European Union's (EU) General Product Safety Regulation (GPSR) is a set of rules that requires consumer products to be safe and our obligations to ensure this.

If you have any concerns about our products, you can contact us on

ProductSafety@springernature.com

In case Publisher is established outside the EU, the EU authorized representative is:

Springer Nature Customer Service Center GmbH
Europaplatz 3
69115 Heidelberg, Germany

www.ingramcontent.com/pod-product-compliance
Lightning Source LLC
LaVergne TN
LVHW010333260326
834688LV00036B/686